"Hall's critical analysis of contemporary cinema is an essential for anyone studying to be, or interested in being, part of the current filmmaking community. This is the first stop for anyone looking beyond the closed doors of the mainstream."

— Josh Koury, Director, Brooklyn Underground Film Festival

"Hall has the ability to put movies into words, and possesses the sheer brilliance as a film critic to allow the reader to understand the filmmaker as well as the film."

— John T. Ryan, Documentary Filmmaker (*Sincerity on the Sunset Strip; Freaks, Glam Gods & Rockstars*)

"Hall is one of the few film critics working today who tells it like it is. His knowledge of film, both commercial Hollywood, indie, underground, and international cinema trends, puts him towards the top of the list of people whose opinion I trust implicitly. "

— Peter M. Hargrove, President, Hargrove Entertainment Inc.

"Phil Hall's enlightening descent into the oft-overlooked contemporary celluloid/digital underground makes for a fun, fascinating read—a must for cinephiles!"

Joe Kane, *The Phantom of the Movies' VideoScope*

"We could use more critics like Phil Hall. The passion and knowledge he displays for cult and underground movies is truly impressive."

— Scott Weinberg, editor, *Daily-Reviews.com*

"Brilliant, fascinating, witty, insightful. A must-read."

— Jed Dylan, editor, *The Movie Times*

"If your idea of underground cinema is early John Waters or snuff films, you're in for an awakening. This book will dispel any preconceived notions you may have regarding underground films."

— Kent Turner, editor, *Film-Forward.com*

"If it's a film that flummoxes conventional critics — not to mention moviegoers hypnotized by Hollywood's dollar-driven tricks — the intrepid Phil Hall has tracked it down, looked it boldly in the eye, and grasped the secrets of its outlandish soul. His news and views are as adventurous, unpredictable, and liberating as the best of the incredibly strange movies he loves."

— David Sterritt, film critic for the *Christian Science Monitor* and author of *Screening the Beats: Media Culture and the Beat Sensibility*

"*H.R. Pukenshette? Jesus and Hutch?* Boldly viewing where few cinephiles are willing to ogle, the intrepid Phil Hall separates some of the cinematic wheat from the schlocky chaff in this wide-ranging and entertaining guided tour through subterranean filmmaking that highlights off-the-beaten-Hollywood-path dramas, comedies, documentaries, and genre films (and filmmakers) that make the entries in *The Psychotronic Video Guide* resemble staid *Masterpiece Theatre* drawing room fare (did I mention *Midget Nun?*). A one-of-a-(admittedly weird)-kind, this should find a welcome home in the hands of budding filmmakers and on the shelves of public and academic libraries."

> — Randy Pitman, editor, *Video Librarian*

"Phil Hall's fascinating introduction to Underground Cinema is an invaluable guide book. With care and obvious affection, Phil tells the strange and often inspiring stories behind the production of these celluloid underdogs, as well as helpful tips on how to get a copy of these hard-to-find films for yourself. I highly recommend this well-written guide to those looking for movies a little different than the cookie-cutter tripe put out by Hollywood."

> — John O'Brien, editor-in-chief, *PulpLit.com*

"Phil Hall's determined exploration of ultra-independent, low-budget cinema is to literature what his little-known subjects are to the celluloid-devoted: a goldmine of the unique, the alternative, and the surprisingly urgent. Aficionados of the medium: Pick up Phil Hall's roadmap and follow it beyond the megaplex and video store to underground treasures beyond your imagination."

> — Dave Foucher, editor/publisher, *EDGE Boston*

"Thoughtful, thorough, and well-researched, yet readable and entertaining, Phil Hall's *Encyclopedia of Underground Movies* offers comprehensive insights and information about some of the sadly neglected but most imaginative areas of filmmaking in recent years. Hall's love of these odd, sometimes maddening but often brilliant works is downright palpable."

> — Eric Monder, *Film Journal International*

"Phil Hall's understanding of the many cultural and socio-political undercurrents in Western film critique allows him to comprehend film as much more than just an entertainment medium. For him, film is poetry, the nascent literature of the age, and a snapshot of our times. Rarely have I met anyone with comparable command of and dedication to his medium. "

> — Charles Shaw, publisher/editor-in-chief, *Newtopia Magazine*

"This book is a tribute to that other American dream… the one that says a few people with an idea instead of a big studio budget can create something wonderful."

> — Joshua Tanzer, editor, OffOffOff.com

THE
ENCYCLOPEDIA OF
UNDERGROUND MOVIES

FILMS FROM THE FRINGES OF CINEMA

PHIL HALL

Published by Michael Wiese Productions,
11288 Ventura Boulevard,
Suite #621
Studio City, CA 91604
(818) 379-8799, (818) 986-3408 (FAX).
mw@mwp.com
www.mwp.com

Cover design: MWP
Interior design: William Morosi
Editor: Paul Norlen
Printed by McNaughton & Gunn, Inc., Saline, Michigan

Manufactured in the United States of America
Copyright 2004 Phil Hall

Library of Congress Cataloging-in-Publication Data

Hall, Phil, 1964-
  The encyclopedia of underground movies : films from the fringes of
cinema / Phil Hall.
      p. cm.
  ISBN 0-941188-95-7
  1. Experimental films--Criticism and interpretation. I. Title.
  PN1995.9.E96H35 2004
  791.43'3--dc22
                                    2004009133

Dedication

This book is dedicated to the three most important influences in my life: my mother, who encouraged my love of movies (even when it meant sitting through some of the strangest films ever made), my brother Theo Llewellyn Hall, who always knows how to keep me focused and inspired, and to the memory of my beloved grandmother, who during my childhood years happily put her world on hold to join me for afternoons watching Godzilla flicks on television.

Table of Contents

Acknowledgments

John Donne once wrote that no man is an island, and this was not merely a broad topographical observation. The creation of this book was not a one-man operation, by any stretch. Indeed, this book could not have possibly occurred without the input of scores of supportive individuals, and praise needs to be given before we begin.

First and foremost, thanks must be given to Chris Gore, my dear friend and my editor at *Film Threat*. Without Chris, my opportunity to dwell in the underground cinema realm would never have taken place. Chris, bless you and thank you!

Thanks are in order for Ken Lee and Michael Wiese at MWP Books, who happily accepted the notion of putting my writing into book format and sending my work out into the unsuspecting world. And special thanks to Paul Norlen and William Morosi for making this book look so good! Ken, Michael, Paul, and William made a dream come true for me!

A special thank you needs to be given to my friend and colleague David Nagler, who has been an invaluable source of information, opinions, and encouragement during the writing and editing process. Praise also needs to be shared with Eric Campos, the deputy editor at *Film Threat* who has been a trusted ally in my work.

For my adventures in the celluloid trade and the wacky world of underground cinema, I need to give a cheer to the following heroes (in alphabetical order) who gave me their valued input and inspiration along the way: Mark Adnum, Keith Alcove, Antero & Sylvi Alli, Selena Ambush, Taka Arai, Mike Aransky, Ed Arentz, Rory L. Aronsky, Ace Bannon, Ron Bonk, Ted Bonnitt, Jason T. Bozzuto, Nathan Bramble,

Cameron Kelly Brown, Doug Brunell, Geoff Burlaza, Irene Cascione, Erik Childress, Jaime N. Christley, Victoria Clark, Lloyd Cohn, Ben Coccio, Carla Cole & Tom Edwards, Darren D'Addario, Mike D'Angelo, Christian de Rezendes, Dennis Dermody, Paul DeSimone, Arthur Dong, Dennis Doros & Amy Heller, Chuck Dowling, Rama Dunayevich, Bilge Ebiri, James Eowan, Udy Epstein, John Farrell, Mark L. Feinsod, Dave Foucher, Larry Fessenden, Robert Firsching, Kevin Filipski, Ken Fox, Jonathan and Matthew Friedman, Gregory Gilleland, Carole Goldberg, Nicki Goldstein, Lawrence Grecco, Philip Guerette, Dianne Griffin, Richard Griffin, Shanti Guy, Peter M. Hargrove, Nick Harmon, Phil Hartman, Greg Hatanaka, Kevin Hunt, Susan Hussey, Mark Johnston, Erica Jordan, Brandon Judell, Eli Kabillio, Elliot Kanbar, Joe "Phantom of the Movies" Kane, Young Man Kang, Jeremiah Kipp, Ann Kolson, Josh Koury, Aaron Krach, Ryan Krivoshey, Jon Lap, Bruce Lawton, Jason Leaf, Quentin Lee, Graham Leggat, Donald J. Levit, Dennis Lim, Robin Lim, Patrick Lockley, Mike Lyddon, Paul Lynde, Peter Marai, Brian Matherly, Marc Mauceri, Maitland McDonagh, Andrew Repasky McElhinney, Doug Miles, Terri Minsky, Ben Model, Wilson Morales, Carl Morano, Vincent Musetto, Tim Nasson, Jim Neibaur, Peter M. Nichols, Christopher Null, Dennis Nyback, Suzanne O'Connor, James O'Ehley, the Online Film Critics Society, Josh Pais, Matthew Papertsian, Kit Parker, Dorne Pentes, Eric Phelps, Bill Plympton, Randy Pitman, Dustin Putman, Lawrence P. Raffel, T.C. Rice, Mark Rifkin, Tim Ritter, Debbie Rochon, Jason Rosette, John T. Ryan, Eric Russell, Shaun Sages, Jamil Said, Mike Sargent, Elias Savada, David Schenfeld, Dennis Schwartz, Michael B. Scrutchin, Matthew Seig, Dennis Seuling, Thomas Edward Seymour, Mark Silverman, Alan Simpson, Renaldo and Diarah Spech, Penelope Spheeris, David Sterritt, Eric Stanze, Stuart Strutin, Mike Thomas, Jimmy Traynor, Bradford Trebach, Kirsten Tretbar, Kent Turner, Greg Walloch, Stephen Wang, Scott Weinberg, Sam Wells, Terry M. West, Tracey Westmoreland, Greg Wild, Michael Williams, Zack Winestine, Woody Wise, Caveh Zahedi, Billy Zane and Sande Zeig.

Introduction

The motion picture industry, as it stands today, can roughly be divided into three wildly uneven segments. The first segment is the most prominent: the Hollywood output. Anyone with access to the mass media and a multiplex will know all about these films. It is virtually impossible to escape the omnipresent impact of Hollywood movies, from both a positive and negative standpoint, and the effect of these films on both the American and global cultures is profound to the point of being frightening. Mercifully, this book is not about that segment.

The second segment of the motion picture industry is significantly smaller when compared to Tinseltown's output, but in many ways it rivals and often surpasses its intellectual and artistic results. This is the art house circuit, which presents independently-produced American films and imports from foreign film industries. The distribution of the art house fare is significantly limited: most films open in on one or two screens in one or a handful of cities (usually New York and Los Angeles) and then expand in a city-by-city route which is known in the film world as a "platform release." Sometimes it can take a year or more for a film that opened in New York or Los Angeles to find its way to the art house cinemas in smaller cities, and sometimes these films never make it at all. These films cannot compete with Hollywood's massive openings when thousands of screens are simultaneously carpet-bombed with their flicks, but the art house fare has three things to its advantage: the love of the influential movie critics (who inevitably shower these smaller films with awards and significant editorial cheerleading), a passionate audience base who go out of their way to support these films and thus keep this segment alive, and the good fortune of serving as talent pool for the major film studios, who scout and recruit clever filmmakers and actors from the art house orbit and groom them for stardom in Hollywood. This is a fascinating part of the film world, to be certain, but we won't be considering it here.

Then there is a third segment of the motion picture industry which is generally unknown to most moviegoers, and is also unfamiliar territory to many players in the industry itself. This is the Underground Cinema, a vast and somewhat unexplored territory consisting of thousands of films which rarely find their way to audience, media, or industry recognition. In many ways, today's Underground Cinema represents a parallel universe to the motion picture world. The number of films here is staggering, and it is hardly an exaggeration to think that for every film playing on a movie screen there are hundreds (if not thousands) of films which cannot get into theatrical release. Some of these films have obtained a degree of cult classic status, almost entirely from word of mouth or Internet review praise, and others probably would be celebrated if the right people had access to them.

Today's Underground Cinema is the ultimate hidden gold mine for the true cinephile. Which is not to say that all of the films in the Underground Cinema are great. Far from it. As with Hollywood and, yes, even with the gentrified art house sphere, there are more than a few duds that stink up the place. But overlooking the bad films (and we will, trust me), there is still such an extraordinary wealth of talent, audacity, and inspired lunacy with these films that it is impossible not to pause and wonder why the Underground Cinema has been ignored for so long and continues to be treated with an acute absence of respect.

The concept of Underground Cinema as a sovereign celluloid entity is not new, and actually it has its roots back in the era of the silent movies. During the late 1920s, several artists working in the United States and Europe decided to push the limits of filmmaking to edgier lengths. Eschewing the polished look of the Hollywood productions and usually throwing away the concept of linear storytelling, their films took on a rough and experimental visual quality that offered a surreal challenge to how audiences considered movies. The most famous of these films were the collaborative efforts of Spain's Luis Buñuel and Salvador Dali: *Un Chien Andalou* (1929) and *L'Age d'Or* (1930), which brought a degree of shock effects and playful blasphemy uncommon to the screen.

The only problem with this school of filmmaking was the lack of audiences. Since these filmmakers were working outside of established movie industries (often in the cheaper 16mm format and almost always in the creation of short subjects), they had no access to anything resembling theatrical release. Many of these films remained widely unseen until many years after they were completed; even the Buñuel and Dali films did not receive the level of universal praise until they were rediscovered and resurrected decades later by film societies and museums.

The introduction of sound to filmmaking in the final stretch of the 1920s hampered underground filmmakers, who lacked the budgets to accommodate soundtracks. Even as late as the 1940s, when Maya Deren arrived with films such as *Meshes of an Afternoon* (1943), the relatively few underground films being produced did not include sound or even a synchronized music score. Deren, whose films were shot and originally projected as silent works, aggressively sought to find a wider audience for her efforts. Since she lacked the clout to get into theatrical release, she literally bought her way in: by renting theaters and presenting her experimental films on a single bill. In doing this, she pioneered the concept of "four-walling," in which an exhibitor will rent a venue to films. Today, many underground filmmakers have taken to four-walling to gain theatrical exposure.

Underground Cinema continued quietly through the postwar years, but it was not until the early 1960s that these films finally began to gain some degree of mainstream recognition. The first major break came with *Shadows*, an improvised feature film directed by John Cassavetes. The fact that Cassavetes already enjoyed name recognition as a Hollywood actor gave him and his film more leverage in gaining exhibitor and critical attention, and pushing the film was a major goal for Cassavetes. Rather than be content with barely-attended screenings at obscure film societies, Cassavetes worked to get *Shadows* into theatrical playdates at high-profile cinemas in major markets. His self-distribution strategy paid off nicely. *Shadows* became a surprise hit with the critics when it began to receive commercial playdates in 1961, resulting in Cassavetes being recruited by Hollywood to direct major films for the studios (though ironically, his initial Hollywood ventures *A Child is Waiting* and *Too Late Blues* were so unsatisfactory that he later returned to self-financing and self-distributing with his 1968 classic *Faces*).

The second major break came from another high-profile name: Andy Warhol. With his talent for self-promotion, Warhol emerged in the late 1950s and early 1960s as the most famous American artist. Not the best, by any means, but certainly the most famous. Warhol began dabbling in filmmaking, creating works of a confusing and often monotonous nature (such as 1963's *Sleep*, a 321-minute study of a man sleeping, and 1964's *Empire*, a 485-minute single shot of the Empire State Building over the course of a day). Yet because they were Warhol productions, they received a level of attention which no other film artist could ever dream of achieving.

The Cassavetes-Warhol breakthroughs helped call attention to Underground Cinema, bringing more media and film scholastic attention to artists including Kenneth Anger, Stan Brakhage, Jonas Mekas, Shirley Clarke, and, belatedly, Maya Deren (who died of a brain hemorrhage in 1960, still vastly underappreciated). The raw vitality of their films, which pushed Hollywood-style production and style aside in favor of assaults on good taste and conformist lifestyles, found appeal with prominent film writers and even some filmmakers. Visual experimentation, most notably the use of split-screen techniques, and the willingness to deal with taboo subjects such as homosexuality and racial strife, made these films daring and provocative when held up against typical Hollywood fare. By the late 1960s, many of the visual and conceptual experiments created by these underground artists found their way into mainstream Hollywood productions (but ironically, the filmmakers themselves were not welcomed to the Hollywood studios to helm these works).

The next big hurrah for Underground Cinema came from Baltimore, of all places, in the giddy persona of John Waters. His no-budget features such as *Mondo Trasho* (1969) and *Multiple Maniacs* (1970) were crude in every sense of the word — from the bare-bones production values to the scatalogical humor that laced almost every scene — but Waters' comic screenplays were rich in original wit and his ensemble cast, most notably the oversized drag queen Divine, were uncommonly gifted in turning his grotesque imagination into celluloid gold. The emergence of Waters' 1972 *Pink Flamingos* as a favorite of the midnight movie circuit gave the filmmaker a higher level of recognition.

And here is the schism that separates the traditional concept of independent movies and Underground Cinema: recognition. Any American film which is produced outside of the traditional Hollywood studio system is technically an independent film. Some of these films get into the A-list film festivals and get picked up for theatrical release (usually for the art house circuit, but in rare cases like *The Blair Witch Project* for mainstream multiplex distribution). For those that don't get into theaters and never get seen at major events like Sundance or SXSW, they remain in the Underground Cinema — literally, buried from view.

So why don't these films get picked up if they are so special? It is actually not a question of quality (since plenty of lousy movies are in theaters), but rather it has to do with quantity. Or to be blunt: there are too many films being made today and not enough opportunity for all of them to be seen. And sometimes getting a distribution deal is no guarantee that a film will be shown. Miramax, for example, has a history of acquiring films and leaving them on the shelf. And Artisan Entertainment, which put *The Blair Witch Project* into theaters, acquired but then balked at giving theatrical playdates to the 2002 Abel Ferrara crime drama *'R-Xmas*. Despite the director's fame and reputation, the film was destined to go straight to home video before a small company called Pathfinder Pictures snagged theatrical rights and put it in New York and Los Angeles theaters right before the home video debut.

Further complicating matters is the state of the motion picture industry. After all, it is an industry and the purpose of any industry is to make money. Rising costs plus the death of several significant independent distributors in recent years (most notably the ambitious Shooting Gallery, which tried and dismally failed to bring art house films to wider national release) has made life harder for those who want to take a chance on edgier and unusual titles. Add to that the loss of many theaters devoted to showcasing non-Hollywood fare. With fewer opportunities for films made outside of the Hollywood system to get screen time and less reason to make such films available, it is no surprise that Underground Cinema is growing.

Yet the Underground Cinema titles are not just lying around without anyone seeing them. They are available, if you know where to look. These titles are available on home video and, increasingly, DVD, and many aspiring filmmakers who lack distribution deals have taken it upon themselves to sell their films directly through wholesalers, e-commerce web sites, at special events such as film festivals or specialized film conventions, and even directly off the web sites designed to promote the films.

There is also a growing number of film festivals designed to give Underground Cinema its own special place on the big screen. Most of these festivals are relatively new and poorly publicized, but over time it is not difficult to imagine they will find their attention and wider audiences. And beyond the traditional cinemas is a new exhibition outlet: the Internet. As broadband connectivity becomes more commonplace, the promise of being able to show films online has brought a higher number of Underground Cinema titles to the World Wide Web, thus creating a 24/7 showcase with a potential global audience. The Net is also home to a rather high number of original online magazines devoted exclusively to this genre, as well as the digital mirrors for influential and still-popular publications that were on the subject long before anyone heard of the Internet.

Computer technology has played a crucial role in the expansion of the Underground Cinema. Special software enables aspiring filmmakers to handle all of the postproduction aspects with clicks of a mouse and bangs on a keyboard. Indeed, one can literally shoot a professional-looking film on an inexpensive mini-DV camera and handle all of the editing, dubbing, scoring, and other postproduction chores on a desktop or laptop computer. This technology has cut the cost of filmmaking drastically, and it is not difficult to find feature films created with these tools that were made for thousands or even hundreds of dollars.

Phil Goes Underground

My experience in the Underground Cinema came through two blessed opportunities. In joining the editorial staff of *Film Threat* (www.filmthreat.com) in 2000, I was assigned to review the Underground Cinema productions. This was a relatively easy task in terms of legwork, as the filmmakers passed along videotapes of their work to the *Film Threat* editorial headquarters and they were, in turn, shipped to me. These were films that I never heard about and probably would never have heard about had it not been for my editorial association. As *Film Threat* is one of the relatively few major cinema news sites to devote coverage to Underground Cinema, I've been privileged to see several of the films which I reviewed find their way out of the Underground Cinema into wider distribution.

Concurrent to this was my work as a programmer and host of the weekly Light+Screen Film Festival in New York City, which had its origins in Atlanta thanks to filmmaker Michael Williams, who brought the festival to New York and later returned to Atlanta while leaving me to run the show. This movie series was underground in the physical sense: it took place in the Siberia Bar, a popular watering hole located inside a subway station just north of Times Square that featured a performance space with video projection capabilities. While the Light+Screen Film Festival series offered the usual line-up of retro and classic titles (including, appropriately, John Cassavetes' *Shadows*), it also gave many Underground Cinema productions a chance to be seen by New York audiences. The Light+Screen Film Festival also enjoyed a rather high level of press coverage, thus giving some nice publicity for the films (which the filmmakers, in turn, used to leverage future playdates for their works).

This book encompasses my exposure to Underground Cinema. If anything, it is a labor of love since it provides an opportunity to give attention to some of the most remarkable features, shorts, documentaries, and (in several cases) unclassifiable oddities which would otherwise remain unseen. Many of these films are rich with vibrant imagination, daring intellectual and emotional audacity, and a unique creative vision which makes the best of Hollywood and the art house circuit look puny in comparison. Others have no real brainpower or aesthetic value, but just offer plain old-fashioned entertainment — and Lord knows there's nothing wrong with that!

Since many of the productions cited in this book are not widely available, I have included, where applicable, the web sites for the films. Where no web site exists, a link to the *Film Threat* review or the Internet Movie Database listing for the title is provided. This will enable the reader who wants to learn more about Underground Cinema to go online and find these just-out-of-reach treasures. It really isn't difficult if you know where to look — and truly, it is worth more than just a look.

1: The Artistic Underground

For Eric Phelps, former development director with the Atlanta International Film Festival, the best things about today's underground cinema is the fact it is underground — literally, separate and apart from mainstream movies.

"I think that underground cinema has the advantage of not having to work toward the market," says Phelps. "Scripts can be more edgy and people can take risks with style. Hollywood as such has very little to do with making films. It has to do with making money, and whatever project will make the most dough is good for them. It's been this way from the beginning, and hence directors have always tried to have their own independence from the Hollywood system. John Ford shot out in the desert so that he could stay away from the control of Hollywood's moguls, though he couldn't help but be part of the system as it existed."

In the past several years, there has been a dramatic rise in the number of underground films being created. This has primarily been spurred by technology that is both professional and inexpensive. "The advent of digital video has made it possible for practically anyone with a few bucks to make a very strong short or feature," continues Phelps. "There have been some very innovative and interesting films made by independent filmmakers. Another advantage is that you are not limited by having to be screened at a cinema or festival. You can make smaller films for DVD or video, and we see the distribution of smaller films in this way around the world."

Yet Phelps notes all is not copacetic in this no-budget world. "But at the same time, the lack of resources can result in very poor quality," he laments. "Sometimes that comes in the form of acting (using one's friends and family for cast), and sometimes in the form of the production values."

While acknowledging that there are more than a few underground films with shaky production values and shabby acting, for the most part this world is rich with strikingly original films that dare to take risks with both style and substance. Indeed, the worst underground films are the "safest" in the way they tow the line of traditional filmmaking. For obvious reasons, we won't bother with those films. Instead, we will enjoy the creative gambling and the impressive returns that many underground filmmakers have brought forth.

Classic Sources

One of the most audacious experiments in the underground cinema has been the challenge to bring literary classics to life, albeit without the grand trappings one associates with film versions based on such celebrated sources. Several films have gone far back in time and brought out bold new concepts in literary adaptations.

The story of Boston filmmaker's John Farrell attempt to create a film version of Shakespeare's *Richard the Second* is as memorable as the tale of the doomed monarch. Farrell's film was put into motion in 1987. A $50,000 budget was planned and raised. Location shooting in England and Ireland was obviously out of the question, but that didn't matter. "We all knew the location we wanted — the decrepit and isolated Fort Strong on Long Island in Boston Harbor," recalls Farrell. "It was like having your own studio lot, right in the middle of the Harbor islands, complete with half a dozen 'sound' stages, ready to order for this kind of cinematic story. And no one was allowed out there to bother us while we were shooting."

With this go-round, *Richard the Second* finds its royal court and rival regents wearing battle fatigues and sporting Uzis as they travel through lush, overgrown wooded areas around the fort, which offers a cold and towering central edifice which balances nicely off the heated intrigue of the story. In capturing the tale of an indecisive king whose poor judgments and talent for making enemies leads to his downfall, *Richard the Second* provides a stunning tale of how not to run a kingdom. By waging costly wars financed by excessive taxation on an increasingly disgruntled population, coupled with the foolish banishment of vengeful one-time friends who join forces with other powerful enemies, the story reads as a textbook for disaster whose lessons transcend time and geography.

Much of the strength in the film's political struggle is fueled by Matte Osian's rugged performance as Richard. The actor presents a strong mix of smug self-assurance as the crown rests on his head and tragic, belated redemption once his kingdom is lost and he is locked away in a dark dungeon (the film actually begins with the imprisoned Richard contemplating his downfall and fate). Speaking of dungeons, those sequences are quite jolting. The fort which served as the principal location lacked electricity, forcing Farrell to shoot these sequences with illumination from torches. The result offers a grimy yet hypnotic visual power which brilliantly captures the despair and doom that faces the fallen king (and, of course, this would approximate the darkness which the real Richard experienced in his final days... not a pretty picture, to be sure).

For the sake of economy, Farrell opted to shoot the production on video rather than film, which would have doubled the budget. "The original intent with *Richard the Second* was to shoot in broadcast 1" format and transfer to 35mm," he says. "We shot with an Ikekami camera and used Sony reel-to-reel. I even did a test trailer in the edit suite which we sent to a place in Los Angeles called Image Transform, which sent us back the trailer on 35mm — this was when laser transfer was the new thing for video to film (no scan lines!). I still keep the reel in my office."

The production sped at a fairly rapid pace: the preproduction casting, rehearsals and the actual shooting at Fort Strong spanned March to September 1987. From October to mid-December of 1987 Farrell was involved in the offline edit and then the online edit for a 97-minute one-inch master. And then, it all stopped. Costs associated with the online postproduction video editing and sound mixing were higher than Farrell had planned and no additional funds were available. There was also the need to pay for a 35mm film transfer that would be necessary for theatrical presentations.

"The project basically died on the vine right there," says Farrell. "We had spent all of our $50,000 on securing the location, paying the cast, renting the equipment, and for costumes and weapons. So I felt stuck for quite a while."

Unable to proceed further, *Richard the Second* was shelved and over time the project was soon forgotten. Farrell went on to other projects, including work in broadcast and cable television and writing three novels, six screenplays, several short stories, and articles for *National Review* and *Salon*. *Richard the Second* laid dormant until the late 1990s when the introduction of low-cost MPEG (pronounced M-peg, an acronym for Moving Picture Experts Group), a family of standards used in coding audio-visual information for movies, video, or music in a digital compressed format, allowed Farrell to revisit and recut the movie in purely digital format.

By September 2000, Farrell finally completed the film and even created a trailer which he posted on the Internet. The trailer led to an inquiry and then an article in *DV Magazine*, a tech trade journal. More press coverage ensued and Farrell was invited by the Two Boots Den of Cin, a video projection venue in New York, to theatrically present the film in the summer of 2001, where it received supportive reviews.

Farrell actually kept updating and improving the postproduction on *Richard the Second* after its New York theatrical engagement. "After 2001, when I could afford the equipment upgrade, I re-mastered the entire movie in full-screen DV format, which I finished in November 2002," he said. "The film was finalized using Final Cut Pro 3.0, on a couple of Mac G4s. I also used After Effects 4.1 for some of the modest special effects sequences in the movie (when Bolingbroke wanders off into exile in a wide shot, I airbrushed out an inappropriately distracting telephone pole and also added a harvest moon). Sound mixing and effects were done with Macromedia's trusty old Sound Edit Pro 2, as well as Bias Peak DV."

Richard the Second finally found a wide audience in the summer of 2004 when it debuted on DVD. Unlike Richard the Second himself, Farrell enjoyed a much-deserved and long-overdue happy ending.

Farrell has also been responsible for bringing the 1495 morality play *Everyman* to life and modern dress. The play, whose author is unknown, seems quite timely today. The eponymous *Everyman* of this film is a typical modern guy (played by an appropriately nondescript Robert Kane) with a good job, a nice circle of friends, and a satisfied life. One day, however, Everyman is confronted on a highway by Death (depicted here as a vulturous yuppie in a blue business suit and dark shades and carrying an ominous briefcase). Everyman is informed that his time is up and his grave is waiting. Unable to bribe or cajole Death into taking a raincheck, Everyman desperately races to find someone who will join him on his pending one-way trip.

Needless to say, there are few takers: the gregarious ale-guzzler Fellowship refuses to come along, and the checkers-playing Kinsmen also turn their back on him. Everyman then confronts his highly-valued Riches (brilliantly depicted as a talking PC), but Riches rudely informs Everyman that he never loved him. Everyman then tries to find Good Deeds, who is lying alone and forgotten in a hospital. Heartsick that he has ignored Good Deeds for too long, Everyman makes rapid amends by seeking out Knowledge (depicted as a brainy lass with a bright red backpack). Knowledge brings Everyman to a church where he receives blessings, and then discovers Good Deeds immediately recovered. Together with Knowledge, Good Deeds, and a pair of new friends named Strength (who doesn't look all that powerful, to be sure) and Discretion, Everyman sets off to meet his final destination.

As morality plays go, *Everyman* is more than a little peculiar. Imagine Bunyan's *Pilgrim's Progress* as an episode of *Twilight Zone* and you have an idea where this is coming from. Filmmaker Farrell deserves praise for bringing intact the lessons of this 15th-century work into the 21st century. Similar to *Richard the Second*, Farrell has a genius for guerrilla-style filmmaking which makes remarkable use of public settings (the streets and pubs of Boston and the autumn wilderness of New Hampshire are the playing fields for Everyman's journey). Unlike his other film, however, *Everyman* has something of a problem in terms of keeping the original dialogue intact. The film's cast of Boston-area actors are frequently not comfortable with the ebb and flow of the 1495-style dialogue and there are passages in the film when the conversation hops and flops awkwardly as the actors fail to fully embrace their lines. One might question whether it would have made more sense to update the original text into contemporary lingo rather than force the cast to ride

Barry Smith and Robert F. McCafferty as Bolingbroke and Northumberland in John Farrell's modern dress version of Shakespeare's *Richard the Second*.

Thomas Roache as Demetrius is condemned to death by Nigel Gore's Titus in Richard Griffin's *Titus Andronicus*.

a medieval vernacular for which some are not well-trained. (Strangely, the talking PC with its coldly mechanical voice provides the finest line readings in the film.)

Elsewhere in New England is Richard Griffin, who in 2000 unveiled his Rhode Island-based feature film based on Shakespeare's *Titus Andronicus*. Griffin is a producer/director for the cable TV provider Cox Communications, where he co-produced and co-directed the award winning magazine show *Rhode Trip* and directed a monthly hour-long live jazz/blues show called *An Evening at Chan's*. Griffin has been making short films and an occasional short feature for a dozen years prior to *Titus Andronicus*, but never quite secured a position of high recognition.

Griffin's film ran nearly three hours and was filmed in DV on a tiny $12,000 budget. To keep costs in line, he took a similar route to John Farrell and updated Shakespeare's tale of gore and revenge in ancient Rome to contemporary times, where the political machinations are just as grisly despite refinements in wardrobe and decor. *Titus Andronicus* secured a theatrical run at the prestigious Cable Car Cinema in Providence, Rhode Island (no mean feat for a digital film without a distributor) and gained excellent reviews and smashing box office. Even the *Daily Telegraph* of London noticed, running a lengthy feature article on the unique production.

But why *Titus Andronicus*, of all plays? Doesn't that play have the reputation of being among Shakespeare's least successful? "When I was studying Shakespeare in grade school, my English teacher told the class not to read *Titus Andronicus* and used the old 'Shakespeare probably didn't even write it' argument," he recalls. "So, being a rather rebellious teenager, it was the first Shakespeare play I read just for the sheer pleasure of it, and being a teenager I loved it because it was so violent and brutal. Today, I love it because it's so violent and brutal, but also because it has a timeless message about how acts of vengeance have no end — and I actually find it to be rather profound, and in a rather odd way, strangely touching. There really are no heroes, just victims and victimizers."

While one does not typically associate ancient Rome with present-day Rhode Island, Griffin had no trouble using the Ocean State for his base of operations. "Oddly enough there was very little problem in making the adaptation work," he says. "This play has a theme of not only vengeance being an all consuming thing, but also of political corruption — and you don't know what political corruption is until you've lived for a few years in Rhode Island. For such a small state, we are surrounded by little Neros and Caesars. So, a great deal of working on the adaptation was pretty much automatic writing."

Griffin's genius for guerrilla cinema rivals Orson Welles' amazing production history on *Othello*. His *Titus Andronicus* takes the councils of ancient Rome and has them replaced by upholstered modern boardrooms; the proverbial corridors of power transplanted into the staircases and hallways of today's buttonholing lobbyists. The exquisitely tailored and groomed cast is dressed and coifed to kill, reminding us that the thirst for power and its corrupting influence on the judgment process has not changed whether the uniform of the day is a toga or a double-breasted Armani. *Titus Andronicus* is also rich in visual wit which complements the absurdities of today's tastes. The vanquished Goths of Shakespeare's play are presented in the make-up and clothing of today's Goth music subculture, and the Emperor's coronation is offered as a "Rome TV" live broadcast. The bloody execution of the son of the Goth Queen Tamora is shot in a home video format, with the executioner babbling idiotically into the shaky camera on the pleasure he took in mutilating his helpless captor. Griffin has brought, for the most part, an excellent cast of Rhode Island-based actors to his work. Nigel Gore offers the perfect blend of noble weariness as Titus, while the strikingly beautiful Zoya Pierson reigns as the treacherous Tamora. The actors who play Titus' vicious sons are all strikingly handsome and curiously touched with weak voices, yet their lack of vocal majesty strangely empowers the venality and pettiness of their lines.

Unknown to Griffin while shooting the film, another movie based on *Titus Andronicus* was in the works via Julie Taymor. Griffin initially took the initial shock of her big-budget *Titus* rather badly.

"I must say I was pretty crushed by the whole thing," he recalls. "It's like working your ass off to make a nice little cottage, then having someone build a multimillion dollar mansion right next to it. But, that being said — the reviews of our film were extremely kind, and several pointed out that we tackled the themes of the play in a more down-to-earth fashion. Plus, the fact that her movie was seemingly released by the CIA made matters a little bit more pleasant for us. At least we didn't spend millions upon millions for what amounted to pretty much a direct-to-video film. We did that with only 12 grand!"

Griffin had planned to follow *Titus Andronicus* with film versions of two other Shakespeare plays, *Macbeth* and *A Midsummer Night's Dream*. Shooting was completed on *Macbeth* in 2001, but to date the film has not been finished; *A Midsummer Night's Dream* has yet to get beyond the planning stage.

Another filmmaker, Gil Cates Jr., made his own modern version of *A Midsummer's Night Dream* — albeit without the Shakespearean text. Cates' *A Midsummer Night's Rave* moved the play to a rave just outside of contemporary Los Angeles, with Shakespeare's magical forest turned into the inside of a warehouse where club music, laser lights, a hunt for drug money, and a pill-dispensing Puck add to the chaos. Cates jettisoned the Shakespeare wordplay, which is a shame since it may have been amusing to see how it would've fit into the rave context.

Shakespeare never wrote about Joan of Arc, which is fine enough since the doomed Maid of Orleans has been the subject of many great plays. The transcripts of her trial have survived intact, offering a chilling record of the judicial miscarriage that sent her into flames.

The trial and death of Joan of Arc was the unlikely subject of Sam Wells, a New Jersey-based experimental artist whose first feature *Wired Angel* is a work of such audacious and outlandish originality that viewing it comes as a jolt to the soul and a rush to the mind. An equal mix of madness, brilliance, character, and courage, *Wired Angel* is a stunning reminder of what can be accomplished with the tools of cinema.

For anyone who only prefers a film that drips along from Point A to Point B to Point C and so on, *Wired Angel* will disappoint and confuse. The film jettisons the concept of linear storytelling for an avant-garde series of tableaux which tell about the life, death, and impact of Joan of Arc with a skill and style that leaves one breathless. Indeed, the film often plays like a celluloid Rorschach test, with images of a harrowing, haunting and frequently baffling nature that assault the senses without mercy until the mind is forced to respond. Imagine that... a film that makes you think!

Wired Angel is shot on black-and-white reversal film, which provides a rich chiaroscuro visual appeal that makes the blacks impenetrable and the whites fiery. Recurring images of ominous crosses, balls of smoke, showers of ash, rolling fire, unforgiving iron bars, sacred religious rites, and bursts of hot light flash and crash across the screen with abstract and nightmarish grace, mirrored in a brilliant aural tour-de-force by composer Joe Renzetti's multi-layered score that combines bells, chants, instrumental symphonics, and tonal waves of doom. Beautiful images of a placid garden in Joan's childhood are transposed against the misery of Joan's prison cell, where the faces of her clerical captors peer down at her with stolid contempt.

In a bizarre touch, images of jarring contemporary happenings (a man with a ray gun, neon light sabers) come and go with wicked glee, as if reminding the audience how contemporary society embraces Joan the warrior into a new modern image which suits our heroine-worship needs.

Wired Angel divides Joan's story into six sections, each running approximately 15 minutes. There is no dialogue, although the transcripts of Joan's fatal trial are read on the soundtrack in digitally distorted French and English — clearly the mockery of these words do not demand the respect of a pristine presentation. As Joan, actress Caroline Ruttle wears her fate with stoicism, forcing the audience to read her mind as she confronts her accusers, wastes away in isolation, withstands the challenge to her faith and, ultimately, surrenders to the flames without betraying a hint of emotion. Whereas that great silent portrayal of Joan by Maria Falconetti in Dreyer's *The Passion of Joan of Arc* stunningly recreates the inner turmoils of the ill-fated woman, Caroline Ruttle's performance forces the audience to recreate the very same turmoils. It is a weird experiment which pays off handsomely, literally creating a mental interactive film experience.

In his notes for the film, Sam Welles describes his work as a "psychological and neurological portrait in images and music of Joan of Arc, her milieu and culture." In many ways, *Wired Angel* is also a challenge to a self-satisfied film world to dare and dream in a manner that spins outside of that proverbial and dreadful box.

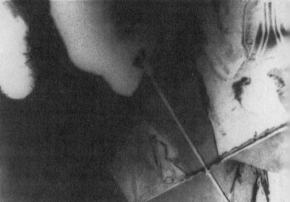

The final days of Joan of Arc as
imagined by Sam Wells' avant-garde
Wired Angel.

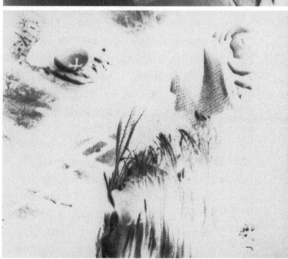

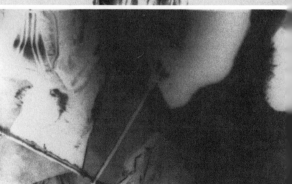

Experimental Outlooks

One of the most striking elements of underground dramatic films is the boldness of visual style. Unlike play-it-safe Hollywood films, today's underground flicks are not afraid to take chances in creating productions that look and sound different from the proverbial pack.

One of the most remarkably stylish underground films of the recent past was inspired from a totally unexpected source. Shanti Guy, a Fort Worth surrealist painter, was listening to his car radio on a hot summer night in 1997 when he heard a tune that literally changed his life. Four years later, the result of this FM-based idea came to life as *Texas Night Train*, a 2001 production that is easily the most hypnotic film to come out of the Lone Star State since Abraham Zapruder took off his lens cap in November 1963.

"I was taking a late night drive in my black 1959 Dodge," recalls Guy. "It was August and had been over 100 hundred degrees for a week. My whole town was in a desperate funk from the heat. I didn't have air conditioning in that little oven on wheels, so I was a little delusional myself. I was listening to a community radio station that had a rockabilly show on for two hours on Tuesday night. There guest host was Mac Stevens. Stevens was showcasing a compilation CD that he had just cut. The first song they played was 'Moppin' the Floor with my Baby's Head.' The song was about a man fed up with his girl and her bad cooking. The man kills her and then mops the floor with her head. The content seemed pretty typical for rap or metal but hearing this country swing version blew my mind. I found the idea of someone totally overreacting to bad potato salad very intriguing. So much so that I couldn't stop thinking about the song for days. I had been outlining different ideas for short films but I didn't really have a handle on who my main character was. I used the song to define the mood of the main character for me. Once I had that down I could write from his point of view and then tell his story."

The story became *Texas Night Train*. The film follows Jake, a transient who simultaneously occupies the hemispheres of vintage and contemporary cool. He drives a classic convertible and speaks in beatnik-inspired prose that tumbles and tears the language with happy recklessness, pausing only for drags of his never-ending chain of cigarettes. His arms are palettes of intricate tattoos and his lithe muscular body moves with kinetic energy, just waiting for something to happen. Something happens, in tenfold, and that something is embodied in sleek, chic Mae. Giving the impression of sexy indifference, Mae takes Jake's invitation for a drink in a Texas honky-tonk and immediately drugs his booze. Jake wakes up later handcuffed to a railroad track while Mae is driving off in his car en route to her day jobs: selling human organs and casting voodoo spells. *Texas Night Train* follows Jake's attempts to track Mae down, only to discover he is not the hunter but actually the prey.

Filmed in DV on a teeny $7,200 budget, *Texas Night Train* is one of the most visually and aurally stunning achievements this year. Guy actually began his career as a surrealist oil painter and he brings an almost Dalist sense of absurdity and horror to his wild story. Tight close-ups, rude blasts of color, unexpected camera blocking and tilted angles, and a seemingly endless series of disturbing images fills the screen like a full-blown nightmare come to horrifying yet dazzling life. To the ear, *Texas Night Train* is laced with a rockabilly score that is equal parts invigorating and haunting, seducing the listener with its vibrancy yet leaving a residue of guilt for having too much fun in listening to songs which carry more than a hint of danger. Running throughout the film is a wired beatnik commentary delivered by Chuck Huber as Jake (in real life, Guy's brother-in-law), who speaks with the voice of an unrepentant cool cat whose ninth life has just begun.

To date, Guy has found a somewhat predictable pattern in response to *Texas Night Train*. "There are three standard reactions that I got," he states. "#1: We are proud of you whatever you do. #2: That was so much cooler than I thought it would be. And #3: So, what was it about?"

Ultimately, Guy believes that filmmakers should focus on what their artistic integrity and not allow their work to be manhandled by outsiders who don't share the filmmaker's vision. "Don't create for glamour," he says. "Concentrate on what you believe in. If producers tell you it should be sexier and more violent, rape them."

Rape mercifully doesn't come into play in Christian de Rezendes' 2002 *Getting Out of Rhode Island*, but almost every other harrowing emotional

★★★★★

"...a masterpiece"
- Phil Hall
Film Threat

GETTING
OUT OF
RHODE
ISLAND

DVD
VIDEO TM

FILM THREAT

experience surfaces. This feature is about a movie project fundraising party designed to create a new indie film capital in New England, but the grand plans to float the concept go terribly awry as jealousies, ego trips, and parallel agendas sabotage the event.

To create this work, de Rezendes experimented with a Dogme-style production that was largely improvised by the 44-member cast. Shot in real time in mini-DV during the course of a single evening and within the confines of one increasingly claustrophobic location (the house that was party central for the film), *Getting Out of Rhode Island* is both an astonishing technical achievement and a daring experiment in pushing visceral emotions to a near-sadistic edge.

"There is a rawness of the image that the viewer cannot escape in Dogme," explains de Rezendes. "There is also a cutting style that exercises their brain muscle to find the storyline and make their way through the muck of real life and make sense of it all. The demands are high when the comfort factor of the artifice is reduced or removed, catapulting the audience into an improvisational universe where anything could happen at any moment and forcefully adapting each viewer to realize he or she had to catch onto its flow to survive the experience. This is sticking them in the emotion, in the comedy, in the dramatic weight of each moment. That's what makes this film unique."

The Dogme style of filmmaking has not been enthusiastically adapted in Hollywood. But for underground filmmakers, Dogme's handheld camera work and natural lighting have helped cover some obvious problems in working with a low-budget (and sometimes no-budget) agenda.

Vladamir Gyorski took the Dogme approach for *Resin* (2002), a harsh feature that questions both the controversial "three strikes" law in California and the American law enforcement community's attitude towards marijuana usage. In following the desperate odyssey of a small-time grass peddler with two convictions to his record (one for a self-defense bonk of a skateboard on the head of a would-be miscreant, the other for pushing a police officer away during a bogus stop and search) and the prospect of life in jail if he gets caught with marijuana in his possession. The filmmaker's fly-on-the-wall approach via the Dogme style gives *Resin* a strength that would've been absent in conventional filmmaking.

Connecticut filmmaker Ben Coccio took the naturalistic Dogme style even further in a found footage video diary which gives a quasi-documentary feel to a dramatic film. This approach was successfully employed in Coccio's 2003 *Zero Day*. Inspired by the Columbine massacre, *Zero Day* tracks the devolving emotional state of two alienated high school students who keep a video diary of their activities in the weeks leading up to the inevitable shoot-out in their school (which is captured on a slightly blurry surveillance camera for the film's jolting conclusion). Found footage is hardly a new idea (*The Blair Witch Project* was clearly the most commercially viable production using this tool), but raw edges of this style of filmmaking gives *Zero Day* a visceral power which was conspicuously lacking in the more conventional filmmaking approach given to another film with a Columbine theme, Gus Van Sant's *Elephant*. (*Zero Day* is discussed in greater depth later in this book.)

A video diary of a very different sort was presented by Josh Koury in his 2000 short *Whores are Expensive*. The title is never explained by anything that happens on screen, adding a mystery to a fascinating video experiment. Koury, who made the film while studying at Pratt Institute, brings unsmiling young men and women into close range with his camera... then closer... then closer. Isolated parts of the subjects' anatomy (eyeballs, teeth, tattooed stretches of arm) fill the screen, literally deconstructing each individual into a part rather than a whole. Throughout it all, a creepy selection of kiddie music (taken from LP records of an early 1960s vintage) warps the soundtrack.

"This film was a piece I made for the moment," says Koury, who later attracted national attention as the director of the documentary *Standing by Yourself* and then as a co-founder of the Brooklyn Underground Film Festival. "It wasn't about making a film as much as it was a kind of self therapy. I remember asking the people shot about their memories and personal history. There was a real exchange and I remember some of them telling me some very extreme things. This film is mostly about secrets, memory, and loss. I think people were just happy that I didn't expose any of the personal issues discussed while we were making the piece."

It's Here, It's Queer

Another area where underground filmmakers have taken a command-ing lead has been in the frank consideration of movies with gay and lesbian themes. While this school of cinema is a subject unto itself (and, indeed, it is the focus of specific festivals), it deserves citation here because underground filmmakers have been uncommonly active in addressing the subject while the Hollywood film studios have been ill-at-ease.

Yet Mark Adnum, editor of the online magazine *Outrate.net*, feels this is simply because of Hollywood's failure to reap green out of lavender. "Why is Hollywood still uneasy and unwilling to make gay-friendly feature films at this late date?" asks Adnum. "Mainly, I think it's that the gay-oriented studio films of the mid-1990s, like *The Object of My Affection* or *The Next Best Thing*, haven't been huge box office suc-cesses, despite having been made in commercial formula with some big name stars. The testing of the gay market in the late 1990s didn't exactly uncover a gold mine. Gay audiences go to see *Titanic, The Lord of the Rings* or *Lost In Translation*, along with everyone else. Activist group calls for more (and more positive) gay big-screen representation put some pressure on Hollywood in the early and mid-1990s, but the modest commercial successes/borderline failures of the few attempts at testing and satisfying the gay audience just weren't enough to start any kind of momentum — the market simply isn't there. And reliably commercial movie templates like romantic comedies and ensemble dramedies aren't engineered for same-sex intimacy and romance. It's not audience discomfort, then, as much as gay content just doesn't really slot into a movie comfortably. Clunky rom-coms like *All Over The Guy* and *Big Chill*-style pieces like *The Broken Hearts Club* demon-strate the pitfalls of jamming gay politik into precise movie formula and hoping it all still works, or that no one notices the transposition. Independent cinema remains, by definition, the place where non-commercial films are generated, and so the few gay-themed films that do emerge through the year are invariably indies. I think the old idea that Hollywood has some kind of inherent aversion to making gay films is true — not because of homophobia though, but because of limited box office potential."

For filmmaker Quentin Lee, the absence of Hollywood has made the genre all the more fascinating in terms of creating productions that stand out on the merits of their artistic imagination and emotional honesty.

"Queer Cinema is a particularly exciting arena particularly because studios are still not touching it as much," he says. "And for savvy independent producers, it could be a very profitable niche with an established and growing queer festival circuit and growing queer theatrical markets and distributors. As an independent filmmaker, I look at queer cinema as an exciting market to explore. But when studios start to take over, I guess we'll have to start looking elsewhere... or make queer studio films."

Lee's 2001 feature *Drift* is a perfect example of the dares being taken with this genre. *Drift* follows a gay love triangle and imagines a trio of conclusions on how the situation would resolve itself. The film's frank yet passionate romantic scenes may not seem uncommon to anyone familiar with such films, yet Lee's decision to make the love triangle interracial and then not offer any superfluous commentary on the cross-cultural mingling is a remarkable example of maturity in filmmaking.

"I believe that the market of gay films is really developing," adds Lee. "Just from personal experience, my generation came out in college between 18 and 21. Kids who are ten years older than me are coming out in high school, between 14 and 18. So even within the decade, gay culture itself is evolving. Quite quickly. With the success of *Queer as Folk* and *Will and Grace*, I believe that the market for queer films will grow. In fact, it has already grown from two decades ago. If you look back at the history of film, a lot of so-called B-movies or indie movies in the '60s, '70s and early '80s are horror. Horror was once a niche/genre that studios didn't touch as much. But now, it has become a hugely profitable genre for studios and indies alike. Or even black cinema. It used to be entirely independent. And of course, now you have *Barbershop, Shaft,* and *Bringing Down the House.*"

Lee's newest film, *Ethan Mao*, is about a gay teenager who gets kicked out of his house and returns to rob his family and ends up holding them hostage. "It's a thriller, a family drama, and a romance — a pretty ambitious film," he says. "As a filmmaker, I try to focus less on the genre or perceived marketability and just try to make a good and entertaining film."

AN UNDERGROUND DRAMA QUAKE

Some of the finest underground features and shorts take a wide variety of approaches to dramatic subject matter.

After an Autumn Day That Felt Like Summer (2003): Film critic turned filmmaker Mark L. Feinsod created this short drama about an amoral young New Yorker who uses the excuse of post-9/11 trauma to cheat on his girlfriend. Web site: http://www.feinsodville.com

The Angel (2002): Uncommonly sensitive adaptation of the Hans Christian Andersen fairy tale about an angel's escorting of a deceased child from this world to the next life. Web site: http://www.darevproductions.com

April is My Religion (2001): A college freshman gets involved with the campus drug scene while falling in love with a mysterious student named April. Web site: http://www.filmthreatdvd.com

Back Up, Please (2002): Two cars meet in a narrow street and neither driver is willing to back up to let the other pass. Tragedy ensues. Web site: http://www.backupplease.com

A Boy and His Fetus (2000): A dark coming of age tale about a man child, his twelve year old lover, his dead father, his catatonic mother, and his partially born brother. Web site: http://www.filmthreat.com/Reviews.asp?File=ReviewsOne.inc&Id=2847

Briar Patch (2002): A thriller about a love quadrangle set in the Deep South. Cast features Dominique Swain and Henry Thomas (the one-time Elliott in "E.T. the Extra-Terrestrial). Web site: http://www.filmthreat.com/Reviews.asp?Id=4063

The Bulls' Night Out (1999): Four retired Brooklyn cops decide to take the law into their own hands and fight the growing crime levels in their neighborhood. Web site: http://www.bullsnightout.com

The Chester Story (2003): Drama about a small town called Chester in which a few unsuspecting souls partner with fate after a disastrous car pile-up. Web site: http://www.geocities.com/seathorne17

Christmas (2000): Based on a short story by Vladimir Nabokov, this short film recounts a father's winter visit to the family summer home after burying his son. Web site: http://www.microcinema.com/ titleResults.php?content_id=318

Con Games (2001): An ex-soldier turned private eye goes undercover in a prison to investigate a series of suspicious deaths, but his own life is on the line when the corrupt correctional officers discover his true identity. Web site: http://www.mtivideo.com

Crazy Jones (2002): The unlikely friendship between a forty-something cemetery maintenance worker with Tourette's Syndrome and a teenage runaway is the focus of this *Sundays and Cybele*-inspired drama. Web site: http://www.filmthreat.com/Reviews.asp?Id=3110

Criminal (2000): A bookkeeper commits an act of embezzlement against his employer, then cracks up and goes on a crime spree when he discovers his wife in an adulterous affair. Web site: http://www.firstrites.com

Drive-Thru (2001): Intriguing experimental offering about an alternate universe where high school geeks are cool. Web site: http: //www.filmthreat.com/Reviews.asp?Id=2483

Final Cut.com (2001): Two filmmakers offer depressed and lonesome people to film their departure in order to immortalize them. Web site: http://www.FinalCutdotcom.net/

Fits & Starts (2002): A young man and woman spend the afternoon drinking orange soda and conversing through cassette recorders. Features a musical number. Web site: http://www.kalmiapictures.com/ html%20pages/fits&starts.html

1st Testament: CIA Vengeance (2001): A CIA operative discovers he has been betrayed and framed by a hitherto-unknown mole working within the Washington spook factory. Web site: http:// www.youngmankang.com

Five Lines (2001): A quintet of stories relating to Washington residents from different levels of the social scale who all meet their untimely deaths on the same evening. Web site: http://www.5lines.com

Free Speech Zone (2002): Described by Ohio-based filmmaker Kasumi as "a psychedelic Dada/techno opera, is a scathing condemnation of the American government's quest for world domination." Web site: http://www.microcinema.com/programResult.php?program_id=%20188

Foucault Who? (2002): A film about the assorted couplings and sordid doings that go on at the local leatherbar on "Foucault Night." Web site: http://foucault.home.igc.org/

Game Plan (2003): A blue-collar riff on *Gaslight*, with a Baltimore mechanic slowly driving his schoolteacher wife to insanity in order to collect her substantial savings. Web site: http://www.traynorfilms.com

Harsh Light (2001): A washed-up boxer finds himself in the middle of a turf duel between a ruthless drug lord and an equally combative police detective. Web site: http://www.filmthreat.com/Reviews.asp?Id=2251

The Innocents (2001): In a small Indiana town in the early 1960s, a high school girl discovers a shocking secret about the life of one of her mother's friends that drastically alters her perceptions of race, gender, and the economic status quo. Web site: http://www.styopa.com

In the Wake (2001): A San Francisco sculptor emerges from a state of professional and personal inertia when she discovers and becomes inspired by the diary of a free-spirited turn-of-the-century actress. Web site: http://www.inthewake.com

The Last Kennedy (2003): The story of a murdered African-American political leader and presidential candidate and his daughter's attempt to confront the tragic events surrounding his death. Web site: http://www.thelastkennedy.com

Milwaukee, Minnesota (2002): A crime drama about the attempted exploitation of a young retarded man who has made a small fortune winning ice fishing contests. Cast includes Bruce Dern and Randy Quaid. Web site: http://www.filmthreat.com/Reviews.asp?Id=4352

Money Bound (2002): A bank robber hides his stolen funds but is apprehended by the police. He endures a brutal jail sentence, waiting patiently for the time to come when he can reclaim his hidden fortune. Web site: http://www.traynorfilms.com

No One Sleeps (2001): A German researcher in San Francisco investigates the conspiracy theory that AIDS was created by the American government and tested on prison inmates who took it out into the world. Web site: http://www.wolfevideo.com

Now Hiring (2002): A movie about the interesting, sometimes twisted, sometimes dangerous staff of a movie theater. Web site: http://www.filmthreat.com/Reviews.asp?Id=2801

Nutcracker (2001): The story of a prominent psychologist whose unorthodox methods and voracious sexual appetite cause a rift with his psychologist wife. A patient suffering from childhood trauma brings the doctor into a psychological battle. Web site: http://www.nutcracke rthrillermovie.com

The Placebo Effect (2000): A Russian cab driver gets mixed up with a squad of Chicago goons planning a political assassination. Web site: http://www.placeboeffectmovie.com

QIK2JDG (2002): Man relives the experiences of those who made their mark in a gas station's bathroom before making his own contribution. Web site: http://www.filmthreat.com/Reviews.asp?Id=4093

Rapid Eye Movement (2001): A nine-minute film featuring a guy wandering around busy streets and subways in a dreamlike state while his voice-over narration describes what it's like to have narcolepsy. Web site: http://www.filmthreat.com/Reviews.asp?File=ReviewsOne.inc&Id =2877

Researching Raymond Burke (2002): John Heard stars as deadbeat superstar Raymond Burke and the relationship between he and his 21-year old nephew Bradley after the death of Raymond's mother. Web site: http://www.filmthreat.com/Reviews.asp?Id=3848

Say I Do (2003): A soon-to-be married couple and their wedding party head out to a ranch in the middle of the desert and they become lost and stranded. Web site: http://www.sayidothemovie.com

Security (2003): A pair of security guards that work the graveyard shift at a candy factory, discover that prototype candy samples are being stolen from the factory during their shift. Taking their job way too seriously, the guards decide to form their own investigation, which ultimately leads them to a dead body. Web site: http://www.filmthreat.com/Reviews.asp?Id=4343

A Sense of Entitlement (2001): Mark L. Feinsod's short drama follows two self-absorbed New York half-sisters who find their vacuous world collapsing when their wealthy father goes broke. Web site: http://www.feinsodville.com

Shut Yer Dirty Little Mouth! (2002): Based on the play "Shut Up Little Man!", this film features the violent rantings and ravings of legendary alcoholics Peter and Raymond. Web site: http://www.shutyerdirtylittle mouth.com/flash.html

Steel Spirit (2001): Dallas McQuaid successfully disappears after a $5,000,000 bounty is placed on his head. Years later, his normal life as a car salesman is turned upside down when his identity is revealed. Web site: http://www.steelspirit.com/

They Only Come Out at Night (2002): A young woman named Honesty takes a job as a temporary employee in a blood collection center, altering her dreams, her marriage, and her future. Web site: http://www.klmltd.com/tocoan.html

Thirst (2003): Jessica Joy Wise's meditation about eating disorders, hunger, and desire, and their relation in regards to our need for identity and control. Web site: http://www.microcinema.com/programResult.p hp?program_id=162

30 Minutes or Less (2001): A short film following a pizza delivery person around the "hell hole" that is the Santa Clarita Valley of California. Web site: http://www.filmthreat.com/Reviews.asp?File=ReviewsOne.in c&Id=2843

Trade Day (2001): In a small Alabama town during World War II, an old man cannot bear to see his lethally injured Army hero son suffering in a local hospital — so he euthanizes his son and buries him in an isolated field. Web site: http://www.tradedaythemovie.com

Tumult (1997): An Ethiopian aristocratic family is thrown into disarray when one of its members is discovered to have participated in a failed 1960 coup against Emperor Haile Selaisse. This film was shot in

Southern California using a cast of non-professional Ethiopian expatri-ates. Web site: http://www.imdb.com/title/tt0177811/

Vakvagany (2002): An experimental feature film constructed from alleged archival home movie footage of a Hungarian family. Features author James Ellroy, filmmaker Stan Brakhage, and music by the Alloy Orchestra. Web site: http://www.vakvagany.com/

Walls of Sand (1994): An Iranian student, unhappy at the prospect of leaving California upon the expiration of her student visa, struggles to find work to gain a green card and lands a job as an au pair for a boy who is at the heart of a bitter custody dispute. Web site: http://www.filmthreat.com/Interviews.asp?Id=21

Warm Blooded Killers (2001): The story of a pair of San Fernando Valley suburban assassins-for-hire who are faced with the task of kill-ing an innocent man, or else being killed themselves. Web site: http://www.bloodbyte.com/

The Water Rope (2002): A young sailor's rudeness to an elderly woman comes back to haunt him (literally) when he meets a mysterious babe who wants to take him out to sea. Web site: http://www.filmthreat.com/Reviews.asp?Id=3739

Woman X (2001): A short film in the tradition of English crime movies about a misanthropic bank employee. Web site: http://www.filmthreat.com/Reviews.asp?Id=3624

INTERVIEW

ANTERO ALLI: UNDERGROUND REIGNS SUPREME

Unless you are a rabid devotee of underground cinema, there is a good chance that you are unfamiliar with Antero Alli. The Finnish-born, Berkeley-based artist concentrates on the creation of lower-budget vid-eofilms which have primarily been seen in alternative venues on the U.S. West Coast. While this obviously denies Alli the access to a wide national audience, it has brought him a devoted cult following among aficionados of underground cinema.

Alli's films are not for the easily distracted. His films are challenging and sometimes cryptic in their dissection of human emotions and societal interactions; repeated viewings, however, reveal layers of wisdom and wit that may not have been obvious in the initial screening.

Alli's versatility as a filmmaker is obvious in the range of films he's created. His documentary feature *Archaic Community* (1992) details a sociological/theatrical experiment in which a group of strangers are brought together via a series of exercises which trace the genesis of ritualistic behaviors. Another documentary feature, *Crux* (1999), uses a similar sociological/theatrical experiment to chart how the symbol of the crucifix weighs on the minds of individuals — not just as a religious symbol, but as a non-sectarian example of the crux of their basic existence. Alli's documentaries will be discussed at greater length later in the book.

But as the creator of dramatic films, Alli is truly in a class by himself. Alli's feature *The Drivetime* (1995), arguably his finest film to date, offers a wildly imaginative tale of a time-traveling librarian seeking to retrieve lost video footage, but the film is infused with undercurrents which focus on how a society obsessed with telecommunications technology is losing the ability to deal in a person-to-person manner. Shot in Seattle, the film culminates with a catastrophic riot that eerily predicted the chaos that enveloped the demonstrations against the 1999 World Trade Organization meetings in that city.

The short subjects *Requiem for a Friend* (1991) and *Lily in Limbo* (1996) focus on the pain of loss — the former visualizing Rilke's elegy to one who is dearly departed, the latter on a bitter artist who isolates herself from the world until she can no longer differentiate reality from fantasy. *Loaded Visions* (made from 1994 to the present) offers abstract and frequently disturbing images inspired by the poetry of such diverse writers as Arthur Rimbaud, Sylvia Plath, and astrologer Rob Breszny.

Alli's more recent features have limned the concept of isolation and how people find their place in a world that seemingly does not appreciate them and might not even welcome them. Religion plays a significant role in *Tragos* (2000), a thriller about the efforts to stamp out a cyber-cult, and in *Hysteria* (2002), which details how religious mania can be taken to horrible extremes when theological devotion warps into an advocacy of violence. The short film *Road Kill* (2001) finds two romantic unions (one between a married couple, one between casual lovers) hopelessly frayed when it becomes apparent the loving partners barely know each other. *Under the Shipwrecked Moon* (2003) visits the persistence of memory, both genuine and recreated, when a dying old man shuts off from the world around him and loses himself deeper into the comfort of his distant past.

Q. It's easy to list the obvious advantages and disadvantages of being an underground filmmaker — the joy of self-expression, the scramble to raise funds, et cetera. But what are the less-than-obvious advantages and disadvantages that you've encountered in your work... issues and concerns that you may not have considered before pursuing filmmaking?

ANTERO ALLI: Since I favor an impartial use of multiple media (film, video, animation, et cetera), I view myself more as a mediamaker than a filmmaker, per se. In my case, it's a relevant distinction, as well as a nod of respect to those working exclusively in film. The advantages to making my own media are both simple and severe. I either do it or die, or worse yet: numb down in that dismal, dreary, consumer sort of way. Sometimes I feel driven by a vengeance for forcing visions upon the world; visions and impressions that have been assaulting my sensibilities for a long time. Mediamaking suits this obsession very well and I think that's got to be the main advantage for me. The chief disadvantage, which may be a dare in disguise, is succumbing to any economic and cultural pressure to compromise your work (and how it's publicized) by conforming to externally defined values, categories, and genres. This clearly sucks. If you've been lucky enough to make this mistake in a way that really hurt you and if you are smart enough not to repeat the error, you can turn this disadvantage to your favor. The greater the disillusionment, the greater the clarity afterwards... the way of the world...

Q. Your films deal with some very troubling subjects — alienation, the breakdown in interpersonal communications, people pushed to emotional extremes. Yet your films are never heavy or depressing. How do you address these mature subjects without getting weighed down in Bergman-style doom and gloom?

ALLI: Probably because I'm not nearly that good yet. Bergman's a genius and he referred to Andrei Tarkovsky, one of my favorite film-makers, as a kind of teacher; if you've seen his work, you'll know why. The pacing, the texture, the editing, and the real time captured in each frame of Tarkovsky's films breathes with so much exquisite gloom it almost brings dying back into style. I die every time I see his epic, *Andrey Rublyov* or his last film, *The Sacrifice*. A kind of ego-death, if you will, that allows for a more fluid passage of real time, the time of my life, to unfold. My own personal style tends more towards the glib and the arch, no matter what the subject matter. I treat my themes as truth-fully as I can. And as I see it, the truth is serious enough as it is; why leaden it any more? This is a complex question due to what I believe to be the subjective nature of truth. What is worth filming or creating a movie about? What is worth saying that has not been said before in a more effective way? It's a humbling process, coming to terms with what and how to write, shoot, direct, and edit but that's how it should be. Otherwise, it may not be worth watching.

Q. You've made documentaries and dramas, features and shorts. Which genre do you prefer to work in... or do you prefer not being restricted to a single genre?

ALLI: This usually depends on what I need to learn next. For example, I might approach a documentary after completing a project that was, for me, a deeply creative and personal vision. There's this need to utterly immerse myself in my own world, as much as there's an equal need compelling me to be free of that world. Some projects are more iden-tity-defined, while others are more devotional to something other than myself. I go for that long-term kind of balance. I also choose projects based entirely on who I get to work with. I've also been known to sign up six months of my life for a new technical challenge, such as an oppor-tunity to edit on equipment I've never used before.

Q. You've created films based on the works of Neruda, Rilke, Plath — not really the traditional source of cinematic adaptations. What draws you to filming literary works which most filmmakers would not consider?

ALLI: Besides being a lover of great poetry, it's easy for me to think of cinema in poetic terms. I'm intrigued by the use of poetic text as oblique narrative. In my first feature, *The Oracle*, a grandfather character is on his deathbed and talking in his sleep. His daughter and the nurse sit there dumbfounded, as his words form these poetically precise questions (from Pablo Neruda's *Book of Questions*); cut to a Bardo-like afterlife scene where his nine year-old granddaughter guides him through the dark woods. With Rilke's *Requiem for a Friend*, the challenge was to narrate the epic lament as a story, not a poem. To keep it cinematic and theatrical, it's important to break down conventional ideas about poetry and how poems should be read and find instead, the story in the poem.

Q. Your films are primarily seen by audiences in alternative venues which specialize in smaller films, especially those shot on video. But when you consider the economics of film exhibition, do you believe these alternative venues and their eclectic fare can ultimately compete (from an economic, not an artistic standpoint) against the multiplexes?

ALLI: I don't think there is any real competition between these levels, especially if we're talking about work that aspires towards commerciality and respectability in that consensus mainstream Hollywood sort of way versus work with little or no commercial value whatsoever. Since my own work leans heavily towards the latter, I don't feel the heat of competition as much as the appreciation from those who seek out alternative media and the fringe-dweller values that define it. Besides, I dig the view from the outer limits, the margins.

Q. All filmmakers encounter negative criticism, and you have not been immune to critical rebuke. *The Drivetime* was dismissed by the (now defunct) *Amazing World of Cult Movies* as a "silly mess" and you were equated with being "a ninny." How do you react to harsh criticism, from both an artistic and an emotional standpoint?

ALLI: Though I often remind myself that any review is only one person's opinion, harsh reviews always hurt. What are you going to do? Stop reading all your reviews? That's just more self-stabbing victim bullshit. Why not pick up some objectivity and identify the bias of the reviewer just to see where they are coming from? Just for fun. When I do this, it's understandable why the *Amazing World of Cult Movies* calls me a "ninny" and my movie a "silly mess." That's very funny. If I were as cynical and jaded as them, I'd probably say the same thing. To confound things, *The Drivetime* was also given glowing reviews by *Wired Magazine*, the Pacific Film Archive and the Northwest Film Forum and these guys didn't even call me names. Of course, their bias and outlook are, for the better part, already more aligned with my own. And I like that. If they had trashed my movie, I'd probably feel more hurt than the cynic who called me a ninny.

For me, the best reviews are instructive and these are very, very rare. Most film critics have seen too many movies and suffer imagination loss, in addition to having weakened their critical judgement for constructive praise. That's a mouthful. The worst reviews must be the most indifferent reviews and, knock on wood, I've not seen one for my work yet.

Q. Critics can elevate a smaller film to unexpected success, but they can also eviscerate a film into financial failure. As a filmmaker, how do you view the power of the critics?

ALLI: Of course, critics can make or break a show in terms of sheer audience attendance; that's their godawful power and responsibility. As for myself, I usually go see those films that have elicited at least two opposing reactions from different newspapers. Why? The best work always confounds genres. It outgrows previous genres while mutating its own. Unless critics are still capable of creative thought, they will tend to pan a movie they cannot pigeonhole and, often enough, to justify their own pet dogmas. In my own mind, critics only have the power I give them and from my ranting, you know that's not very much. In the real world, however, critics are media gods blessing and cursing the fates of filmmakers everywhere.

Q. What advice would you give to aspiring filmmakers and aspiring film critics?

ALLI: I have no advice at all for aspiring filmmakers but heartfelt discouragement. If you cannot or will not throw yourself into this crazy-making process with all your will, heart, guts, mind, soul, and money, then you will never know what it means to realize your dreams in this medium. This medium does not treat half-baked attempts kindly. Most movies demonstrate this in living Technicolor. Here's a warning for you: I go a little more crazy with each and every project but it is going crazy in the name of creation, not destruction. And that kind of crazy I can live with, and live for. As for critics, there may be no hope unless you find ways to teach us as you criticize. You may be able to do this if you commit to learn new ways to keep learning. Know your bias. It always shows, anyway, and you suffer less when you are not the last to know.

2: Frantic Antics

One of the least amusing incidents I ever experienced was the result of an underground comedy movie. Actually, it was called *The Underground Comedy Movie* and it was a feature length version of a Los Angeles public access television program consisting of gross-out skits and vulgar sight gags. I was hired to do the publicity for the film's New York theatrical premiere and I coordinated a press screening for the local critics.

To say you could hear a pin drop during the 90 minutes of the press screening would be trite. You could actually hear the critics seething in their chairs while the screen filled with sequence after sequence of nasty, puerile, and hopelessly off-centered humor that barely coaxed a giggle or harrumph from the audience. Seated in the back of the screening room, I was beneath the projectionist's window and the clickety-clack of the projector unspooling this celluloid debacle chilled my senses.

Following the presentation, the critics who emerged from the screening room all glared at me with a fury and contempt which I've never witnessed before or since. A more hated man could not have existed anywhere else at that moment. My one line of defense was passing the buck. "Please!" I cried. "I didn't make the film! I'm only promoting it!"

Within underground cinema, comedy is the most difficult genre to experience. For a variety of reasons which we will shortly consider, too many underground comedy films don't work. Many of the films are vulgar, shrill, immature, mean-spirited, and vituperative in their concept of what constitutes a humorous situation. This is painfully ironic, given that the purpose of comedy is to bring pleasure and laughter to a world which is constantly lacking in both elements — and when a film designed to bring pleasure and laughter offers neither, something is dreadfully wrong.

But let's not blame underground filmmakers as being the sole culprits for the lack of movie mirth. *Time* magazine's esteemed critic Richard Schickel, in his recent biography on the films of Woody Allen, paused to reflect on the state of the Hollywood comedy film with this rather bold statement: "Comedy in America is now either crass and aimed at an essentially juvenile audience, or it is weary and strained in the way that romantic comedy aimed at an older crowd — *You've Got Mail, Maid in Manhattan, Two Weeks Notice* — has been for many years. If one sees a comedy that is seriously funny about, say, domestic disturbances, it is likely to be French. Certainly it will have subtitles."

On the surface, these comments seem fairly snobbish and elitist — and for anyone who views the French with alarm or contempt, Schickel could also be considered as borderline seditious. Yet, truth be told, the celluloid fun factory seems to have broken down terribly.

Jaime N. Christley, the editor of *Film Written* magazine, has a fairly sophisticated diagnosis for the less-than-jolly state of film comedy: "I don't know how to explain the lack of good comedy in contemporary films. Maybe there isn't one — that is, the drought may not be any worse than it has always been. (Who remembers the horrible, flat, and no-reputation comedies of the 1920s and '30s? Name three.) I do know that comedy can be made from many things — it doesn't have to be strictly verbal, or visual, or character-based. Jacques Tati made my favorite comedy, *Playtime*, and many of his jokes are about architecture and sound! There's very little that's verbal or character-based in a Tati film. Good comedy makes us laugh. But great comedy involves us and operates on us in a manner not unlike a complex symphonic arrangement."

Even more troubling is the state of comedy beyond the Hollywood orbit. While the major studios have the financial ability to stage elaborate chases and special effect sequences or to hire scores of gagmen to yuck up a screenplay, the micro-budget underground film world has to rely on the basic roots of comedy: the ability to make people laugh. Often the roots are growing in stony soil, providing a poor foundation for the film that often withers before reaching full bloom.

"I get the impression that contemporary indie comedies are so desperate to be hip that trying to develop a comic sensibility, or using what they might already have, probably doesn't occur to too many filmmakers or actors," says Christley. "Maybe the talent is there, but it remains untapped. Another possibility is that good comedy has always been hard to find. Look at Olivier's Archie Rice in *The Entertainer*. Back in the vaudeville days, guys on that level of mediocrity must have been pretty hard to escape."

Robert Firsching, former editor of the *Amazing World of Cult Movies* online magazine, provides another approach to the subject. "I would have to agree that most underground comedies are not very funny," he says. "Those which do elicit laughs from an audience are usually provoking shock-laughter more than displaying real wit. The grand majority of them fall prey to the same problems as a comedienne I saw recently who was doing a stand-up routine about her family's drinking. The subject itself can certainly be played for laughs, as Eddie Murphy showed in his 'Barbecue' routine, but this woman was too close to her subject and was displaying so much anger and pain that the routine was not only not funny, but genuinely uncomfortable to sit through. I think that the pointed, emotional material which is the stock in trade of underground comedy requires a certain distance from the subject on the part of the artist in the work. In comedy, much more than in straight drama, I have to be able to relate to something in the work that makes me laugh. For whatever reason, most underground filmmakers seem to be so intent on being earnestly personal, genuine, and true to life that they fail to get a comic perspective. What we get instead are quirky or outrageous situations presented at face value rather than in some way that would touch a chord in someone other than the filmmaker."

We could travel endlessly down this route by finding fault with underground comedy, but let's stop here to consider that not all underground comedies are flops. Indeed, many talented filmmakers have been able find a distinct comic style. Rather than spend the chapter bemoaning the overall lack of good comedy in underground filmmaking, let's put on our miner's caps and dig out the rare gems that are shining within the muck.

Did You Hear About the Two Critics Who Made Movies?

Film critics, who are subjected to umpteen comedies during the course of their reviewing duties, inevitably get an idea of what constitutes an original and entertaining comedy and what offers groans instead of laughs.

Two of the most promising comedy filmmakers are critics who have stepped out of the screening room and on to the sound stages: Bilge Ebiri of *New York* magazine and Jeremiah Kipp of *FilmCritic.com* have crafted some of the most fascinating and satisfying underground comedies of recent vintage.

Ebiri's *New Guy* (2003) is a feature about a young white-collar professional's first day on his new job in an office environment which seems to have been created by the combined input of Jacques Tati, H. P. Lovecraft, and Tex Avery. The new guy of *New Guy* is Gregg (played by newcomer Kelly Miller), a polite but nervous young man who views his surrounding with wide-eyed curiosity and apprehension. He is clearly in a situation, which he cannot imagine or comprehend: his cubicle is covered in yellow Post-It notes and apparently belonged to a worker who went off into the homicidal deep end. His co-workers are an equally weird bunch: an angry mess of a man who hogs the fax machine, two women who discuss their respective sex lives for all to hear, a fellow worker at a neighboring cubicle whose entire day is spent on the phone with a girlfriend, men who watch some hanky-panky at an office across the street via binoculars, a boss who allows his son to run a monster toy car around the office, and a hostile janitor who curses feverishly in Spanish. Even more frustrating are his attempts to get in touch with a woman he is supposed to take out on a date: the phone tag becomes almost Olympian in its dimensions and length.

Ebiri paces his film at a slow but steady level that allows the comic dementia to build at a leisurely pace. His camera is usually just a little off-center and tilted, perfectly reflecting the slightly-out-of-whack corporate world where Gregg finds himself trapped — and during the second part of the film, he is literally trapped alone in the office when he is the last worker to leave but cannot get the front door mechanism to open for him. Or is he alone? This leads to an extended adventure that brings *New Guy* down unexpected dark corners with Gregg turning homicidal by using a jagged coffee pot as his weapon of choice. Initially this section of the film sometimes feels like it belongs in another movie, but by the end of the picture it all falls together quite nicely.

"The unique thing about comedy is that, even though there have been plenty of great comedy writers and great comedy directors, it's probably the most performance-oriented of the main cinematic genres," says Ebiri. "When we think of comedy, we think of actors — be they silent greats like Chaplin or Keaton or Lloyd, or more contemporary ones like the *Saturday Night Live* folks like Adam Sandler or Will Ferrell. So it's hard to write comedy without writing it *for* somebody. That's also why there are so many instances of great collaboration throughout comedy history — be it sketch shows like SNL and The Kids in the Hall or classic troupes like the Marx Brothers, or duos like Laurel and Hardy, and so on and so forth. You don't see 'thriller troupes' or 'improv tragedy' (although, come to think of it, that's kind of a neat idea; I should copyright that)."

"Comedy," Ebiri continues, "more than anything, is generated by the energy of performance. So it was, on some level, really frustrating to write a comedy script — because when you're working at this zero-budget obscure filmmaker level, it's not like you're going to have your choice of great comedy actors to write for; you don't really know what you're going to get. But on another level, it's liberating — precisely because you don't know who you're going to get. You can play make believe. Somebody asked me, if I could choose anybody from film history, whom would I want to play the main character in my film. I replied, 'A young Jack Lemmon.' Lo and behold, that day I got a head-shot for this young, total unknown named Kelly Miller, who had done no film work, and in the picture, he looked exactly like a young Jack Lemmon. It turns out Kelly in real life doesn't really look anything like

Jack Lemmon, but that was what struck me about his headshot at first. And I auditioned many, many people for the part — but in the end, Kelly got the part, and gave an amazing performance that has knocked the socks off just about anybody who has seen the film."

Ebiri has come to appreciate the challenges that arise from writing comedy and bringing it to life for the camera. "Making comedy on paper work on-screen is one of the hardest things in the world," he says. "I mean, just the fact that you're dealing with the physical world, with actualities and tactile objects, changes the nature of what you're doing. A certain composition turns out to not work in the way you expected it to; a certain line uttered after a different line reads funny on paper but falls flat on screen. It happens all the time. Then again, certain things turn out to be funny that you hadn't even noticed before. This is also why comedy is such a collaborative medium. We had a number of shots where Kelly had to lean his face against a glass door. When he did it, it turned out that the glass door contorted his face and eyebrows in all sorts of different directions, resulting in some pretty hilarious moments. It was the silliest little thing, but it worked, and it was a nice touch. You need the people around you to create situations that generate comedy, and you need to be able to recognize it when it comes.

"Another thing I noticed was how much this sort of thing changed during editing. It's a lot like music. You take funny moments in the footage and put it together, and suddenly, it's not that funny anymore; and you have to play with the timing, to see if you can make it work again, or make it work differently. Or you put two shots together that weren't meant to be funny, but suddenly, the combination is funny, That happened a lot to me and my editor Cabot Philbrick. We'd just throw a shot in there and suddenly, we'd have this beautiful comic editing gag that we'd never intended to have in there. Happy accidents. I've often said that filmmaking is the art of making the right mistakes."

If Ebiri sees filmmaking as "making the right mistakes," then people making the wrong mistakes has been the darkly comic focus of the films by Jeremiah Kipp. His 13-minute *Snapshot*, for which he won the Best Director Award in the 48 Hour Film Festival (literally, a challenge to make a film in two days from scratch), provides some serious risk-taking in a truly comic environment.

Snapshot focuses on Cathy and Chris, young New Yorkers whose marriage has suddenly grown stale. Cathy turns for comfort (emotional, then physical) to her half-brother Stan; they explain away the incestuous stigma by blithely stating their actions are only "half-bad" since Stan is her half-brother. Chris winds up in search of understanding from his friend Magnus. Their relationship gets physical also and the men calmly define themselves as being lovers but not being gay. Yet Magnus also has the hots for Cathy. So where can this romantic quadrangle lead?

For a film that was literally cobbled together without serious preparation, *Snapshot* is a remarkably smooth venture with a distinct personality and sophisticated style. The joy of *Snapshot* is its refusal to explain or analyze why the characters are doing what they are doing. The Cathy-Stan relationship, clearly the ickiest of sticky wickets, is stated in a positive and unapologetic manner. The characters not only know the nature of the relationship has societal problems, but they actually enjoy stepping on the taboo. Likewise, the bisexual Magnus and Chris are blithe in dismissing their mano-a-mano actions. To them, their relationship is a typically normal buddy kinship with nothing (pardon the expression) queer around its edges or within its core. When all four characters decide to merge into a romantic foursome, the film seems more like it belongs in Paris than New York (is Richard Schickel listening?); rarely does an independent American production have such an airy and uncomplicated vision of sexuality.

Kipp did not write *Snapshot* (that honor went to Suzanne Bachner), but he was taken by the script upon first reading it. "When I read it, I found the premise to be quite daring," he says. "It's about a quartet of unhappy people who find temporary relief by drawing together into a romantic foursome. I knew that the moment when the four characters decide to sleep together was comical because it's uncomfortable — and instead of trying to goose up the humor, make it wacky, we played it straight. The actors reacted naturally, in character, and believably. By not trying to make it funny, we had characters taking an absurd situation very seriously. As an audience member, we watch it and recognize something in ourselves that is ridiculous. That's very personal, and the funny bone is a very personal part of us. Jack Lemmon said: 'Comedy is a serious business!'

"Upon my initial reading of the script, my greatest concern was that the characters not be played as grotesques. One of the first lines in the script is a character proclaiming that he's been fucking his sister on and off since he was a child — but they justify it by proclaiming that she's only his half-sister, so it's only half-as-bad. That line cracked me up, but if we pushed it as a funny line it would probably have felt leering and grotesque. Again, the actors and I stressed the idea of 'keeping it real.' I wasn't sure the movie would be funny, since I treated it like a tragedy while working with the cast. Ultimately, we're dealing with painful stuff. The relationship doesn't work out and the characters so desperately want to hang on to it. ('I've never felt so loved,' one of them opines. 'I don't want it to end!') By emphasizing their desperation, trying to hang on to this thing, I felt there was a bit of pain to go along with their antics during the montage (popping the champagne, walking through the park all linked together arm-in-arm). I'm pleased that audiences laugh at the film when we screen *Snapshot*. But we weren't going for overt slapstick or satire or even dazzling wit. I think they laugh because of the situation being a ridiculous and strange one, and that it's presented warts and all, without judgment. Because the situation is so odd, people react nervously and laugh at these poor, hapless souls trying to hold on to something. I know Suzanne Bachner was responding indirectly to 9/11, and the shellshock that so many of our friends were going through. But rather than make a movie about a tragedy that touched all our lives, we preferred to gently laugh at ourselves, and our times of confusion. And laughter can be a soothing balm in times of crisis."

Kipp's next film was *The Christmas Party* and it is even more daring by holding religion up to the light and finding it lacking — albeit in a subtle but amusing way. In this film, a young boy named Gabriel lives with his grandparents because his alcoholic mother is unable to properly care for him. To liven the boy's spirits, the grandparents arrange for him to be dropped off at a children's Christmas party hosted by a local minister and his wife. At this party, however, the holy duo decide to put the "Christ" back into Christmas and arrange for Gabriel to be "saved." The boy, who is none too certain just what is going on, agrees to go along with this and is rewarded for his efforts with extra chocolate cake and a pretty paper angel made by a girl at the party. But on

Kelly Miller uses a coffee pot for homicidal purposes in Bilge Ebiri's *New Guy.*

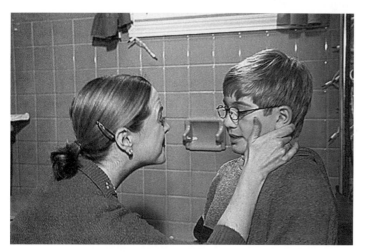

Renee Heitman as the preacher's wife who gives a bathroom sermon to Austin Labbe as the vulnerable child in Jeremiah Kipp's *The Christmas Party.*

Philip Guerette and Thomas Edward Seymour are up to no good in the Hale Manor production *Everything Moves Alone.*

the ride home, Gabriel's grandfather glumly informs the lad that God is in the same category as Santa Claus and the Easter Bunny — pleasant fairy tales with no connection to real life. Gabriel, who was riding with the paper angel in his hands, drops it into the darkness of the car floor as the vehicle speeds off in the night.

The Christmas Party is not a laugh-out-loud comedy, obviously, but it serves well as a dark satire of manners and morality. Everything here is a touch off-base: the mother's telephone conversation with Gabriel in which she swears her love while balancing a full wine glass, the "I Saw the Light" melodrama of the minister's wife leading Gabriel in prayer on the bathroom floor, the unctuous manner in which the minister explains the miracle of the Nativity with a tad excess of condescension to his audience of children, and the grandfather's unexpected shedding of his folksy Norman Rockwell demeanor to expose a sour atheistic core that unapologetically deflates whatever religious connection Gabriel may have experienced and enjoyed.

Okay, anyone expecting a Christmas film laced with sentiment and sweetness will get a cold shock here. Yet *The Christmas Party*, with its enigmatic characters and sense of foreboding (especially when the melodramatic minister's wife preaches to Gabriel on the bathroom floor), is both creepy and challenging. Insincerity rings throughout the film: the child's seemingly insincere acceptance of Christianity, his mother's false claims of devotion while balancing an overfilled wine glass, even the minister's surprisingly less-than-enthused oration on Jesus' birth gives the impression of a world where it is easier to play along than take a genuine stand. The grandfather's seemingly callous declaration of God being a fairy tale should be wildly out of place, given this is a Christmas film, but at the very least it is the one honest statement made in the film.

The strength of Kipp's films are the unusually solid story foundations, and that is not a happy accident. "Most filmmakers have lost touch with the basics of storytelling," decries Kipp. "Comedy is about situations we can relate to that are often ridiculous or absurd. It's delicate stuff, and absolutely depends on presentation, style, craft, and timing. Whether you're dealing with the highbrow comedy of witty banter or the low-brow of physical slapstick, it all depends on the performer or filmmaker knowing how to visually sell the gag or the pacing of the one-liners. Romantic comedies have lost sight of what makes up the physicalness of romance. We often don't buy that the characters actually belong together, or that the actors possess any chemistry. Black comedies and farce have been done in by political correctness, when comedy never should be played as safe or easy. Nothing kills humor faster!"

Why does Kipp feel it so difficult for filmmakers nowadays to make a genuinely funny comedy?

"Part of it may have to do with laziness," he says. "Filmmakers just don't seem to push the envelope very much nowadays. Whatever happened to the gusto of Donald O'Connor during his song 'Make 'em Laugh' in *Singin' in the Rain* — an artistic credo towards entertaining your audience by any means necessary? Many gags have become rote, or cliché. Take that time-honored gag we've seen a million times: kicking somebody in the nuts (or whatever variation you want — a dog biting someone in the nuts, a golf club to the nuts, etc.). It happens so often all the life has been drained out of it. Ditto the 'old person busting a rhyme' gag, where grandma smokes a joint and launches into a spontaneous rap. Filmmakers slap on these gags without forethought."

Kipp adds that *Saturday Night Live* is also responsible for the overall dismal state of comedy. "They are one of the worst offenders, because they aren't creating gags or set pieces anymore (in the show or its spin-off movies)," he comments. "They're creating familiar characters who recite the same familiar lines every week. Or, even worse, they attempt to cook up one-joke skits that go on for five minutes too long when they could easily be summed up in 30 seconds — the running time of your standard TV commercial."

THE HALE MANOR METHOD

Three of the brightest young comedy filmmakers have the good fortune of not only being the best of friends, but also harmonious partners in cinematic endeavors. Thomas Edward Seymour, Philip Guerette, and Mike Aransky make up Hale Manor Productions, a Connecticut-based indie outfit designed to bring their versatile sense of humor to the screen.

The Hale Manor trio began their filmmaking efforts in high school with a series of short films that, admittedly, brought more amusement to the threesome than to anyone they could corral as an audience. Realizing they needed to be a bit more serious if they wanted to film comedy, they concentrated on a wonderfully loopy take-off on direct-to-video B-flicks called *Thrill Kill Jack in Hale Manor*, which they completed in 1999 after a year's worth of weekend shooting and postproduction.

Thrill Kill Jack in Hale Manor stirs in all of the wonderfully inane clichés and tricks of the B-genre and serves up a happily hyperactive kick. The title character is a mystical, monosyllabic tough guy entrusted with a powerful hand-made gun crafted around a magical ancient Indian arrowhead. The gun is stolen by Hale, a grandiloquent wizard who runs a freakish mini-empire in a mansion populated by gimps and creeps. Thrill Kill Jack scales the mansion's walls and finds himself going room to room in search of his weapon, encountering endless threats on his life and sanity behind each new door.

Produced on the barest of shoestring budgets, *Thrill Kill Jack in Hale Manor* nonetheless offers witty and wise tributes to adrenaline-inducers such as Roger Corman, Larry Buchanan, John Woo, and even Hitchcock. The film speeds with the required nervous camerawork, outlandish sound effects, and staccato editing one expects from the genre, and the inanity of action never ceases. Vats of acid, drill guns, chained-up prisoners, flashing lights, deadly lasers, and wild chase scenes populate the film, all used with the appropriate amount of good humor that gently mocks the thrill-kill conventions of this school of filmmaking.

As Thrill Kill Jack, slender Philip Guerette lacks the muscular bulk one associates with B-Movie action stars like Dolph Lundgren or Brian Bosworth, but he offers the right touch of stoic indifference to his hostile surroundings with occasional surprises such as a whimper when a weapon is slapped from his hand or an Oliver Hardy-style slow burn when a bucket of water falls on his head after he pushes through an open door. Thomas Edward Seymour camps it up in the best Vincent Price style as the nefarious Hale, clearly enjoying his miscreancy the way a glutton enjoys a steak. Mike Aransky shows up in a supporting role as a weird gimp determined to wrestle Thrill Kill Jack into submission despite a complete lack of athletic ability.

For such a wealth of imagination, *Thrill Kill Jack in Hale Manor* was shockingly cheap to create. "The film only cost about $700 to make," admits Seymour. "We shot it on a Hi-8 that we had and did the editing on a crappy PC. The real cost of the film was video tape and renting a Beta deck to make our masters on."

Despite its threadbare roots, *Thrill Kill Jack in Hale Manor* gained screenings in several film festivals and positive reviews in cult movie sites including *Hollywood is Burning* and *Undergroundfilms.com*. It also appeared on the Independent Film Channel's *Split Screen* during that program's coverage of the annual Fangoria horror gathering. A commercial home video release was almost inked but the intended distributor abruptly went out of business; Hale Manor subsequently handled the video release itself and the film has since made a $100 profit.

Buoyed by their experience, the Hale Manor trio aimed higher and deeper with their next feature. Their budget was a mere $9,000 (inexpensive even by underground standards, but a monumental leap from their first effort) and the video production equipment was replaced with 16mm cameras. The resulting film, *Everything Moves Alone*, was almost everything *Thrill Kill Jack in Hale Manor* was not — polished, mature, sensitive, character-driven — but it also shared one attribute with the earlier feature: it was great fun.

Everything Moves Alone opens in a sleepy New England town where Scotch (Guerette), a recently discharged soldier, arrives at a bus depot with the vague plan of crashing with his long-estranged older brother. Scotch spies a creepy yet interesting character stealing luggage (Seymour), who then offers Scotch a ride into town if he will assist in dropping dirt and a frog-shaped flower pot into another man's car. Scotch, who is clearly several cards short of a full deck, complies and immediately earns the wrath of the car's owner, McDunley (Matt Ford, in a wildly funny performance). McDunley is a bearish sourpuss who runs the local video store and who has a mysterious long-running feud with Anderson, the luggage-thief who quickly becomes Scotch's new best friend.

Scotch's brother (Aransky) is a hostile weirdo who puts numerical tags on each item of food and harbors an unnatural fan devotion for videos starring the Olsen Twins (this was when the girls were still very much underage, and mercifully the film doesn't explore that angle too deeply). The siblings barely tolerate each other but stay under the same roof, inevitably ironing out the kinks in their relationship. Scotch and Anderson spend a great deal of time together in rambling conversations ranging from the mystery of women to the pointlessness of fishing. The duo take breaks in their palaver to direct harmless yet annoying mischief at the ill-tempered McDunley, who takes to chasing Scotch with a baseball bat. Scotch and Anderson also try their hand with the ladies. Scotch finds himself on a disastrous date with a cutie who harbors a bizarre anti-Semitic mindframe while Anderson eventually finds a connection with a waitress who keeps him hydrated with an endless supply of orange juice and Coca-Cola at his favorite diner. Eventually, the root of the Anderson-McDunley feud is unearthed and all warring parties find a common ground on which to build a new future.

For relatively tiny films, the Hale Manor casts are surprisingly large and no one (even the smallest of bit players) is on-screen without some connection to the story. "The comedy I like almost always involves actors playing off other actors," says Seymour. "I believe the best kind of comedy is not self aware. I always thought people like the Coen Brothers and Monty Python were in a way the future of comedy. At times they are very subtle but not afraid to stoop to dick and fart jokes. Though I think especially in the case of the Coen brothers films, their characters are almost never in on the joke. Much like a comic who laughs too much at his own routine, I believe that putting too much emphasis on comedy or obviousness of a punch line ruins comedy."

But creating comedy is not the funniest course of action to pursue. "Sometimes the jokes I thought would be the funniest in my film were awful," continues Seymour. "So we cut them out. I believe you can never be afraid to cut out what is most precious to you. For filmmakers it's hard to "Kill the baby," a phrase my fellow filmmaker and friend Mike Mongillo (*The Wind*) uses. Meaning it may be the best thing you ever wrote but if it doesn't work on film it needs to go. It's hard to see clearly by yourself so luckily my partners Mike Aransky and Phil Guerette are there to filter out the crap.

"The scripts come very slow. I write down ideas on scraps of paper until I get a few hundred or so of them and all the while I try to piece together the plot in my head. Then I write over about a six month period until I get a first draft. I show it to Mike and Phil. Mostly they concentrate on what they don't like about it. I have five or so other people look over it. I leave it alone for a month. Then I tear it apart and re-write it over and over. I've done five drafts of my last script and we will still tweak it during rehearsal. Ultimately Phil and Mike decide what's not funny in scripts, they however have input as well. What ruins comedy are bad jokes, lines, or skits. So they're good editors in that sense. We do have an equal share in what stays and goes but since I create nearly all of it I guess you could say I determine what the script will be and they determine what it won't be. We're all pretty reasonable though."

The latest Hale Manor offering takes on a fantasy element as a plotline and a much more mature tone in character. *The Land of College Prophets* finds Seymour and Guerette as a roughneck duo whose inability to pass up a good fight creates endless problems. One day their brawling goes too far and they somehow reactivate a dormant well that begins to pump toxic water that brings a reign of violence to their community. The comedy is darker than the previous Hale Manor efforts, with more sarcasm and even elements of sadistic humor, particularly in a sequence when Seymour's character (who is employed in a college audio-visual lab) is intentionally hostile to an excessively polite professor who is totally unaware he is being treated with a rude attitude.

"It's a bunch of mystical elements, mixed with violence, mixed with comedy, mixed with sci-fi, mixed with drama, mixed with horror with an 'independent' heart," says Seymour. "It's a great big untraditional comic book. If anything it will be noticed no matter what happens. Not everyone will like it but I'm sure it will have a loyal following and that's my goal. Hey, I'm not trying to make *Pretty Woman* here! I believe in making comedy accessible to some but not all. When you try to get too wide of an audience you're compromising your message. It's a lot like politics: if you don't take a stand in your writing or your beliefs people will think you're full of shit. I'd rather have 700,000 loyal fans than an audience of five million who will forget my film next week."

One new loyal fan to the Hale Manor school is actor Eric Russell (*Cherry Falls, The Contender*), who plays an English professor in *The Land of College Prophets*. Russell's character is transformed in the course of the story after the brawling protagonists bring the toxic wishing well to life, setting off a chain of events in which they realize the world has been broken. Russell details the distinct sense of humor that laces this new production as it relates to his character.

"When we first meet my character Professor Gray, he is lecturing to the class in a very professional straightforward tone," says Russell. "He takes his class very serious and does not take kindly to being mocked by his students, especially by the ones he feels have talent and ability. Gray really likes the boys (played by Seymour and Guerette) and is disappointed that they don't live up to their potential. He punishes them when they curse in class by making them pay fines to his 'potty mouth' jar, but in a very fatherly manner. Then sends them on their way; most teachers would have just kicked them out for disrupting the class. When the boys return to the classroom after they have 'broken the world' they find that their professor, who was very well-grounded, is now not so grounded. He is going on and on very intensely about writing, as if it was a form of religion. On the set the day of the shooting, Seymour and Guerette told me they really wanted this to be a very over-the-top presentation, like fundamentalist preacher — you know, very fire and brimstone and 15-piece back-up band. Okay, so where do I find a character like that? Fortunately I live in Virginia, where the Tabernacle Channel is on all-basic cable, so I had an idea of how Gray might deliver his 'you need writing or you will go to hell' class lecture that day. I felt a little silly at first, especially since I had not seen that part of the script till I got to the set (the script changed on me without notice). So — thank you Fort Lee Theater Company for those improv sessions — I just had Professor Gray let his hair down and let loose. When Gray stops his lecture to speak with the boys and they apologize for breaking the world, Gray is now more Donna Reed/Fred Rogers. When Seymour goes: 'I kinda messed up my writing hand' (which is now a bloody stump with a tin can on it) Gray responds in a 'that's nice dear and wait till your father get home' attitude. A real switch from fire and brimstone. But Gray does not see the boys as having changed — he sees them as kids and not two young adults who are trying to save the world. He even makes them pay a fine again and scolds them like a mother hen for cursing. But when Gray is given a letter from them apologizing for breaking the world, he reverts back to normal. He understands what has happened and he gains a small sense of pride in what they've done!"

From LDS to LSD

Washington-area filmmaker Jamil Said made an extraordinary splash with his 2002 debut, the short comedy *Byromania*. The film took fairly tasteless concepts, including a crazed fortune teller trying to open a serial killer-inspired amusement park and a group of Mormon missionaries seduced by a transvestite prostitute, and exploded it into a bold, harsh, breathlessly effective satire of morality and evil.

"I was rarely worried about offending people, but I was consumed with the fear that no one would laugh," says Said. "I figured if someone was offended by something in the movie, they could leave or turn it off. It's very simple. Viewers too often disapprove of a piece because it does not abide by their own morality. A primary influence for *Byromania* was early 'offensive' John Waters movies, especially the use of the drag queen. In fact, the drag queen's deception/seduction of the Mormons was based on real events so sometimes reality pushes the limits of good taste!"

The *Byromania* subplot with the Mormon missionaries concludes when one of the young men, after unknowingly ingesting LSD, is confronted by Byron dressed as Jesus. But rather than the Jesus of love and compassion, this is an angry and wrathful Christ. This segment came to the film by way of Said's personal experiences with missionaries.

"My entire life, from Miami to Jerusalem and Baltimore to Cairo, people have been trying to convert me to either non-denominational Christianity or to the Church of the Latter Day Saints," he notes. "I consider attempts at converting the unwilling to be the most violent form of non-physical rape. Many religious missionaries are cunning because they know how to approach you, take advantage of your current psychology, and make you feel comfortable with them before they lower the hatch. The victims most often tell the missionary flat out they are not interested in converting, but the missionary never stops and pursues until the very end. On the surface, I was poking fun at these people in *Byromania*, but deep down I was trying to blast them out of the water — which is an action these people would consider "typical" of a lost soul. Apart from my personal feelings, one of the reasons I used these aspects of religion was because they are the antithesis of what Byron believes, thus establishing the villain of the movie. Byron calls the missionaries 'killjoys' because he believes that everybody should be happy and entertained. He feels missionaries take away that happiness because they essentially tell you that your life and your beliefs are incorrect and you will be punished in the afterlife if you don't join their team. Although organized religion is most often very comforting to believers, it tends to separate barely different people which is unfortunate. Byron wants 'everybody' to come to his serial killer theme park to have a good time.

"The executive producer of *Byromania*, Jesse Lovell, was worried that Mormons who saw the movie would be offended. He stopped me from sending an advertisement for the first screening to a large Mormon temple in Washington, D.C. I was looking forward to seeing a line of boys with their book bags scurrying down the aisle and back up ten minutes into the movie. The subplot of the Mormons being seduced by the drag queen is actually a combination of three real stories my friends told me about so their use in the movie is also based on fact. I considered Mormons the safest target just because other people have criticized them in the past on women's rights, most people know who they are, and plenty of the civilized world have been victims of their conversion attempts.

"Some people have misunderstood the Angry Jesus who swears at and kills one of the missionaries. They tell me it is blasphemy. However, it is the opposite because that which the Angry Jesus accuses the missionary is what the real Jesus was promoting: love and acceptance of others different than yourself, and selflessness as demonstrated when Angry Jesus says '(people) don't want to be defiled by your arrogance.' And there lies the irony in the accusation. I was very aware of this irony when I wrote it in the script and I knew that people would accuse me of this and I was laughing inside because I knew that *they* were the ones actually misunderstanding the real tenets of Christianity. Seeing an angry Jesus is probably a missionary's worst nightmare, especially when unknowingly tripping on LSD. Jesus is the person the missionary is supposedly promoting and is fully dedicated to so for him to turn on the missionary is absolutely terrifying. Jesus represents the very existence of a missionary, his reason for living, his life's work, his identity. It is ironic that the personification of Jesus kills the missionary with the very tool (his guitar) he uses to spread the word of Jesus! The missionary's identity is killing him, a forced suicide in a way. What is more frightening than that?"

Reaction to *Byromania* has been often funnier than the film itself. "A few people, after seeing the movie, were actually scared of me because they thought I really was Byron, the psychotic murderer who wants to create a serial killer theme park and is willing to kill people to do it," recalls Said. "Some positive responses were accidental. There was a screening of a few movies set up at a nightclub in Washington, D.C. by local filmmakers. I brought what I thought was a videocassette copy of *Byromania*, but when the projectionist pressed Play, an episode of *Little House on the Prairie* came on the screen. I had to run home and bring back a real copy. People thought this mix-up was intentional and told me I was Dadaist. I said: 'What's a Dadaist?' I am also hearing about positive responses through the grapevine. I have been recently informed that a group of girls in D.C. (who I don't know) get together every week, smoke up, and watch *Byromania*. This makes me so happy because I always wanted *Byromania* to become a cult film. If I hear that people start timing the movie to Pink Floyd's 'Dark Side of the Moon' while tripping on LSD, that would be an even greater compliment."

WHISTLIN' DIXIE

Further south on the movie map (in North Carolina, to be precise) is Dorne Pentes, who may be among the finest filmmakers in need of major recognition. His 1992 short *Confessions of a Southern Punk* was named to the Top 25 Underground Films of All Time list by the *Film Threat Video Guide*, and his 1996 *The Closest Thing to Heaven* was championed as one of *Film Threat*'s "Ten Best Films of the 1990s Which You Never Saw." His films have won awards and applause on the festival circuit, albeit primarily at happenings within southern states... but north of the Mason-Dixon line and west of the Mississippi, Pentes' films are often viewed with less enthusiasm.

Pentes, whose family roots can be traced back to pre-Civil War North Carolina, describes his films as "ethereal, character-driven and loads of fun," and for once, this is a slice of self-praise which is totally on-target. Focusing on contemporary Southern culture, Pentes happily kicks away the encrusted cinematic Dixie stereotypes to present a raw, hilarious dissection of a region rich with acute individualism and mind-boggling solutions for solving life's simplest and deepest problems. *Confessions of a Southern Punk* offers a visceral sub-culture clash with a teenage punk couple whose decision to abort an unwanted pregnancy raises the ire of right-wing nutcases who torment them into prison and revenge. *The Closest Thing to Heaven* offers a sublime quintet of interconnecting stories following denizens of Charlotte, North Carolina, on the single worst days of their respective lives. Pentes' films aim mercilessly at subjects of sexual, political, racial, and economic fissures within today's South. (His other features, *The Great Unpleasantness* and *Lullaby*, are closer to the dramatic with their focus on severely dysfunctional families, although each has winning underplayed humor running throughout.) Anyone looking for Miss Daisy, Tennessee Williams' operatic neurotics or the *Steel Magnolias* beauty parlor set in Pentes' films will be in for a wonderfully rude surprise.

"I love working far removed from New York and L.A. — the scenes there are so intense, so product- and profit-driven, that it's amazing to me how anyone can think straight," says Pentes. "I love living in my little neighborhood in my mid-sized town where I can't throw a hundred rocks and hit another film director."

Pentes' visceral image of the contemporary Southern culture in *Confessions of a Southern Punk* is invigorating in its undiluted anger — and it stands in very sharp contrast to the Hollywood concept of today's South. Why won't the Hollywood productions serve up a contemporary South with your bite and fury? "You'll have to ask Hollywood why they portray the South in such cliched, stereotypical terms," he says. "Part of the reason I began making 'Southern' films was that I wanted to give the world a version of the South it had never seen before: the truth of it, at least through my eyes. Hollywood (and it's fascistic multicultural spin-off, IndieWood) has, as it does with all indigenous culture, stereotyped, dumbed-down, and caricaturized the South. And as a Southerner it truly makes me very sad and angry to see the South so misrepresented. Hollywood simply does not have the will or the expertise to make decent Southern films, period. (With the exception of Billy Bob Thornton of course — but he's a true, real Southerner.) There also seems to be a very large, pervasive, anti-Southern bias in L.A. and New York — and if films are made that don't conform to stereotypes, such as *Confessions of a Southern Punk* or *The Closest Thing to Heaven*, then they're vilified. We couldn't get a decent review in L.A. for *The Closest Thing to Heaven*, and all of the reviews we did get were politically tinged against the South. It's as if the reviewers feel some hip, '60s liberal multicultural bullshit responsibility to trash Southern films as their own personal revenge against all the sins the South has committed. If a film doesn't criticize, stereotype, or vilify the South, then it must be bad."

The Closest Thing to Heaven, a truly undiscovered masterwork, tells five interconnecting stories of a day in the life of Charlotte, North Carolina. The stories range from tart (a would-be Lothario tries to impress a put-upon single mother attempting to bring bags of groceries and her wise-mouthed little daughter home by bus) to the ironic (the pastor of an African-American church has an affair with a woman in his parish — whose husband is a white man that accidentally discovers the unholy union) to slapstick (a pair of stoners try and fail repeatedly to raise cash via petty theft, and even set an ATM on fire by mistake).

Perhaps the most extraordinary story in *The Closest Thing to Heaven* was the emotional but strangely humorous depiction of George, the elderly Greek diner owner whose dementia and his longing for a vanished heritage and loved ones creates serious problems for the family business and emotions. What could have been tactless or maudlin becomes warm and bittersweet. "George's story actually is a composite of a number of stories I had grown up with," says Pentes. "My grandfather was indeed a Greek immigrant who ran a number of restaurants across the South, though he was unhappily married to my grandmother, a Southern belle in the finest Tennessee Williams tradition. My grandfather died when I was very young, but my father

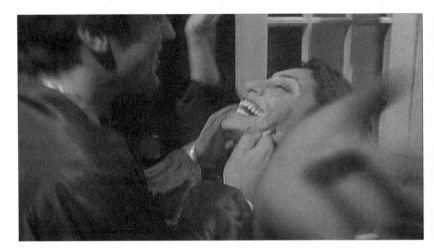

A zany dance leads to disaster in Jamil Said's *Byromania*.

Ohio filmmaker Jim Bihari, who gave up cinema to become an optometrist.

The recently deceased arrive in New Orleans for *Zombie! vs. Mardi Gras*.

told me many, many stories about his life, how he came to America with nothing, and made something of himself — plus how he drank, womanized, and was generally an ornery, ass-whippin' cuss of a dude. My grandmother actually lived much longer, into my late 20s, and she had Alzheimer's and dementia which I experienced first hand and up close for a long time. There were times when I visited her when she would tell me that General Lee had just been by to visit. I loved her dearly, though she blew my mind. So I had a deep, personal, specific connection to George's character and troubles — it was a pretty easy character to write."

From Movies to Optometry

During the mid-1990s, Ohio-based Jim Bihari established a reputation for his droll, Altmanesque comedies which weave an intricate web of botched communications, skewered misperceptions, and colorful characters trapped in bizarre situations. *I Didn't Think You Didn't Know I Wasn't Dead* (1994) offers a kooky mystery with an extraordinary line-up of suspicious miscreants. An obsessed humane society worker is convinced that a diner is the front for a cockfighting operation and she hires a very reluctant private eye to keep a surveillance watch on the eatery. Under their eye, a young woman searching for her brother and his okra farm (which may be home to a very different and very illegal botanical) comes upon an old boyfriend she assumed was deceased. Throw in some Russian black marketeers and a gang of moth-collecting criminals and this comic gumbo really starts to boil. His second feature, *My New Advisor* (1996), offers a wild road trip with three unlikely passengers — a burned-out graduate student, a cantankerous professor and the professor's rebellious teenager daughter — on their way to a Midwest conference in a perpetually unreliable 1960 Oldsmobile. When the car up and dies, the trio winds up hitching rides through rural Ohio and encounter a crazed biker, a presumed-dead artist, a gun-toting waitress, and various members of the agricultural proletariat.

Sadly, Bihari has been absent from filmmaking after his second film. "I haven't done any other films since *My New Advisor*, he says "Someday I still hope to. I've just been running a production company for the past five years doing boring stuff like wedding videos, industrial videos, and vintage car videos. Doing all this video production work made me so busy and poor it made it impossible to even think about making another film. I'm pretty much hanging up the video work for now because this fall I started optometry school and also decided to try to finish up a dissertation in science education I never finished (with the hope of finishing my PhD by 2005 and my O.D. by 2008). I'm just so tired of being poor that I decided I need to be something like a rich doctor and makes lots of money and then waste it all on independent films. So maybe I'll make my third film in 2010 or something!"

Bihari, whose films played in festivals but were not theatrically released and had a limited video release (they have not been released on DVD yet), is practical about the state of filmmaking and where a talent like his can take root. "I think the market can accommodate a certain number of independent films of any type," he comments. "One film like *Stranger than Paradise* can make it (relatively) big, but the next 100 similar films that come along probably won't be so lucky. I'm more of the opinion that if you want to make films you should just gear your life to do whatever you can to both make a lot of money and be in a situation in which you have time to make films. Then just make those films you want to make with your own money (or be good at schmoozing with folks who have money) and don't ever concern yourself with marketing the films or ever trying to make money off of them. If the films were meant to be seen then somehow, somewhere, sometime (maybe after you're dead), the films will gather their own life and make themselves seen. I don't think comedy tastes or comic styles really change that much over time."

Jimmy Makes Laughs

Whereas Bihari has only made two films, Jimmy Traynor created more than 100 over the course of a decade. Working in Baltimore, his films have been both shorts and features and cover nearly every genre. Comedy is where Traynor shines, though he's made relatively few comedies.

Traynor is a winning comedy force, working both sides of the camera with equal aplomb. Two of his Christmas-related shorts resonate with this special brand of mirth. In *Billy's Christmas* (1995), Traynor plays a petulant youth given to bouts of miscreant behavior. At one point, he invents a piñata-style game which involves hanging a playmate from his wrists off a basketball hoop and whacking him with a golf club. A timely visit from Santa Claus eventually rights the bad Billy of his nasty ways... almost (Billy replaces grocery bags stolen from a neighbor by raiding his mother's refrigerator of its contents to replace the loss, then denying knowledge of where his mother's food has gone). In *Billy Saves Christmas* (1996), Traynor revives his Billy character as a stand-in for an ailing Santa, but his appearance creates such anger and agitation among children (who scream in horror when he arrives with his toys) that he finishes his chores by running through the streets and throwing gifts through windows, smashing glass and Yuletide cheer in the process.

"Comedies are hard because what you think is funny doesn't always get a laugh," remarks Traynor. "It's the most honest type of filmmaking. People can't lie: if they don't laugh they didn't like it. Horror is the easiest to make: throw some blood on someone and you have a movie."

The cheese element of Traynor's no-budget productions (many of which were literally filmed in his basement) is often spun into a special brand of cinematic caviar. Not unlike the early John Waters, Traynor takes the most obviously absurd anachronism and turns it into a small treasure of nudge-in-the-ribs fun. In *Billy Saves Christmas*, a small black dog is placed on the table and identified as a "baby reindeer" without any comment or contradiction; compare this to Waters' *Multiple Maniacs* with the timid child in extravagant robes who abruptly wanders on screen and is hailed as the Infant of Prague. For his sci-fi flick *The Weird Thing*, an omnivorous alien bears more than a passing resemblance to a large black garbage bag; compare that to *Multiple Maniacs* again when the blatantly mechanical and virtually inert giant lobster is pushed on screen to ravage Divine.

In recent years, Traynor curiously placed a greater emphasis on the creation of horror flicks and crime dramas and has made fewer comedies; his last comedy to date, the *Charlie's Angels* parody *Jimmy's Devils* (2003), deliciously warps the giggle-jiggle private eye franchise.

Traynor relocated from Baltimore to Los Angeles in 2003 to seek out an acting career and, to date, has not directed or written any additional films since heading west. Hopefully he can return to generating laughs in the very near future.

Legge Work

Up in Boston, Michael Legge has been turning out no-budget comedies of a fey nature. Legge's first film *Loons* (1991), shot on Super 8, delightfully displays his talent for finding the satirical in the least likely places. *Loons* opens in the days of the Salem Witch Hunt, when Judge August Loon makes the mistake of condemning a real witch named Hepzibah Crowley to death. Hepzibah places a curse of hereditary lunacy on the judge and all of his male descendants. The curse carries into the present when Jeff Coukos, a carrier of the Loon blood, learns of the curse. His attempts to break the spell on his bewitched bloodline goes to wild extremes, including raising the condemned Hepzibah from the dead (completely against her will and pleasure)! His next film, *CutThroats* (1994), was also shot on Super 8 and focuses on a minor white-collar worker whose days are spent in the mix of downsizing jitters and extreme office politics and whose nights are plagued by insomnia. He attempts to cure his sleep-deprivation problems by using a recording of ocean waves, and it works... too well! As he is finding peace in slumberland, his office environment goes from bad to worse and soon he cannot differentiate between the real and surreal.

Legge's early films were primitive in their production values and the acting was uneven (although the filmmaker himself had a natural, breezy, on-screen charm). More recently, his films have enjoyed a more polished production value but, oddly, seem more conventional in concept. *Braindrainer* (2000) is a homage to B-grade sci-fi of the 1950s. It follows a seemingly harmless meteor that drops to Earth, but anyone who touches it has their intelligence drained in a matter of seconds. Dr. Belinda Garland of the Pointless Research Institute tries to find a beneficial use for this "brain drainer," but her efforts are interrupted by the mad hypnotist The Amazing Jacques and his co-hort, The Spiderwoman. The title character of *Honey Glaze* (2003) is a perfect little girl who minds her Daddy, plays with her toys, and stays out of trouble by never leaving the house. The trouble is, she is 30 years old. And when her father, a government agent, is killed, Honey is pulled into a perilous plot of intrigue and danger. With the help of special agent Dash Hope, Honey starts to grow up fast in her attempts to stop the evil Dr. Sum Thaim and his nefarious assistant Nurse Tarika.

Who's Laughing Now?

While Legge's films have enjoyed a small but devoted cult following, the sole collaborative film by the triple team of Mike Lyddon, Karl DeMolay, and Will Frank has become something of an anti-cult classic. The 1999 *Zombie! vs. Mardi Gras* was shot for $5,000 in black-and-white 8mm on the streets and in the clubs, hotels, and diners of New Orleans. In this utterly bizarre film, a paralyzed occultist and an evil go-go dancer combine their magical forces to raise Zombie! (yes, spelled with an exclamation point) from the dead to prey on the Mardi Gras celebrants. As Zombie! shambles about killing people, he is completely unnoticed by the hedonistic crowds. However, word of Zombie! begins to spread quickly and soon he is pursued by a trio of bickering documentary filmmakers (a forerunner of the Blair Witch bunch?), an overweight ninja, and, incredibly, Galileo (having been sprung from Purgatory to catch Zombie!). Throw in scenes of gratuitous female nudity, a weirdo rock group, drug-dealing cops, rude waiters, stupid tourists, devotees of the New Orleans horror novelist "Anne Gravy," and a subtitled tribute to Jean-Luc Godard, and you have some idea of what this film is all about.

What magical influences came together to build the foundation of this extraordinary film?

"Predominately a love for psychotronic culture: Corman, Jean-Luc Godard, Robert Anton Wilson, free masons, UFOs, Mardi Gras satire, sick puppetry, porn, cockroaches, pagan rituals, psychoactive drugs... I could go on and on," says Mike Lyddon. "The feel and look of the film revolves mainly around paying homage to Roger Corman and French filmmaker Jean-Luc Godard (do a career comparison, you'll find remarkable similarities). Shooting was pretty loose, over about one-and-a-half years and two different Mardi Gras festivities. We just filmed when we had money, which was kind of rare. Strangely, filming on Bourbon Street amidst wall to wall drunkards was fairly easy (but fucking exhausting). We were able to move about and get shots rather quickly, as well as ask people if they'd be in a scene (usually to get attacked by Zombie!), and that went very well! And yes, I've never filmed so many breast shots in my life, but I wouldn't mind beating that record!"

The breasts were quite inspiring, to be certain, but perhaps the most inspired sequence in "Zombie! vs. Mardi Gras" was the appearance of Galileo in purgatory being assigned to hunt down the zombie. How in the world did Galileo turn up in a New Orleans-based zombie comedy? "As you recall, the Pope pardoned Galileo several years ago," recalls Lyddon. "So we figured, 'Hey, let's get Galileo in as a main character, who needs to kill the zombie before he's totally pardoned!' The actor did a decent job looking like Galileo but we had to bring in another guy to overdub his voice, which worked out great — not to mention Rusty Jackson as the snide Angel sent to give G-man the news."

Zombie! vs. Mardi Gras inspired intense passion from critics who've seen the film — for the wrong reason. Many reviewers barbecued it as being the worst film ever made. Yet Lyddon is not losing sleep over horrible reviews. It opened for a brief theatrical engagement in New York in 2001 and *New York Times* critic Lawrence Van Gelder sniffed the film's "juvenile ideas of comedy run to toilet humor; the acting seems unworthy of the name, and as a whole the film is sluggish and starved for style and originality." Robert Firsching of the *Amazing World of Cult Movies* was more succinct, dubbing it the worst cult movie of the 20th century.

"Ah, we deal with morons every day, and this is no exception," he sighs. "Some lame jerk-off actually complained about the end credit sequence where Zombie! runs slow motion into the arms of a beautiful girl in a lovely green field. He couldn't believe the evil Zombie! got the girl at the end of the film?!? Good God, what an idiot... which proves film critics are usually filmmaker wannabes who lack both the intellectual and physical fortitude to make a film, so they wallow in uneducated opinions about other people's work. Pretty sad, really. Another loser from *Videoscope Magazine* used an entire page to rant about how bad the film is, and in reality people who read the review were more intrigued about the film afterwards. Ha! *Zombie! vs. Mardi Gras* is cinema of the absurd, it works along a line of abstract thought and humor, and is definitely not your typical plot oriented film... BUT... If you are knowledgeable in cinema history and possess a brain, you will catch onto the film's cryptic sensibilities."

Lyddon and his Mardi Gras co-conspirators went their separate ways after their film was made; none of them have yet returned to the comedy fold.

An Underground Laugh-O-Rama

Comedy is served funny-side-up in underground cinema. While the humor sometimes get edgy, rude, and demented, the laughs are hardly in short supply. Some of the most memorable underground comedies include the following:

Agent 15 (2001): Originally produced for online viewing, this take-off on James Bond stars Paget Brewster as a sultry lady secret agent who can turn heads in a bikini and sever heads with a ninja sword. Web site: http://www.filmthreatdvd.com

Ape Canyon (2002): The character of Bigfoot is revamped as a Don Juan who intrigues the ladies and makes the guys jealous. According to Joe Bob Briggs, the movie is "the finest Bigfoot rape-revenge flick ever made by people with WAY too much time on their hands." Web site: http://www.normalpeoplelikeyou.com/Ape_Canyon.htm

Arnold Schwarzenegger is Completely Insane (2003): A compilation of all of Arnold's kills throughout his entire movie career (total score: 463). Web site: http://www.filmthreat.com/Reviews.asp?Id=5149

Arrowhead Beer (2000): A compilation of three faux commercials for Arrowhead beer. Each spot features Steven Lance, president of Arrowhead, touting his product near Arrowhead Lake (water from which the beer is made) and ends in a calamity. Web site: http://www.filmthreat.com/Reviews.asp?File=ReviewsOne.inc&Id=2841

Bad Dates (2001): The story of a man and his spastic colon. Web site: http://www.filmthreat.com/Reviews.asp?Id=2553

Battleship Contempkin (2002): Parisian lovers, trapped in their Left Bank apartment on a rainy afternoon, play a humorously perverse version of the popular American board game. As the consequences of the losing escalate, Battleship becomes not just a game of strategy and fun, but an instrument of love and death. Web site: http://www.apollocinema.com/filmcatalogue/filmdetail.asp?Title=Battleship%20Contempkin

The Best of the Ricky Mestre Show (2004): The Connecticut-based public access comedy show is presented in a feature-length collection of its funniest skits. Web site: http://www.rickymestreshow.com

Billy Jones (2001): A dark satire that follows a 1950s youth's attempt at being cool by adopting a lethal chain-smoking habit. Web site: http://www.filmthreat.com/Reviews.asp?Id=1615

Bored of the Rings (2002): No hobbit spoofing here. This is a lampoon of the dullness of the Olympic Games, as exemplified by the introduction of the event "Olympic Penmanship." Web site: http://www.filmthreat.com/Reviews.asp?Id=3131

Boxhead Revolution (2000): The story of what happens when an American space probe crashes on an undiscovered planet where love cannot be openly displayed. Web site: http://www.findartfilms.com

Boy@nt (2001): The rise and fall of a severely untalented boy band is the focus of this music industry parody. Web site: http://www.atlscript.org/asgprod/boyant/

The Confetti Brothers (2001): A mockumentary about two confetti-manufacturing brothers and their quest for the perfect confetti. Features Rip Taylor (which is reason enough to see the film). Web site: http://www.filmthreat.com/Reviews.asp?File=ReviewsOne.inc&Id=2875

Cupid's Mistake (2001): Made for only $980, this charming romantic comedy follows the rough edges of a love quadrangle where the person in love finds the object of their affections in love with someone else, but that person is also in love with another person. Web site: http://www.youngmankang.com

Darth Vader's Psychic Hotline (2002): This parody of the Miss Cleo/ Psychic Friends Network, with various characters calling "D.V." with their problems and wanting advice. Web site: http://home.usit.net/~f-shysa/Vader.html

Dead Guy (2001): Twisted and comic short film about a mild-mannered zombie who is goaded by a walking and talking television into eating his girfriend. Web site: http://www.filmthreat.com/Reviews.asp?File=ReviewsOne.inc&Id=2853

Dear Julia (2001): An effectively creepy and seriously funny short film about a man with an acute Daedalus complex and the oddball who helps him achieve his obsessions. Web site: http://www.tonyoursler.com/dearjulia.html

The Discreet Charm of Don Bourgeois (2002): Faux TV sitcom about Don Bourgeois, an adult-acting boy who works at an office and is fighting for a promotion. Features cursing, drinking, and erectile dysfunction. Web site: http://www.filmthreat.com/Reviews.asp?Id=3725

Don't Ask Don't Tell (2002): The 1954 cheapie sci-fi *Killers from Space* gets a sassy new dialogue track that creates a new adventure about gay aliens trying to take over the hetero Earth. Web site: http://www.lser.net

Dr. Fred's Episode III: The Phantom Movie (1999): Parody of *Star Wars Episode I: The Phantom Menace* featuring characters from the original *Dr. Fred's Amazing Exploding Cow Show* cable access series. Web site: http://orangecow.org/phantommovie/

E=MC3 (2002): After it is discovered that E actually equals mc3 instead of mc2 and that the universe will implode and time will begin to run backwards, former astronaut Captain Zeno travels forward against the backtracking time, as everyone else is moving backwards in order to meet up with Einstein and tell him that his calculation is false. Web site: http://www.gulliver.cc/zeno/

Enemies of Laughter (2003): A comedy about a TV writer played by David Paymer. Directed by Joey Travolta and featuring Judge Reinhold, Peter Falk, and Marilu Henner! Web site: http://www.filmthreat.com/Reviews.asp?Id=4839

Extreme Man and Insane Boy (2000): Cartoon about the angry Extreme Man and his straightjacketed sidekick Insane Boy going up against a zombie. Web site: http://www.filmthreat.com/Reviews.asp?File=Revie wsOne.inc&Id=2844

Farmer McAllister's Thinkin' Machine (2001): Movie about a man who attempts to prove his self-worth by building a robot with a copper nozzled-penis, which quite excites his wife. Web site: http://redsrobots.tripod.com/main.htm

Fashion Victim (2002): Several women exact revenge on a nymphomaniac boutique owner after it is discovered that she sold them all the same outfit. Web site: http://www.filmthreat.com/Reviews.asp?Id=4387

First Movement Form (2002): A Mozart-obsessed lunatic's attempts to share his passion for classical music is met with stony silence from the world around him. Web site: http://www.filmthreat.com/Reviews.asp?Id=2883

Fly Me to the Moon (2000): A *Goodfellas* homage that focuses on Tony Mancoti, lounge singer extraordinaire and the troubles that show business has thrown his way, such as his pothead guitarist father and the fact that their family name has been spelled wrong on the marquee as "Manicotti." Web site: http://www.filmthreat.com/Reviews.asp?File=R eviewsOne.inc&Id=2849

42K (1999): Four would-be rockers come into possession of a mysterious necklace and suddenly find themselves being sought after by four beautiful women who can't get enough of them. Throw in three ninjas, two evangelical Christians, one gansta rapper and a dozen machete-swinging vampires and you have the wild mix that resembles an episode of *The Monkees* as reconfigured by George Romero. Web site: http://www.b-movie.com

Gas 'n Fuel Employee Training Video #4A: Makin' It Happen (2003): A faux-training video for new employees of a fictional gas station convenience store that follows the exploits of Shelly, an annoyingly perky crew trainer, and Chris, her enthusiastic but dim trainee. Web site: http://www.cine-magic.com/gasnfuel.html

Gavin's Way (2000): Three cousins in a Boston-Irish working class family experience respective misadventures in love in this light romantic comedy. Web site: http://www.gavinsway.com

Generation Z: The Movies of Nick Zedd (2000): A collection of eight short films by the off-beat Brooklyn filmmaker, whose comedy runs towards the more scatological side of the surreal. Web site: http://www.musicv ideodistributors.com

George Lucas in Love (2000): An Internet cult favorite, crossing the *Star Wars* trilogy with *Shakespeare in Love* to show what may have given the college-age George Lucas some of the inspiration for his classic sci-fi movies. Web site: http://www.filmthreat.com/Reviews.asp?Id=738

Hairdo U (2002): A pair of gruff construction workers who are arrested for an act of homophobic violence (throwing a gay hairdresser through the window of his place of employment) get a very unusual sentence: community service working as beauticians in the hair salon where their crime took place. Web site: http://www.yorkentertainment.com

Honky: The Movie! (2001): A Pythonesque comedy shot on video about a man named Honky (born Hank Halloway the 11th) who wakes up to find a dead guy on his porch. Features a super villain (Tire Man) as well as a love interest (True Love). Web site: http://www.filmthreat.com/ Reviews.asp?Id=2545

H.R. Pukenshette (2001): A man who loses his girlfriend gets advice on the world from a very unlikely source: a pool of vomit that comes to life and calls himself H.R. Pukenshette. We are not making this up! Web site: http://www.jointfilms.com

Ice Scream (1995): Conrad Brooks (of *Glen or Glenda* and *Plan 9 from Outer Space* infamy) plays the nutty owner of a failing ice cream parlor who boost sales by hiring an all-girl staff in extraordinarily revealing uniforms. When a maniacal killer comes to town, the girls prove their mettle as crime fighters. Web site: http://www.b-movie.com

If Spielberg Made a Snuff Film (2001): A fake documentary of the making of a Spielberg film in which actors (i.e. victims) actually die in real life on screen. Web site: http://www.lowtotheground.com/snuff.html

Inbred Rednecks (1999): Good ol' boys Billy Bob, Joe Bob, Clovis and Bubba and their supersized poultry Bigass Rooster become the kings of the North Carolina-Tennessee cockfighting circuit until rivals steal their prize bird. The film's satiric view of rural life includes a jolting reminder of why it is never a good idea to urinate on an electrical fence. You have been warned. Web site: http://www.b-movie.com

Jesus and Hutch (2001): The man from Galilee returns — as an urban cop? Eric Stoltz is the red-headed, gun-and-handcuff-toting Jesus. Web site: http://www.filmthreat.com/Reviews.asp?Id=1616

Joyful Partaking (2000): A bittersweet, Altmanesque story of a day in the life of Walter Majeski, a former TV weatherman whose young son perished in a freak snowstorm that Walter failed to forecast. Web site: http://filmthreat.studiostore.com/product/DVFTD0102/s.lfTb9vT7

Keisha Vs. Geisha (2002): Ethnic humor laces the tale of Keisha and Geisha, two sisters that were separated at birth. Features exploitation movie fighting and the opening of a sushi & waffle house. Web site: http://www.filmthreat.com/Reviews.asp?Id=4120

Killing Michael Bay (2002): The title suggests a hidden wish of many a critic, in this short action parody about two digital filmmakers who plan to kill Bay for being the worst director in Hollywood. Web site: http://www.killingmichaelbay.50megs.com/

Kung Phooey (2003): A spoof of the stereotyped Asian actor and kung fu movies by writer/director/producer Darryl Fong. Web site: http://www.kungphooey.com/

Lucky (2001): Hermitic and alcoholic cartoon writer Millard Mudd's life changes when he meets Lucky the talking dog. Their co-dependent relationship leads to Mudd becoming well-acquainted with his dark side. Web site: http://www.themovielucky.com

Midget Nun (2002): A shot-on-video offering about penguins and intercourse. What were you expecting, midget nuns? Web site: http://www.filmthreat.com/Reviews.asp?File=ReviewsOne.inc&Id=2851

My Life with Morrissey (2002): A dark comedy that chronicles the adventures of an off-kilter office girl whose life unravels when she meets her idol (British rock icon Morrissey) and sets off on a journey of obsessive self-delusion. Web site: http://www.mylifewithmorrissey.com

North Beach (2001): A San Francisco artist's one-night indiscretion with a stripper visiting from New Orleans literally becomes the talk of the town. Web site: http://www.northbeachthemovie.com

Of Bass and Men (2003): Short film that focuses on the relationship between college buddies Willie and Richie, after Willie starts drinking bleach with the local hillbillies, melting his brain, turning into a hillbilly himself, and becoming best friends with singing sensation Big Mouth Billy Bass. Web site: http://www.zabbazabba.com

Only in Venice (2001): An astrologer from Venice, California, is swept off her feet by a chef from Venice, Italy. Web site: http://www.onlyinvenice.net

P.A. Wars (2000): The story of Sponikan Sponewalker, movie "production assistant" and Jedi apprentice, who goes to war after endless abuse and thankless duties. Web site: http://www.theforce.net/theater/shortfilms/pawars/index.shtml

The Paper Mache Chase (2003): A mockumentary about the ridiculously rough admissions process of a fictional nursery school. Web site: http://www.filmthreat.com/Reviews.asp?Id=4335

P.E. (2002): A trio of malevolent seventh grade girls take the news of a potential failing of their physical education class by plotting to kill their gym teacher. Web site: http://www.pe-themovie.com

Pedro + Tony (2002): Animated short film in which Pedro (a dog) and Tony (his rooster boyfriend) find their relationship has hit a rocky patch. A pair of wise lesbian bears who live next door help sort out the heartache. Web site: http://www.filmthreat.com/Reviews.asp?Id=2611

Plan 10 From Outer Space (1995): Not an Ed Wood sequel, but instead this Utah-based feature details how Brigham Young's 22nd wife was actually an extra-terrerstrial — and she has returned to Earth (in the form of Karen Black!). Web site: http://www.cc.utah.edu/~th3597/kolob1.htm

Raping Steven Spielberg (1998): A disgruntled aspiring actor attempts to rape Steven Spielberg in order to become the hottest ticket in town. Web site: http://www.filmthreat.com/Reviews.asp?File=ReviewsOne.inc&Id=3023

The Real Third World (2000): A take-off on the MTV reality series, with the house full of self-absorbed young people living in a fancy house in Bangladesh! Web site: http://www.filmthreat.com/Reviews.asp?Id=1532

Reflections of Evil (2002): An experimental comedy in which the viewer gets to experience the childhood of a paranoid and disturbed man who sells watches on the streets of Hollywood Blvd. Features angry homeless people, rabid dogs, skate punks, and even a young Steven Spielberg. Web site: http://www.reflectionsofevil.com

Robot Bastard (2001): Robot Bastard must fight zombie-monsters and insecurity in order to complete his suicidal mission of rescuing the President's daughter from the clutches of the brilliant super-criminal Blood Mamba. Our money is on Robot Bastard. Web site: http://www.robotbastard.com

Room Tone (2002): Film critic-turned-filmmaker Rachel Gordon wrote and directed this short charmer about a sensible young woman who is ready to move on from a terminated relationship with her fool-around ex-boyfriend, while he is insistent on another chance. Web site: http://www.filmthreat.com/Reviews.asp?Id=3609

Runaway Gossip (2002): A bride-to-be heads to a lesbian bar on her wedding day after learning that her fiancé is gay. Web site: http://www.filmthreat.com/Reviews.asp?Id=3687

Safety With Scissors (2001): Fudgeco Educational Film #24: Playing With Scissors! In less than two minutes, Billy will help teach you the hazards of mishandling sharp objects! Fun for the whole family, but not for the faint of heart. Web site: http://www.fudgefilms.com/films/swsps00.html

The Scary Side of Randall Coombe (2001): A dark comedy about a lifeless marriage and an obsessive relationship. http://www.filmthreat.com/Reviews.asp?Id=2544

Schneider's 2nd Stage (1999): A short film starring Kenneth Branagh (of all people!) as a man who discovers what's the worst that can happen to his sperm sample once it is given to a clinic. Web site: http://www.filmthreat.com/Reviews.asp?File=ReviewsOne.inc&Id=2839

Soap Girl (2002): A Hollywood massage parlor is the unlikely setting for a band of women who find their self-empowerment in a unique brand of girl power. Web site: http://www.youngmankang.com

Sorority Boys (2002): Raunchy college movie about three frat guys falsely accused of stealing who dress up in drag in order to collect a videocassette with the proof of their innocence at the Delta Omicron Gamma sorority. Web site: http://www.filmthreat.com/Reviews.asp?Id=2917

Star Geeks (1999): A comedy that pits *Star Wars* fans against *Star Trek* fans. Web site: http://www.filmthreat.com/Reviews.asp?Id=116

Star Whores: The Phantom Anus (2000): Scatalogical humor reigns here, with a minimal amount of *Star Wars* references and a maximum amount of shenanigans that Luke Skywalker never got around to enjoying (on-screen, at least). Web site: http://www.filmthreat.com/Reviews.asp?Id=1393

The Strange Case of Señor Computer (1999): a robot discovers the joys of contemporary American culture, including telephone sex lines and TV soap operas, and takes it upon himself (itself?) to improve the lovelife of his misfit inventor. Web site: http://www.worldartists.com

Superguy: Behind the Cape (2001): A Discovery Channel-style mockumentary about the life of a superhero. Web site: http://www.superguy.net

Tankup.us (2003): A 'mockumentary' that features an 'infotainment' television program about America's love with a really big passenger vehicle. Web site: http://www.tankup.us

Tatooine: Episode 1.5 (2000): A combination of the Lucas-inspired mania with MTV's *The Real World*. Web site: http://www.midnightstrikes.tv

Temporary Hell (2001): A comedy about the absurdity of the office temp life. Web site: http://www.filmthreat.com/Reviews.asp?File=ReviewsOne.inc&Id=2881

Trailer: The Movie (2002): Based on a true story, the story of two film-makers who decide to decide to cut together every half-decent shot into a misleading trailer to dupe audiences and save their careers. Web site: http://www.trailer-themovie.com/

The Truth About Beef Jerky (2001): Lured into the woods by a fake ad boasting a phony Phish reunion, a bunch of hippies find themselves reluctantly engaging in an event inspired by the film *The Most Dangerous Game*. Web site: http://www.thetruthaboutbeefjerky.com

Vampires Anonymous (2002): Another wacky vampire movie in which a troubled vampire joins an anonymous 12-step program that helps the undead control their appetite and blend into society better. Web site: http://www.filmthreat.com/Reviews.asp?Id=4378

Welcome to Purgatory (2001): An animated short a la Monty Python about the high school in Purgatory, a seaside town where dead celebrities live and shop. Features animated versions of Frank Sinatra, Janis Joplin, Kurt Cobain, Jim Morrison, and the arm of Def Leppard's drummer. Web site: http://www.liebography.com

We Three Kings (2001): Mockumentary about a trio of Elvis impersonators on a mission to spread Elvisness to the world. Web site: http://www.filmthreat.com/Reviews.asp?Id=2950

Whipsmart (2002): Displays the troubles a professional dominatrix goes through when she brings her diaper-clad clients to the home she shares with a couple of bitchy roommates. Web site: http://www.filmthreat.com/Reviews.asp?File=ReviewsOne.inc&Id=2830

William Shatner Lent Me His Hairpiece (1999): A short film about William Shatner's jealous hairpiece and how it led to his success. Web site: http://www.filmthreat.com/Reviews.asp?Id=574

With Nobody (1997): Grand Rapids, Michigan-based novelist Michael Joshua helmed this sweet, fragile film about single people looking for a possible soulmate to fulfill their emotional needs. Web site: http://www.imdb.com/title/tt0145578/

Winner (2002): A completely improvised short comedy about a contest winner who uses her sudden fame to turn the taping of a TV promotional commercial into a documentary about her importance as a sculptor and conceptual artist. Web site: http://www.filmthreat.com/Reviews.asp?Id=4130

The World of the Erotic Ape (2001): A distant planet is home to a tribe of dominant women who've banished all men to a Forbidden Zone and made apes their love slaves (yes, you read that correctly). A *Planet of the Apes* spoof for the truly demented. Web site: http://www.b-movie.com

The Year X-mas Almost Wasn't (2002): An adult-themed parody of the Rankin/Bass classic *Rudolph, the Red-Nosed Reindeer,* (that uses actual footage from the 1964 television special) in which kids all across the world have suddenly lost interest in toys, due to a sudden rise in self-gratification. Ho ho no! Web site: http://www.liebography.com/xmas.html

Zebadiah the Anthropophagus (2002): Nine-minute short featuring a battle against a squirrel with a butthole face (or something like it — we're not too sure about this one). Web site: http://www.filmthreat.com/Reviews.asp?File=ReviewsOne.inc&Id=2852

INTERVIEW

THE BROTHERS FRIEDMAN GET MOVING

Moving is one of the funniest underground films ever made. Conceived by Virginia-based filmmakers Jonathan Friedman and Matthew Friedman starring L. Derek Leonidoff and Terry Jernigan, *Moving* is an original, genuine laugh-out-loud packed from start to finish with truly inventive situations and screamingly hilarious dialogue.

Mixing equal parts of Kafka and Beckett with healthy pinches of Abbott and Costello, *Moving* begins with the most bizarre concept imaginable: Ron Fervent (Leonidoff), a would-be novelist who makes a living writing user manuals for VCRs, returns home from a publishing convention to discover his house is stolen. No, not a robbery in the house... but the house itself, uprooted from its foundation and carted away with nary an eyewitness. Through a variety of miscommunications, it is assumed Ron is trying to pull of an insurance scam when filing a claim on his stolen house and is soon being chased by various law enforcement agencies. His sole salvation is his friend John (Jernigan), an ebullient nutcase writer for a supermarket tabloid which promises news you can't find anywhere else (including sightings of Bigfoot in Central Park and photos from Heaven via the Hubbell Telescope).

Ron and John track the house thieves via a network of flea markets, where Ron's belongings inevitably wind up for sale at prices far below their genuine and sentimental value. With the assistance of various oddballs including a bearded man whispering cryptic clues, a rifleman who takes target practice on ants and a shadowy army of neurotic rebels, Ron and John track down the men behind this edifice-snatching ring.

Much of the joy in *Moving* comes from a series of out-of-nowhere conversations between Leonidoff and Jernigan which move ceaselessly between the ridiculous and the sublime. With a wild-eyed gaze and a rat-a-tat-tat delivery, Jernigan fires off hilariously smutty one-liners ("Flattery will get you underwear"), inane confessions (the admission that the Central Park Bigfoot was a co-worker in an ape suit… but only because he spilled Kool-Aid on the Bigfoot suit), and flights of philosophical lunacy ("You ever think about stuff? I mean, there's so much stuff!"). When confronted by the worst that life can offer, he responds with sharp, edgy cracks that will appeal to the inner wiseguy in everyone: a hotheaded intellectual female rebel is cooled off with "Ease down, Dorothy Parker!" while a rifle-pointing hillbilly's demand "You think I'm stupid?" is met with a Jack Benny–worthy pause, a slight widening of the eyes, and a sincere response of "Honestly?" Jernigan's hijinks are supported brilliantly by Leonidoff's bedraggled everyman experiencing the worst possible mishaps in the realm of the cosmos. When taken for a ride by a pair of sexy gas station bandits, Leonidoff tries sheepishly to find a possible explanation for the bag of cash dumped in his lap by inquiring: "Did you pay for this money?" When his steering wheel is stolen from his automobile, he answers his partner's call to "get a grip" by using a pair of pliers in lieu of the missing wheel. The sight gag is priceless in itself, and Leonidoff's embarrassed scowl and cranky apology to fellow motorists ("I'm driving with pliers") ices this incredibly rich comic cake.

The Friedmans never miss an opportunity to pack a scene with as much fun as possible, either with *Airplane!*-worthy sight gags (the rebel leader fires her gun skyward to silence a room and is met with a shower of plaster smack on her head) or intense dialogue (the rebel leader's mother keeps a running commentary on how clever her daughter is in certain areas and lacking in others). Politically incorrect humor is tossed about at unexpected moments, but the results are more joyfully bizarre than offensive (why is the flea market shopper who purchases the stolen goods an African-American wearing an Arab kaffiyeh?). Endlessly creative and brilliantly conceived, *Moving* is a happy surprise from opening to closing credits.

How did the Friedmans make such a funny film? Let's find out.

Q. What do you view as the essential ingredients for a successful comedy film?

JONATHAN: I would say the script, the actors, and the editing. The script is the most important ingredient, because without a solid screenplay, you have nothing. Assuming you have a good script (and I'd like to think that we did), finding the right actors is essential. We were very lucky to find Derek and TJ for our film. Without their talent and chemistry, the comedy in the script would never have shown through. I found during auditions that the wrong actor for a part can really kill the humor in a script, no matter how well-written it is. When the right actors are cast though, it really comes to life. And of course, editing is incredibly important. When I edited *Moving*, I found that too long a pause here, or too short a pause there could easily ruin a joke. Even one frame makes a difference.

MATTHEW: Parsley, sage, rosemary, and timing.

JONATHAN: Ignore his answer please.

Q. I will try. So, do you find most indie comedies funny or not?

JONATHAN: I don't find most indie comedies all that funny. I actually prefer mainstream comedies. Comedy is probably the most difficult thing to pull off (so of course we had to try it), and the amount of talent involved on every level is essential to making it work. Hollywood really does have access to the best comic writers and actors, so I personally think Hollywood comedies are in general funnier than most indie films.

MATTHEW: Most mainstream comedies are dumb, despite what my brother says. For this reason alone, if an indie film tries to be like a mainstream one, it will probably suck. But then again, if it tries to be like an "indie," it will probably also suck, because a lot of indie comedies are just trying to out-hip each other. Any film festival programmer will tell you how sick she is of Kevin Smith and Quentin Tarantino clones. Be yourself, man! Don't you watch soda commercials? The best comedies defy comparison. *Being John Malkovich* and *Punch Drunk Love* made their own rules, and didn't give a mug of hot piss what anyone thought. All comedy needs is the absurd and the unexpected.

JONATHAN: I think the absurd and unexpected are great, but if it's not funny then you have an absurd and unexpected film that no one laughs at. Can you believe we work together?

Q. Not really, but that is not an issue. So, what was the genesis of *Moving*? And how long did it take for the film to travel from the first draft of the screenplay to the first public screening?

JONATHAN: I first started writing the screenplay in my college scriptwriting class. (I was 20.) It was so well received by both the class and my screenplay professor at James Madison University that I decided to make it my first feature film project. Don't ask me how I came up with the idea about a person's house being stolen, because I'm not really sure. I think it just came to me out of nowhere one day, and I thought it would be pretty funny if something like that actually happened. It would have been a lousy movie if that was the only joke, so we had to follow it with a real plot. We didn't want the movie to just be a gimmick. The script wasn't finished until about five years after I was out of college. It was a collaborative process with my brother. He's a better writer than me, so with my ideas, and his ability to flesh them out, we really came up with something special. By the time the script was done, we'd developed it so far that the house-stealing part became the least funny thing in the movie. It took as long as it did to finish the script and shoot the film because I wanted to make sure I had the time and money to do it all myself; I wanted complete creative freedom. I spent those years setting up my life to allow that to happen. I saved money and ran businesses that let me make my own hours. All in all, it took nine years from the moment I first started the screenplay until the premiere in March of 2002.

MATTHEW: Don't listen to him. He bought the idea on eBay, and then I did all the work. Nine years of my life wasted.

Q. Did you create the film with your lead actors in mind or were they already envisioned for the film?

JONATHAN: I had no idea who the lead actors were going to be when we wrote the script. All I knew was that they had to be damn good, or the movie wouldn't work. We were incredibly lucky that Derek Leonidoff and Terry Jernigan volunteered their time and talent (without pay) to our film because they believed in it so much. Without them, the movie could have been a major disaster.

MATTHEW: I haven't told my brother this, but I actually thought of Derek a lot when I was writing. I didn't think he'd actually be in it or even audition, but I've known him since high school and laughed at him for years, mostly behind his back. Katherine Poirier (who has third billing) was a surprise, even though we were already friends—she looked perfect and has a great voice. Several other roles were inspired by people I hoped would play them, but none of those panned out except for Michael Lemelle, who's so cool it's spooky. That rounded out the four principal roles. I actually wrote the part for him after being in a play with him.

JONATHAN: It's nice to find these things out A YEAR AFTER THE MOVIE IS FINISHED!!

MATTHEW: Maybe you shouldn't print that.

Q. Too late. So... talk about the casting of the film. How did you find your cast and how did you determine who was right for the comic parts in your films?

JONATHAN: The first thing I did to cast our film was take the standard route. I called several local talent agencies and asked them how much it would cost to set up an audition. They all wanted to charge me over $500 just for one day, so I told them "no thanks." Luckily, my brother does a lot of local theater and knows most of the talented actors in our area. With word-of mouth coming from him, and a small ad in the local paper, we ended up bringing in over 150 local actors (more than the talent agencies would have brought!), and the auditions lasted two days. We were looking for actors for so many parts that it was very fortunate we had so many people show up. Almost everyone ended up getting offered some kind of role in the production, even if only as extras. We taped the auditions and sat down over the next several nights, watching tapes and debating about everyone. For the most part, John (our cinematographer), Matthew, and I agreed on almost every role. Derek was without a doubt who we wanted for the part of Ron, but John was a little harder to cast. At first we cast someone else in the part, but that didn't work out. We had already begun shooting when the original actor playing John decided he didn't want to commit to the project. I was devastated because I knew this would delay us (and we were on such a tight schedule). But, it turned out to be the best thing that could have happened. Once TJ stepped on the set and started working with Derek, the movie truly came to life.

MATTHEW: We love our actors. Everyone who auditioned for the movie is in the credits.

JONATHAN: It's true. The credits are longer than the movie.

Q. How much improvising do you allow in your films?

JONATHAN: I'm pretty flexible with that. With *Moving*, TJ did a lot of improv and it was almost always funny. Most of the time he would actually come to me with an idea before we started shooting that day. I would always give his ideas a chance, because you never know what's going to work, and because the guy is just so damn nutty. His improv almost always added to the humor of the film, so I always allowed it. And Derek has since started his own improv troupe, so he's got the chops too. A genius with subtlety. He was in a previous short film I made, and I followed pretty much the same formula — if I thought something didn't work, I would simply tell the actors to follow the script for a few takes, and I would decide later (in editing) what I would keep and what I would discard.

MATTHEW: Actually a lot of what people thought was improvised was strictly scripted — we were blessed with a truly gifted screenwriting team.

JONATHAN: I was just going to say that.

MATTHEW: So it sounded more improvised than it was, but nonetheless Derek and TJ are brilliant improv comics and filled out every spare second with bits and taglines we didn't think of ourselves, because we were always drunk on the set.

Q. Did you shoot any scenes that ultimately had to get cut because they were not as funny as you thought they would be?

JONATHAN: Believe it or not, that didn't happen. The finished film is almost exactly like the script we wrote. Four scenes ended up being discarded, but not because they weren't funny. We had to cut them because the film was just running too long.

MATTHEW: I'm still pissed that we had to cut those scenes. Can I say "pissed"?

JONATHAN: Yes.

MATTHEW: I wasn't asking you, asshole.

JONATHAN: Can he say "asshole"?

Q. No, but hopefully our copyeditor won't notice. So... what was the audience reaction like when you first screened the film?

JONATHAN: It was amazing. My brother talked me into renting out a 900-seat theater for the "World Premiere." I thought that was crazy because I didn't think more than 300 people would show up. But that night, we ended up having to turn people away! The audience was laughing and cheering, and as I watched, I truly couldn't believe it. I knew we had made a good film, but to see people enjoying it like they did was fantastic. I made *Moving* for people to enjoy, and nothing more. I just wanted it to entertain. Most filmmakers try to make some kind of statement with their first film, or attempt to tackle some important issue. I wanted to do just the opposite. I wanted to make a film that had no point and no message. I just wanted it to be a joy to watch. The audience reaction was beyond anything I had expected.

MATTHEW: Actually, they started out kind of angry because it was raining outside and the admission tickets had gotten locked in my car and we couldn't let them in. A lot of things went wrong that nobody knew about. But once everyone got inside, the nitrous oxide we were piping through the ventilation system took care of the problem. It was the first sellout in the history of the theater, and we got a standing ovation, and we told everyone to dress up, so they all had a blast. We sold a couple hundred VHS copies of the movie, which at the time were still cheaper and quicker to produce than DVD. One month later, the UN passed that resolution making everyone suddenly switch over to DVD. Oh well.

Q. How have festivals and distributors reacted to the film?

JONATHAN: We got into about eight smaller film festivals and I didn't attend any of them. They were all too far away. If we had gotten into Sundance I would have gone of course, but I really didn't expect a film like *Moving* to get into that festival (and it didn't). I talked to everyone who organized the festivals though, and they all told me that people really enjoyed the film. All the distributors I sent the film to basically told me the same thing — they really liked the movie, but didn't think they could sell it. Because it had no "name" actors, and didn't fit a particular market niche, no one wanted to take a chance on it.

MATTHEW: Our movie is neither Hollywood-style nor mainstream — it's far too clever for that. But it isn't strictly "indie" either, because it has no agenda. What it is, is something I think all films ought to try to be: unique. What's happened to "Independent Film" is like what happened to "Alternative Music" — once it's given the name, it ceases to be the very thing it was named for. "Independent," or "Indie," is now a marketing category. Instead of a distinction, it's an affiliation. So festivals and distributors look for films that fit the Independent niche and then often find themselves compelled by market forces to ignore films that are, ironically enough, independent of it. We've found ourselves victims of that — people love our movie like crazy, but don't know what to possibly sell it as. We don't really care what people call *Moving*, as long as it doesn't rhyme with "gritty."

Q. Knowing what you do today, would you consider making another comedy?

JONATHAN: I would definitely make another comedy. If I had it my way, my next film would be a "fantasy-comedy" and I would start shooting it tomorrow. It'll cost a fortune, though, so it will be a while until we get to it. So believe it or not, our next movie is going to be a drama. My brother wrote the script, and the first draft was accepted into the 2003 Sundance Screenwriter's Lab. Matthew was there in January 2003 and is now working on revising and finishing the screenplay.

MATTHEW: Yeah, I'd do a comedy again, if someone else was paying for it. You can't spend your life savings twice. Mind if I spend yours?

Q. Don't bet on it, toots!

3: Real Life/ Reel Life

Truth, we've been told countlessly over the years, is stranger than fiction. Thus it should come as absolutely no surprise that the most bizarre aspect of underground cinema comes out of the documentary or nonfiction film genre. After all, these are films made by reel-life outsiders celebrating the antics and ravings of real-life outsiders.

In many ways, this is the least thankful of the genres within the underground cinema orbit. Not in terms of the quality of productions — the majority of the underground documentaries are actually quite superb. Actually, the problem is inherent to the documentary genre as a whole.

Up in the real world of mainstream cinema, documentaries are the toughest sell at every level: for filmmakers trying to sell their flicks to distributors, for distributors trying to sell their newly acquired titles to exhibitors, and for exhibitors to sell audiences on the idea of paying to see a nonfiction movie.

Very few documentaries ever make it into wide theatrical release, and the relative handful (when compared to the mass quantity being produced) which get a distributor are generally pegged for limited release in the art house circuit frequented by the culture vultures with access to small theaters in large cities that give such titles a screen. There are occasional exceptions, such as Michael Moore's Oscar-winning *Bowling for Columbine*, but those are few and increasingly far between.

Yet documentaries do have something of an advantage: the non-theatrical market, which includes screening opportunities beyond traditional cinemas, can be lucrative. Educational institutions, museums, and film societies have often been more receptive to documentary programming than commercial venues. Several distributors, including Bullfrog Films and First Run/Icarus Films, almost exclusively target non-theatrical distribution channels for their extensive catalogs of documentary features.

One might guess that television, especially the cable networks, would be receptive to documentaries given the uncommonly high level of nonfiction programming that appears on the air. For filmmakers, however, this is not the panacea they might expect.

"Television, particularly the specialty cable channels, has built up the consumer interest in documentaries," says Peter M. Hargrove, a film distributor who has released several documentary features in theaters and home video. "But all of the channels want to produce their documentaries so they could own the back-end (consumer video, educational, et cetera). The risk a filmmaker faces includes concepts being stolen blatantly or finished projects being used as templates for in-house production operations. Television no longer takes any chances with thought-provoking documentaries."

This is something of a shame, since underground documentaries offer more thought-provoking imagery than the most over-the-top Hollywood fantasy could ever dream of conceiving. These films are not shy about celebrating iconoclastic behavior and eccentric causes without demeaning their subjects (let alone audiences) with exploitative presentations. In the realm of underground documentaries, there is nothing odd about a septuagenarian punk rocker backed by a band young enough to be her grandchildren, or a drag queen dropping vile parodies of Gordon Lightfoot's tunes, or a neurotic filmmaker giving his father Ecstasy pills for Christmas, or a narcissistic bodybuilder showing off his strength by lifting automobiles off the ground, or small-town volunteer firemen raising money by auctioning horses, or an amateur inventor determined to bring economic self-sufficiency to an African village by way of creating a peanut-shelling machine. After a short time in this world, you begin to wonder where the normal people are. But as you delve deeper and deeper, you are glad the normal people are nowhere to be found.

The music of the underground documentaries is the proverbial different drum. The subjects of these films have no clue about the chaos they are creating or the astonishment they unleash. Unlike so-called "reality" programming which tries to push the limits of good taste and good sense, underground documentaries are not self-conscious in their presentation of odd people thriving in worlds that make Lewis Carroll's Wonderland seem like a Rotary Club luncheon in a dull suburban community.

THE DOCTOR IS WAY OUT!

Take the medical profession as viewed by New York filmmaker Eli Kabillio, who has made a significant film career producing and directing documentaries on alternative health practices. To most people, the concept of "alternative health" would be defined as using homeopathic remedies or visiting a naturopathic physician or an acupuncturist. But through Kabillio's lens, the spirit of alternative health practices involve treatments which seem closer in spirit to John Waters than to Dr. Andrew Weil.

Kabillio's films have included *A Hole in the Head*, which explores trepanation, the science of drilling holes in the skull for physical and emotional therapeutic value. There is also *A Matter of Life and Breath* and its focus on Leonard Orr, a charismatic and controversial guru who espouses Rebirthing, an extreme form of prolonged hyperventilation which aims to return the patient back to the birth stage while helping to cure diseases ranging from cancer to AIDS. These are actually fairly mundane subjects compared to *Urine: Good Health*, which considers a somewhat unlikely health elixir that is currently not for sale in any known health food store, supermarket, or pharmacy (and probably won't be any time soon!).

Yet Kabillio, like many of his peers in this field, helms his films with complete and total seriousness. His subjects would seem at home in any supermarket tabloid or exploitation television talk show, but there is nothing exploitative about his films. Rather, Kabillio seeks out an intelligent and complex presentation of procedures which few people would immediately identify as intelligent or complex.

"In my approach to the documentaries, I purposefully avoided a dismissive approach to our subjects," says Kabillio. "I have seen short pieces on trepanation since *A Hole In The Head* was broadcast, and while they have been shocking and fun to watch there is absolutely no educational value as the discussions are one-sided with the filmmaker/journalist in the paternal role of preaching the stupidity of the practice. I think that most (if not all) viewers will understand that they shouldn't drill a hole in their head — but without respecting the subjects and interviewing top doctors to rebut the claims made in the piece, all we would be doing is creating more 'shock TV' without much depth."

Inspiration for such films came to Kabillio from unlikely places. "My business partner, Cevin Soling, came up with the idea for *A Hole In The Head* after reading an interview with Paul McCartney that mentioned the subject," he continues. "*Urine: Good Health* came from years of hearing about Urine Therapy, originally from my father and then one day hearing an alternative practitioner discuss the subject. After a little bit of research, I realized how many people were using their own urine and I was on the next flight to Los Angeles to start shooting. *A Matter of Life and Breath*, our documentary about Rebirthing, was not planned. We were interviewing Leonard Orr, the main subject of the documentary regarding the practice of Urine Therapy, and literally stumbled over his alleged 'cult' and the small-town religious controversy surrounding him."

Inspiration for another New York filmmaker, Josh Koury, came closer to home. In fact, it was literally in his home: his teenage brother Adam and Adam's best friend Josh, a pair of gregarious outsiders who feel isolated on all possible levels (from their school peers, their families, even their small-town upstate New York community). Koury began videotaping the boys as they happily went about destroying their young lives. The resulting film, *Standing by Yourself*, details the youths' astonishing spiral into narcotized self-abuse and defiant anti-social behavior. The behavior initially seems fairly benign by the standards of juvenile delinquency: the boys hurl lame insults at slow-moving adults, get mildly stoned by gulping bottles of tussin cough mixture and apple juice, and smoke cigarettes while keeping an eye out for tsk-tsking adults who've heard enough public service announcements from the American Lung Association to make sure young lips don't kiss Philip Morris' product line. While Adam was able to pull himself out of this lifestyle before it turned into a maelstrom, his friend Josh was less fortunate and found himself sinking quickly into a private hell of drugs, alcohol, and a stint in jail.

"What I originally intended was very far from what I ended up with," says Koury, whose film played to rapturous reaction at the Slamdance and New York Underground Film Festival and even snagged a well-reviewed New York theatrical gig (a rarity for films in this genre). "The first 20 minutes of the piece is closer to this original idea. It was more about being young and angry, and in this I was reliving my youth a bit. I mean, I grew up just like Adam and had some of the same problems as the boys when I was their age. It was knowing that these kids were hard on the outside, but that they really did have something else to say... this is what made me want to shoot. Of course, as the piece grew and developed it moved into other levels."

Koury, who initially planned a 20-minute short on the subject, expanded *Standing by Yourself* into a feature in order to prevent the boys from being seen as malcontents on the fringe of their society. "I mainly decided to keep shooting because I felt the kids weren't really being properly represented in the first 20-minute version," he says. "People saw them as faceless, rage-filled kids and I had to keep telling them: 'No, there's a lot more to them, they're actually good kids, just confused and maybe a little lost.' I think that this point of view is seen as the piece moves past the first section, and into the rest of the work. An important element was that I began to film more of the people surrounding them, their pains and struggles. These feelings of confusion and isolation that never really leave you, they just change sometimes. I feel that the first section of the film is absolutely essential, people need to see that hard faceless side before they learn more about them as people, and find that maybe their first judgments may have been too hasty."

Another documentarian who found his inspiration at home was Caveh Zahedi, whose 1994 feature *I Don't Hate Las Vegas Anymore* followed a Christmas vacation with Zahedi, his Iranian-immigrant father, and his snarky teenage half-brother to the gambling capital. Intended to encourage a sense of family bonding, the trip turns into an emotional disaster when Zahedi gives his father an Ecstasy pill as a Christmas present. While the ingestion of the Ecstasy pill itself was not shown on screen (and it was not even clear from the film whether Zahedi's father took it or pretended to take it to appease his son), the idea of a person swallowing Ecstasy in a nonfiction film was too much for many exhibitors, who pointed to this scene for refusing to show *I Don't Hate Las Vegas Anymore.*

"Well, it doesn't surprise me," says Zahedi in retrospect. "People shooting each other is considered fantasy, but actually trying to get someone to take Ecstasy in the context of a documentary film impinges on people's comfort zones. I mean, that's why I did it. I like to impinge on people's comfort zones, and I like it when works of art impinge on my comfort zones. It's just an aesthetic predilection."

Whereas Zahedi's camera captured how his family made a mess of the family ritual of bonding during a vacation, the Berkeley, California-based filmmaker Antero Alli has used the documentary format to dissect the concept of rituals and how they shape society. Employing "paratheatrical research" (a level of dramatic role playing taken to a higher sociological understanding), Alli has used the documentary format to see how rituals come together, either uniting a community or breaking down an individual's identity in the process.

Archaic Community (1993), Alli's first documentary, followed an intensive experiment in ritual building. From October 1 through December 1 of 1991, 11 strangers in Seattle underwent a ritual training process three times a week at four hours per session, under Alli's direction. The idea was to explore how rituals might work without externally imposed dogma. *Crux* (2000) took the paratheatrical concept both deeper and wider. This film was fixed to August 11, 1999, when astrologers noted a rare interplanetary configuration called a Grand Fixed Cross (a heavenly equivalent of a cosmic crucifix with the Earth spinning through dead center). *Crux* documented the movements, thoughts, and emotions of a group ritual exploration of non-sectarian crucifixion archetypes for five weeks (three times a week) which lead up to the grand fixed cross of August 11, 1999. Alongside Alli's narrative, the film featured the seven ritualists through interviews and voice overs excerpted from their private ritual journals. What unfolded, however, was not so much about

Antero Alli's documentary *Crux* dissects the crucifixion motif via paratheatrical sessions.

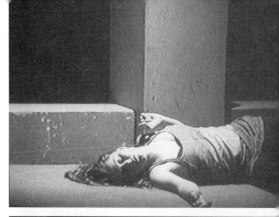

astronomy, astrology, or ritual building. Rather, it became a rich series of highly personal confessions and frequently dramatic confrontations between each person and the crux of what they are living for. Or, as Alli noted, what it means to be crucified to the cross of one's own existence and to wake up to that.

Needless to say, these are not your typical connect-the-dots films. And even in the edgy underworld cinema orbit, Alli's films have provoked considerable debate.

"Audience reactions have been unpredictable," says Alli. "Besides upsetting audience expectations about what a documentary is supposed to be, the subject matter seems to be charged with emotion. People seem to love it or hate it. Depending on your point of view, these paratheatrical video documents come across as either hopelessly pretentious or strangely exhilarating by their sheer honesty. At the very least, they offer a window into a world that most people would never have seen otherwise or never knew existed. I have been directing group ritual dynamics since 1977 and it's only been since 1991 that I have decided to document the process and chiefly in non-performance settings where the rituals unfold without an audience."

The heavily emotional nature of Alli's documentaries makes the production process fraught with intellectual peril. "The chief challenge of making a doc would be finding something I believed was worth documenting which usually means there's something I perceive of great value that would disappear without preserving it somehow, like a lost art or culture or an endangered species," says Alli. "Then, the challenge for me is to shoot the action, meaning, not just talking heads but find a way to capture the heart and soul of whatever process we're shooting. It's not really a creative process as much as it is a kind of journalism."

Alli plans to bring the audience into his next documentary, literally. "I hope to break this cycle by creating a docudrama of a public performance of this work and capture audience reaction to the live event as part of the video document," he says. "I don't have a title for the performance yet but it will probably revolve around the creation of initiation rituals."

PUMP UP THE VOLUME

One documentary which took the notion of public performance and turned it into near lunacy was Michael D. Moore's 1994 *Dika: Murder City*. Growing old gracefully was not the motto for septuagenarian, Richmond, Virginia-based punk rocker Dika Newlin, whose leather-clad performances of venerable pop standards shatter all concepts of good taste and good music (you've not lived until you've seen and heard Dika's astonishing rendition of "These Boots Were Made for Walking"). Tearing into songs like a wolverine attacking a carcass and occasionally finding a connection between her throaty vocalizing and the energetic (though somewhat off-base) melodies of her youthful back-up band, this documentary literally left an audience at New York's Light+Screen Film Festival so shaken that people exited the venue with glazed expressions while muttering "Scary! Scary!" to anyone who would bear witness.

Not as far on the fringes as Dika, but still significantly underground enough to escape detection by mainstream cultural media, are the glam and goth music scenes in Los Angeles and New York. John T. Ryan, a New York-based filmmaker, created stunning time capsules of these respective musical orbits with *Sincerity on the Sunset Strip* (1999) and *Freaks, Glam Gods and Rockstars* (2001).

The stars of *Sincerity on the Sunset Strip* are a scruffy line-up of cheerful leather-clad eccentrics whose music literally throbs and pulsates with a sense of acute individuality and distinct personality. Even if you are not inclined to listen to glam and goth music, one cannot help but fall in love with the wild line-up filmmaker Ryan corralled for his production: The Mistakes, Rebel Rebel, Willow Wisp, Guttersluts, Spiders and Snakes, Kommunity Fk, and the Peppermint Creeps introduce themselves in cheeky and sometimes rude interviews and then roll into their performances with a sense of mission that would suggest the fate of mankind rested on the intensity of their musicalness. Visually, there is no MTV-style fussiness: the flash is kept to a careful minimum while the intelligent camera placements and subtle editing capture the soul of the performances as they happily unfold. The film is a relatively short affair, running only 40 minutes, although Ryan believes the running time is more than adequate.

"It clocked in at 40 minutes because that's how long it took to tell the story," says Ryan. "I was making a documentary, not filling in numbers on a bingo card. However, the production on the 40-minute *Sincerity on the Sunset Strip* took a year and a half to complete, although the filming itself only took a week."

Freaks, Glam Gods and Rockstars is somewhat more flamboyant than *Sincerity on the Sunset Strip*. Even the beginning of the film, with a helicopter tour across the New York skyline, announces something fabulous is happening. Indeed, the film dives deliriously into the vibrant and raucous world of the New York underground music scene, circa 1999-2000, captured with a treasure trove of outlandish performances by an assembly of outrageous rockers who would never be allowed into the increasingly bland and safe worlds of FM radio or MTV offerings. Much of the film pays particular attention to gender-bending performers with predominantly gay audiences, with a surplus of attention given to the foul-mouthed drag queen The "Lady" Bunny (whose act includes off-color versions of Gordon Lightfoot songs, if you can imagine that!). Ryan shot much of the concert footage at Wigstock, a New York cross-dressing extravaganza featuring outlandish performers in excessive costumes, but to provide a hetero balance he also included sequences devoted to the rock duo Daddy and the model-actor-filmmaker-singer Donovan Leitch (who is, to date, the only "name" to appear in Ryan's works).

"The challenge in filming a musical performance is to be honest with the camera," says Ryan. "The camera is a wall between you and the artist; you have to break that wall. Music is sexy, no matter what the style, and if you find the sweat on someone's chest sexy then don't be afraid to shoot it. It is possible to share, in a short few minute clip, someone's emotions — their pain, their joy, their desires to be whomever they want to be without even having to say one word. Some feature-length films don't even begin to touch on that after two and a half hours."

Ryan's films are emotionally closer to classic concert films like *Woodstock* and *Stop Making Sense* rather than to contemporary music videos, which he has also directed and produced. Yet the music video style is not what Ryan was going after. "I'm not aware of what MTV is up to these days," he admits. "Actually, John Waters' *Pink Flamingos* was a major influence — there is certain honesty to John's shots that have an excitement of 'Wow, that really worked!' I will always admire him for that."

Flex Appeal

Another pursuit that mixes a different sort of extreme performance with a lifetime devotion to athletic focus is the sport of bodybuilding. This sport has always been something of an underground endeavor and, not surprisingly, has brought about a subculture of documentaries known as "lifestyle videos." Unlike straightforward documentaries that cover bodybuilding competitions or offer an in-depth perspective into the minds and souls of the athletes (such as the 1977 classic *Pumping Iron*), the bodybuilding lifestyle video is somewhere between a video diary (showing the athlete in training and at home) and the old-fashioned "posing films" that were sold in mail order 8mm reels back in the 1950s and 1960s (which show the athlete flexing and showing off for the camera). As the general interest in fitness in general and bodybuilding in particular began to expand in the 1980s, the lifestyle videos made an effort to lean closer to the concept of documentaries with their focus on the athletes at home and the gym.

"I think along the way the marketing of this product had to expand from the fetishist to a more mainstream audience to keep the cost of doing business in line," says Ace Bannon, president of Xco Media, which produces and distributes bodybuilder lifestyle videos. "So the audience was expanded when the producers added informational content to their videos and started pushing sales toward readers of mainstream bodybuilding magazines. The audiences for the magazines ultimately became the customers for these videos, which is a very mixed group: gay fetishists, gay bodybuilders and gym-goers, straight bodybuilders and gym-goers, and straight guys into sexual fantasies involving bodybuilders and muscle guys. There have historically been very few women consumers of these videos, since the vast majority of women find muscular guys to be freakish in appearance and not at all attractive — to the eternal frustration of the straight bodybuilders!"

A young rebel in search of a cause in Josh Koury's teen alienation documentary *Standing by Yourself*.

The next very big thing: reaching for new heights is bodybuilding champion and documentary filmmaker Paul DeSimone, the creator and subject of *The Underground Lifting Video*.

Curiously, many of the bodybuilders who star in these lifestyle videos are not the reigning champions of the sports. In fact, many are either up-and-comers seeking recognition within the community despite the lack of trophies and competitive honors. (One bodybuilder who took the initiative to create and distribute his own documentary, Paul DeSimone, is profiled later in this chapter.)

"It helps create a larger fan base for a particular competitor," says Bannon. "And those fans can turn into support for the athlete in many different ways: encouraging comments, financial support, and cheering at shows being just a few of them. There is a potential down side, though, and that is that if the bodybuilder's image is presented in the video as too sexy/available, fans can turn into stalkers and show judges (who, interestingly, would have to be either customers who bought the video or unrelenting gossips!) can withhold their best marks as a puritanical (and hypocritical) scolding for the athlete being too 'out there.'"

THE BEST OF UNDERGROUND DOCUMENTARIES

For those seeking an alternative take on reality, here are some great places to start.

Alcatraz is Not an Island (1999): The 1969-71 occupation of the abandoned Alcatraz Island by Native American activists during the height of the so-called "Red Power" movement is recalled with rarely-seen TV news footage and interviews with the participants in this forgotten landmark of the American Indian civil rights struggle. Web site: http://www.turtle-island.com/docu.html

Alzira's Story (2000): Christian de Rezendes' documentary on his grandmother's odyssey from rural Portugal in the 1920s to a new beginning in America and her belated late-life return to her birthplace is a warm, winning celebration of the American dream come true. Web site: http://www.christianderezendes.com

Barry Harris: Spirit of Bebop (2000): A much-needed celebration of the modern jazz pianist/composer and his unheralded impact on the mainstream American musical experience. Web site: http://www.cinemaweb.com/rhapsody

Black Indians: An American Story (2001): The rarely-told story of how African-American and Native American cultures combined through interracial marriages during the 18th and 19th centuries, and how the Afrocentric focus virtually buried all knowledge of the indigenous heritage in many people of mixed race. Web site: http://www.cinemaweb.com/rhapsody

Burying the Past: The Legacy of the Mountain Meadow Massacre (2003): On September 11, 1857, a wagon train heading from Arkansas to California was attacked in an isolated Utah meadow by Mormon settlers dressed up like Indians. This scalding documentary details the horrendous bloodbath and the shameful cover-up by the hierarchy of the Mormon faith in the years that followed. Even today, Mormon leaders refuse to offer any apology to the descendants of the massacre survivor and will not publicly identify the culprits behind the massacre as being Mormons. Web site: http://www.buryingthepast.com/

Champion Blues (2003): Mickey Champion was a top jazz and blues vocalist on the Los Angeles club circuit during the 1940s and 1950s. The film finds her turning 70 and still belting out tunes with a raw power and emotional heft that no youthful vocalist could ever dream of creating. Web site: http://www.championblues.com/

Cul de Sac: A Suburban War Story (2002): In May 1995, an unemployed plumber named Shawn Nelson stole a tank from a California National Guard compound and drove it wildly through the streets of a San Diego suburb. Nelson destroyed property and parked cars and got the tank stuck on a highway divider. The police surrounded the immobilized tank, pried it open with bolt cutters, and opened a fatal volley of gunfire into the tank when he refused to surrender. This bizarre story is recalled by witnesses to Nelson's life and deadly drive. Web site: http://www.frif.com/new2002/cul.html

Das Bus (2003): An experimental documentary featuring bus drivers, passengers, and people with bus phobia which investigates bus culture as modern urban myth. Web site: http://www.dasbus.com

EverQuest Players LFG (2002): A visit to the annual Fan Faire in Baltimore, in which die-hard devotees of the EverQuest computer game arrive in the costume of their favorite characters. This insightful study on the personalities who find themselves hooked on this intricate EverQuest game (to the point of preferring the game to being out in the real world) provides a stunning glimpse into addictive behavior. Web site: http://www.dvdocumentaries.com

Falun Gong's Challenge to China (2001): This jolting and often heartbreaking study of the Communist Chinese government's brutal campaign against the practitioners of the non-political Falun Gong spiritual movement includes photographs and video footage smuggled out of China plus interviews with Falun Gong members who were subjected to imprisonment and torture for attempting to exercise their rights to free assembly and freedom of faith. The film, not surprisingly, has been banned in China. Web site: http://www.hargrovetv.com

Haitian Slave Children: Forgotten Angels (2001): An estimated 300,000 children are abandoned to live and fend for themselves on the streets of Haiti, and many of these children are sold into slavery, where they often suffer from severe abuse resulting in disfigurement and death. This documentary highlights the important humanitarian work undertaken by Michael Brewer, an American registered nurse who runs the Haitian Street Kids Inc. and provides Haiti's abandoned children with the rare opportunity to enjoy shelter, food, and security. Web site: http://www.haitistreetkids.com

The Highwaymen (2000): From the 1940s through the 1970s, a number of self-trained African-American landscape painters traveled the Florida highways and sold their art either from the road or through door-to-door stops at private residences and professional offices. All of the art was cheaply sold, with many paintings later retrieved from junk shops and flea markets for as little as $1 per picture, but today these works are highly popular among some collectors of Florida regional art. Web site: http://www.damicofilm.com

Horns and Halos (2002): The ultimate publishing industry horror story, this documents the controversy surrounding the repeated attempts to publish the unflattering George W. Bush biography *Fortunate Son*. After being withdrawn by St. Martin's Press almost immediately after its first release, the book was picked up tiny Soft Skull Press but was dogged by lawsuits, lingering negative publicity, and ultimately the suicide of author James Hatfield. Web site: http://www.hornsandhalos.com

Kid Protocol (2001): A short documentary about a guy who sneaks into movie-related events by making admission bracelets out of old newspapers, dressing like a caterer, sneaking in unmanned doors, scamming limos, and enacting a process he calls "Chicken Monkey." Web site: http://www.filmthreat.com/Reviews.asp?Id=3222

Lee Priest: The Blonde Myth (1999): The gregarious Australian bodybuilding champ stands a mere 5′4″, but his astonishing physique (including 21-inch biceps) has literally cut his competition down to size while making him one of the most photographed and revered figures in professional bodybuilding. Priest clearly loves being on camera and alternates between macho and playful with brutal displays of his weight-lifting prowess and hilarious explanations on his fixation with Superman memorabilia. Web site: http://www.mocvideo.com

Letters to Uranus: The Hidden Life of Tedd Burr (2001): With his platinum blonde pageboy hairstyle and flowing red gown barely covering a considerable girth, the Ohio-based actor/raconteur Tedd Burr bears a striking resemblance to late-life Peggy Lee. In recounting his long struggle to come to terms with his homosexuality and his quest to raise the culture bar for community theater audiences, Burr spans the range from the sublime to the ridiculous. This single-take documentary makes Burr's storytelling all the more absorbing. Web site: http://www.letterstouranus.com

Mandrake: A Magical Life (2001): Canadian magician Leon Mandrake spent 60 years in the entertainment field without achieving A-list stardom, but his endless path from vaudeville to nightclubs to fairs and carnivals (with an occasional appearance on Canadian television) offers a unique look into the grittier side of second-tier show business. Web site: http://www.makebelievemedia.com/

Mau Mau Sex Sex (2001): Ted Bonnitt's jolly profile of Dan Sonney and David Friedman, the pioneering producer/distributors of exploitation shlock during the 1950s and 1960s. This celebration of vintage grindhouse cinema offers exquisite examples of deranged films where Cambodian women marry gorillas, men turn into goldfish so they can watch women undress over their fishbowl, and rather old-looking teenagers inhale a few puffs of marijuana and experience mind-blowing dementia. Web site: http://www.maumausexsex.com

Not Nude Though: A Portrait of Rudy Burckhardt (2001): The Swiss-born Burckhardt was a pioneering figure in 20th century avant-garde photography, painting, and filmmaking, challenging his fellow artists to push their imaginations further while provoking audiences with his strange and dangerously playful commentaries on American cultures and protocol. The film offers a rich collection of rarely-revived film clips and classic photographic images from Burckhardt's extraordinary output. Web site: http://www.filmthreat.com/Reviews.asp?Id=2461

On Six-Mile Pond (2002): A documentary set in Florida about "mud bogging": the act of driving a truck into a series of muddy ponds. Web site: http://www.filmthreat.com/Reviews.asp?Id=4122

Peanuts (2003): Canadian amateur inventor Jock Brandis took it upon himself to create a hand-operated peanut-shelling machine to help the peanut farmers in Mali prepare their cash crop for market. This might seem like an easy assignment, but Brandis went through countless prototypes in his self-funded quest before finally getting it right. The documentary is both a winning study of bringing economic self-reliance to a dismally poor country and a tribute to the human spirit's unwillingness to take "No!" for an answer. Web site: http://www.bullfrogfilms.com/catalog/pnuts.html

The Real Spider-Man: The Making of the Green Goblin's Last Stand (2002): The documentary about the proliferation of Dan Poole's ill-conceived Spider-Man film, *The Green Goblin's Last Stand*. Web site: http://www.al phadogproductions.net/greengoblin.html

Saltwater Cowboys (2001): The Chincoteague (Virginia) Volunteer Fire Department raises its entire annual operating budget from the proceeds of their annual Fireman's Carnival, which is highlighted by annual herding of the wild ponies of neighboring Assateauge Island and driving them through the waters of the channel separating Assateauge and Chincoteague, where they are put up for auction. While the wild ponies were immortalized in the classic children's book *Misty of Chincoteague*, this documentary offers the human side of the story in providing the single most bizarre and unusual volunteer fire department fundraising operation imaginable. Web site: http://www.fire-police-ems.com/videos/vs1400.shtml

Saving Sheba (2001): Eli Kabillio, who was previously cited in this chapter for his documentaries on outlandish alternative medical treatments, gets autobiographical in this video diary of how he used alternative treatments to aid his 12-year-old cancer-stricken dog Sheba, who was given only three months to live, and to fight his own physical discomforts brought about by years of rough-house athletics. Sheba responded well to homeopathy and acupuncture and lived a year-and-a-half beyond the gloomy three-month prognosis, but Kabillio's ventures into gong therapy and shiatsu massage left him with more aches than he began with. Web site: http://www.maddogfilms.com

Skitzo's Vomitorium (2001): A documentary of metal band Skitzo, which features a great deal of lead singer Lance Ozanix puking on willing women on stage. Web site: http://www.sonic.net/~funkybiz/sk/index2.html

Screamin' Jay Hawkins: I Put a Spell on Me (2002): The veteran blues singer was captured on film during his concert tour across Greece in October 1999, which proved to be uncommonly good timing as Hawkins died four months later. The film details Hawkins' raucous and rowdy life, with the singer speaking freely and often bitterly about his peers while spinning tales on his own adventures which others calmly contradict as being a trifle overcooked. Web site: http://www.screaminjayhawkins.com

UFO File: The Hudson Valley UFO Sightings (2000): If this documentary is to be believed, UFOs have been a common site around New York's Hudson Valley as far back as the 17th century. Footage which is presented as evidence of out-of-this-world visitors (plus, in fairness, hoax footage identified as such) and interviews with those claiming to have close encounters is featured in this balanced and often intriguing film. Web site: http://www.laurient.com

Webcam Boys (2001): A campy collection of gay and gay-for-pay guys who find minor league celebrity and major financial compensation as the stars of Internet webcam sites. While the guys themselves are not the most intriguing group to swish and bump for the camera, the film provides a unique opportunity to explore how the Internet helped bring the gay culture out of the proverbial closet and how a seemingly inane concept with cheapo production values has raked in the digital dollars for many men willing to take it all off. Web site: http://www.webcamboys.tv

What About Me: The Rise of the Nihilist Spasm Band (2001): Canada has given the world such musical talents as Anne Murray, Gordon Lightfoot, Robert Goulet, and Celine Dion. Fortunately for fans of rude music, the Canucks have also exported the Nihilist Spasm Band, who turn their instruments into lethal weapons designed to attack the aural senses. In one priceless moment, R. Buckminster Fuller (of all people!) somehow finds himself in their audience and turns down his hearing aids in order to preserve his sanity. Web site: http://www.subversivemedia.com

White Hotel (1996): The effects of the AIDS pandemic on the people of Eritrea, a small republic in East Africa, is detailed in this harrowing documentary. Web site: http://littlemunk.com/WhiteHotel/

INTERVIEW

PAUL DESIMONE: THE NEXT VERY BIG THING

The first thing you notice about Paul DeSimone is... well, everything. And that is strictly by design and hard work. DeSimone, a 24-year-old Boston-area actor/filmmaker, is also a nationally placed bodybuilding champion. The winner of the Mr. Massachusetts competition, among other honors, possesses one of the most chiseled and well-muscled physiques of any person in the independent cinema realm.

But rather than wait for someone to borrow his muscles for a movie, DeSimone took the initiative to create his own production that works his body to the max. On the surface, DeSimone's documentary diary *The Underground Lifting Video* might seem like just another bodybuilding documentary or DV calling card. But instead, this feature provides one of the most refreshing surprises to come along in ages. Mixing equal parts fly-on-the-wall observations with unexpected chunks of absurdist humor and topped with a sense of genuine sincerity and humanity, *The Underground Lifting Video* is an absorbing gym odyssey where pain and pleasure are served in heaping amounts.

Whether pushing himself too far in weight training (at several points DeSimone complains of nausea and cramps after excessive routines) or indulging in sight gags worthy of Buster Keaton or Jacques Tati (DeSimone inexplicably walks into a parking lot and begins lifting automobiles off the ground), DeSimone's film captures the genuine personality of a driven athlete enjoying his regimen to the fullest. Indeed, not since *Pumping Iron* brought Arnold Schwarzenegger's real-life persona to movie audiences has a sports documentary captured the quirky soul of a competitor building his hunger for success.

While *The Underground Lifting Video* is a remarkable viewing experience, even more amazing was how DeSimone began to distribute his film: by selling the title on eBay, the online auction site. Incredibly, word spread quickly about the film, and not just among bodybuilding enthusiasts. The feedback from the viewers of *The Underground Lifting Video* encouraged him to begin production on a second documentary.

Q. What inspired you to make a film about yourself?

PAUL DESIMONE: In August 2001, I had taken a trip to California and decided to videotape it. It was my first time in California. I had been competing in bodybuilding since 1996 and I had done really well. I had taken two years off from competing to get really big and I wanted to show people how big I had gotten. I went from 230 pounds to 290 pounds in about a year and two months. I gained all that weight naturally.

But don't get me wrong, I was not 290 pounds ripped; I looked more like the guys you see on World's Strongest Man competition. When I went to California, I was almost in shape, enough shape to get noticed, and I knew something was going to happen. So I competed in the Iron Man, a natural NPC event. I finished in third place, so I needed to be a little leaner. During the competition I had talked to many people and two companies that were there showed some interest in sponsoring me: Dorian Yates' company, and ProLab. I ended up signing with Yates and they helped to sponsor the movie.

Q. What was the budget for this production and in what format was it produced?

DESIMONE: The video was shot on small digital cameras. The full budget was around $8,000. Dorian Yates' company basically helped with the budget, but a lot came out of my pocket, too.

Q. Did you attempt to get the video picked up for distribution by companies that specialize in bodybuilding films, like GMV or Repetrope, or did you always consider self-distributing?

DESIMONE: At first I considered selling it to television, but when I went over all the footage that we shot I thought about doing it differently. I wanted to use this movie as an appetizer — this is just a glimpse of me. I know that I can make a much better video with a bigger budget and more help. So I wanted to produce something that gave you an idea, but not the big picture, of what I am about. That's why there is no real one-on-one interviewing.

At one time I did consider selling the video to GMV Productions, but I know that once the second video goes out and is sold that people will want to see the first video. In fact, nearly everyone who purchased the first video wants to see a second.

Q. How and where do you sell the video? And what is the suggested retail price? And where have most of the sales come from?

DESIMONE: The video is sold from both my web sites. It is also sold on eBay, on occasion. I produced a special version of the video that is limited to only five copies; at the moment I have three left and they are being sold for $100 a piece. The video itself is sold for $28.00 and that includes shipping. I sell to people all over the world as long as they have an NTSC-capable VCR. I do not produce copies in PAL, though I could, but it's just too much of a pain in the ass. California and New Jersey are my biggest selling states, with New York and Pennsylvania not too far behind. But if someone cannot afford a video and really wants one, I sometimes send them one for free.

Q. Why did you opt to release your video on eBay and what has the response been from eBay shoppers?

DESIMONE: Actually, everyone who got a copy on eBay loved the video. I think there was only one person who did not like the video because he said there wasn't enough talking. But I have gotten amazing e-mails from some younger viewers who told me I have inspired them to compete and get in shape. I really love those e-mails because they help me to "keep the eye of the tiger."

Q. How many copies have you sold to date?

DESIMONE: So far I sold around 100, but I've given away about 100 so there are around 200 copies out there somewhere! That's not a lot of videos, but if one person watches the video with some other people it really gets things going.

Q. In self-distributing the video, what were the major challenges that you faced and how did you overcome them?

DESIMONE: Oh jeez, there are so many obstacles. First, if you have not attended film school, don't even try. Second, if you don't know anything about marketing, it's not going to work. I know I had a great package (my body) and I needed to market it in a manner so people who don't know me would know me. So I ended up creating a web site targeted towards bodybuilding.

I told all the people I knew about it and I started promoting it in chat rooms. Then I entered my video in many different film festivals. After that, I started doing some advertising and I even got a few stores to advertise for me. The real major challenge is getting people to notice your product when you're not a pro bodybuilder who is famous from the bodybuilding magazines. But all of those years training in the gym really paid off for me.

Most people do not know that I am a 100% drug-free bodybuilder; in fact not many people even believe that. People said it was impossible to be 230-pound all-natural ripped and I did that at age 22. Now I am 24, working on 245 ripped all-natural, and people still think it can't be done. You can accomplish anything that people say you can't, as long as you believe. Just being all natural wouldn't make me a great body-builder, but it's the training and diet that really makes you grow.

The hardest part is getting ripped because using drugs would really get me there a lot faster and easier. So it wasn't so much the getting my name out, but more of getting my body and pictures ready and then letting people access those pics. My body did the advertising while my name was attached to the body.

Q. What advice can you give to others who might want to duplicate your experience in making videos and self-releasing them?

DESIMONE: First you need to get an idea and figure out where you want to go with it. Figure out what is your main objective. Then save some money up to get a good camera and find some good people to work in the production. Build a web site and work around the web site. Then start shooting and don't stop shooting. Get organized and finish the project; don't let things unwind — do it and don't stop till you're satisfied. When you're done, advertise for as long as it takes on your web site. Then try eBay or Yahoo. From there, the sky is the limit. But beware, on eBay people are looking for a bargain, so keep your prices consistent.

Q. What is your new video about and how are you planning to release it?

DESIMONE: My new video, which is being shot now, features my new training principles along with my new body, bigger and leaner. But there will be a more personal approach like contest info, workouts, eating and diet, interviews, and I introduce a few new characters. This video is going to be great! The stuff that we shot so far is really interesting and it will be better than the first video. This is going to be something that will really get you motivated.

But the first video, of course, has me lifting cars. I have not picked up a car yet for the new one, but may pick up some people and do some crazy lifts. I did a 600-pound bent-over row in the new video and no one in history has done that. I may do an Incredible Hulk gag in the video where I'm painted green and I run around the mall scaring people. If any one is looking for a good-looking bodybuilder to play a role in their movie, e-mail me at xxtralargemuscle@aol.com.

I sold one minute of the movie to Fox Sports to put on one of their shows. I also am talking to PBS about doing a documentary on bodybuilding, sort of a *Pumping Iron* type of sequel. People call me "Young Arnold" and I like that a lot. But I prefer "Big Pauly D."

4: Rod Serling's Children

There is an awful lot of horror and science fiction in today's underground cinema. And, truth be told, there is also a lot of awful horror and science fiction.

Horror and sci-fi dominates the underground cinema, perhaps more than any other genre. There are many production companies and distributors who focus almost exclusively on these type of films. With the glut of such films comes a high quantity of media (both in print and online) which celebrates underground horror and sci-fi.

But quantity is not the same as quality, and the level of quality control is a major problem here. Quite frankly, too many titles are spilling an excess of blood and gore without creating the emotional and intellectual groundwork that makes classic horror and sci-fi so intoxicating to the senses.

"Most of the current underground horror and sci-fi efforts merely try to copy what Hollywood is currently doing, but without the budgets," observes James O'Ehley, editor of the *Sci-Fi Movie Page*. "Sure, some horror movies may be more 'hard core' in that they feature more blood and gore, but this seems to be missing the point. The point is to make the sort of movies Hollywood isn't making: intelligent and clever. The problem always with cheapie straight-to-video sci-fi movies is that they try to exploit a particular film's box office success. If *The Terminator* did well, then a host of films will feature killer androids and so forth."

What are the roots of this problem? O'Ehley notes that many filmmakers in this genre are not well-versed with the classic literary roots that drive the classic movies. "Few of these filmmakers actually bother with trying to film science fiction novels and short stories, of which there are many good ones out there," he says. "Maybe it's because today's kids spend more time playing video games than they do reading, but like most Hollywood offerings their movies aren't really pure sci-fi. Instead they are action movies with sci-fi trappings."

Lawrence P. Raffel, film editor for the online magazine *Monsters at Play*, joins O'Ehley's comments by noting the absence of a basic element that goes into filmmaking: talent. "The major problem is that everyone who has a camera thinks they are a filmmaker and this is just simply not the case," he opines. "There's more to making a film than just operating the equipment — and some indie filmmakers can't even get that part right! There has to be vision, you have to be able to tell a story or evoke some kind of emotion (good or bad) out of your audience. I know as a reviewer myself, I tend to cut the indie filmmakers a bit more slack, and I think that these guys use this handicap as a crutch. I'm reminded of this each time I see an indie film that impresses me so much, I begin to rethink my stance on films I had seen previously.

"I understand how hard it is to put together an indie production and I'm aware of all of the effort that goes into it. However, this does not make a good movie. All of the effort in the world will not turn a bad film good and in this instance kudos are NOT warranted. I've seen some indie films that are just terrible and wind up seeing a lot of attention somehow. Then there are those indie films that are simply spectacular and they never see the light of day. Just another reason why quality outlets are so important for bringing these flicks (good or bad) to the public's attention."

But are today's underground horror/sci-fi filmmakers doing a good job in getting a high level of scares and creeps out of their traditional low budgets? "Some are and some aren't," continues Raffel. "As far as the scare factor goes — no, not really. I don't think I've seen many (if any) recent indie flicks that I thought were particularly scary except for maybe *The Collingswood Story* or *13 Seconds*. Some do retain a certain level of creepiness and then there's always the disturbing factor, which I think can be equally as important, but not necessarily scary. I will say that the film-makers who are getting a certain expected reaction out of their audience are doing their job well (and there are quite a few accomplishing this). Considering the ultra low-budget film levels of today's films, I'd say that some of these filmmakers are doing something right and these artists would probably work wonders with larger budgets."

On the other side of that argument is Alan Simpson, editor of the horror film review site *Sex Gore Mutants*, who believes low budgets should not be synonymous with low quality. "While I'm sure some indie filmmakers would love endless funding to create their visions I don't actually think that budget should be a major stumbling block," says Simpson. "In fact sometimes lack of funding could work to their benefit as they need to be more creative rather than lazily kick back knowing that they can pay for the right look or effects scene. Poverty-row filmmaking inspires creativity; an artist with a hunger has fire in their belly and hence will want to make sure every shot means some-thing. A filmmaker with a burger in one hand and access to CGI effects will always take the easy way out — get the shot in the can, job done. While I'd be the first to put my hand up and state my love for splat-ter and gore the true classic horror filmmaker can scare the pants off a viewer by 'not' actually showing the 'money shot' — often what we don't see is far scarier then what we do - and the clever low-budget film maker can use this to their advantage."

Nathan Shumate, film critic and editor for the cult movies review mag-azine *Cold Fusion Video*, echoes Simpson's sentiments. "CGI has greatly expanded what is possible to be shown on the big screen," he says. "Some of the effects may still be dodgy, but filmmakers forget special effects should be in aid of the story and not the other way round."

However, Shumate comments the nature of the genre has always deter-mined that high quality classics will be in eternal short supply. "There is a lot of rubbish in sci-fi," he says. "Always has been and always will be. It is difficult to say whether better sci-fi movies were made in previ-ous decades or not, but I am a huge fan of pre-*Star Wars* 1970s cinema — an era in which both Hollywood and indie producers took a lot more chances. Also, those movies had an attitude about them which is out of step with today's very conformist and conservative times. Some favorites include *Death Race 2000, A Boy and His Dog,* and *Dark Star.* What is needed are some intelligent and clever screenplays. Let mainstream Hollywood do the big action stuff."

Since creating an inventory of the junk side of the genre would take up a book unto itself, let's focus instead on the talented filmmakers and provocative films that shine here. Underground horror and sci-fi is hardly lacking for gems, although sometimes it seems that you need to dig through a mine full of muck to locate a few diamonds. Fortunately, we've done the digging for you.

Eric Stanze: The Ghoul, the Bad and the Ugly

The low-budget horror film has been the creative testing ground for an extraordinary number of directors who have either graduated to A-list mega-stardom or have achieved a global cult following thanks to the sting of their B-Movies. The challenge is easy enough to recognize: creating a work of celluloid art in a genre happily denigrated by critics and audiences alike for its intellectual and financial poverty. Even some of the more outlandish schlockmeisters of the genre such as Edward D. Wood Jr. and Larry Buchanan have been toasted as champions of rib-tickling camp — honors which are conspicuously absent from the no-talent directors of other low-budget genres such as B-Westerns or B-Comedies.

While it is easy enough to trace the rise of a Francis Ford Coppola or John Carpenter or celebrate the oeuvres of Roger Corman or George Romero, it is perhaps more satisfying to locate the heirs to their cinematic heritage. One clear heir seems to be St. Louis–based filmmaker Eric Stanze, who has created an astonishing output of jolting, original low-budget horror flicks which provide an intellectual and artistic shock.

Based in St. Louis ("Five minutes from that big Arch thing," he jokes), Stanze completed his first feature at the age of 18 with *The Scare Game* (1990), in which a wizard's apprentice is transformed into a demon who forces unsuspecting people into a deadly game which results in the forfeiture of their souls. This was followed with *The Fine Art* (1994), with a college student who engages in a lethal cat-and-mouse chase with a psychotic assailant; *Savage Harvest* (1995), where the spirit of a murdered Cherokee shaman is accidentally released from its resting place, with devastating results for the descendants of its assassins; *Ice From the Sun* (1999), an astonishing work rich with experimental film-making techniques in which the angels and Satan find the balance between Heaven and Hell disrupted by a third force; *Scrapbook* (2000), which follows a serial killer who kidnaps and tortures a woman and forces her to record the experience in a diary before she is executed; and *I Spit on Your Corpse, I Piss on Your Grave* (2001), in which a serial killer's prisoner overpowers and executes her captor, but in her madness assumes the role of captor and tortures other abductees who were being held in captivity.

Unlike many films in this genre, the films of Eric Stanze stand out for their audacity and imagination. Yes, the blood and gore of the genre are present — but the true horror here is the casual cerebral sadism which offers a disturbing parallel universe that truly makes the viewer uncomfortable in the right way. *Savage Harvest* frames its tale in the miserable historic treatment of the Native American people, offering a historic weight which questions whether the vengeance -seeking spirit or its historically-indifferent victims are the true monsters.

Ice From the Sun finds its hero in the unlikely state of a woman brought back from a fall into suicide into a role she never expected against a foe she could never have possibly imagined exists. *Scrapbook* takes the Catharsis 101 ploy of keeping a diary to record one's progress and uses it to cruelly document an inevitable demise. While it is one thing to be scared by a bogeyman with a hatchet, it is far more terrifying to see the basic tenets of civilized life turned slightly to reveal a nastier existence which rests quietly around us.

"Probably the biggest lesson that I've learned is that movies are art... so you will never please everyone," says Stanze. "Art is viewed differently by everyone, so one person's tastes in movies may align with mine, but the next guy will think my movies really suck. My distributor, Sub Rosa Studios, really supports what I do. But I've had other distributors ask me why I even bother to make these angry, nasty, upsetting films! So the point is, fuck trying to please other people. I try to make movies that please me while I'm shooting them and please me when I watch the finished product. If I ever get to make a decent living at this, perhaps this attitude will change slightly. Ironically, the movies that I've made where I've been most in the mode of "who cares what other people think?" have been the movies that have become most successful! Fans say they like these movies more and the reviews are better. Look at *The Scare Game*, my first movie. That is one of the worst movies I have ever seen! But when we made it, I had no intention of pursuing home video distribution. And I had that "who cares what people think of this movie?" attitude. We didn't try to do anything with that movie except have fun while we were shooting it. We weren't thinking about marketing or genre or distribution then. But people liked that movie and it got picked up for distribution, hitting video stores all over the U.S. and in a bunch of foreign countries. To this day I have people tell me that *The Scare Game* is their favorite movie of everything I've made! That astounds me."

Unlike other horror and sci-fi filmmakers, Stanze fills his work with disturbing theological subplots and contexts: the disruption of Heaven and Hell in *Ice from the Sun*, the revenge of the murdered Cherokee shaman in *Savage Harvest*, the self-deifying wizard-turned-demon of *The Scare Game*. Even Stanze's music video for the comic song "Put Your Feet in the Wedding Cake" by the band Hotel Faux Pas (which was included in the anthology film *The Severed Head Network*) took on a religious feeling by having the video shot in an empty church. Ironically, religion does not play a major role in Stanze's work beyond the set.

"I am agnostic, so I approach theological story points in a 'what if?' mode," he explains. "Religion to me is just mythology, but certainly still fascinating. I just think there are so many interesting stories that can come out of religion. I think what attracts me to using religious images and concepts is that it is an opportunity to explore what I believe to be fantasy but many other people really believe in. People generally don't believe in vampires or zombies, so the emotional impact of that kind of horror movie is not as great. But a story takes on more weight if you introduce devils or angels or God or hell. Because you may actually believe in those things, or someone else in the room may truly believe. It personalizes the drama. I used to think that I should place limitations on where I take religious concepts. While I am not religious, I do not have a desire to offend religious persons. But a few of the guys who make these movies with me are Christians and they actually like the religious concepts in my movies for the same reasons I do. They aren't offended. They like the fact that these concepts carry the emotional impact that they do. They like the fact that movies that carry these concepts make the religious viewer challenge their faith, which makes their faith stronger. They like that these concepts make intelligent people think about what they believe in."

Some reviewers have found the level of horror and bloodshed in Stanze's films to be a bit too much. For *I Spit on Your Corpse, I Piss on Your Grave*, Stanze filled the screen with situations that rarely turn up in any film, underground or mainstream. As a genuinely shocked Michael B. Scrutchin of *Flipside Movie Emporium* describes it: "You've got full-frontal nudity from nearly every cast member, including a few minutes of sex and masturbation that venture into hardcore porn territory, along with the requisite graphic violence, gore, shit-eating, and masturbating with broom handles (yes, Emily Haack goes all the way). Finally, there's that insufferable scene with (Haack) going to work on a guy using her trusty broom handle. Damn, that's something I never needed to see. Ever."

Reaction to such sequences divided journalists who cover the genre. On one hand, there is Eric Campos at *Film Threat* who declared: "I've seen a lot of over-the-top gross-out stuff, but this movie features some of the most brain-searing graphic violence that I've ever had the pleasure of being witness to. Boundaries are definitely broken through here, not only for violence, but for sexual situations as well. Up until this point, the only place I can recall ever seeing "insertion" in a movie is in a porno, but in *I Spit On Your Corpse, I Piss On Your Grave* there's a scene graphically showing Sandy giving herself the old poke with a broom handle. Whoah! Wasn't expecting that one! And that's just a small sample of the many ways this film is bound to surprise its audience."

On the other hand, there is Christopher Null of *FilmCritic.com* who kept his thoughts brief but succinct: "A true low point in cinema."

Does Stanze have boundaries where he says: "No, that's going too far!"? Says Stanze: "The concept of 'too far' depends on the project. Things we did in *Ice From the Sun* would have been going too far for *Savage Harvest*. Things we did in *Scrapbook* would have been going too far for *Ice From the Sun.* So nothing is out of bounds if it is appropriate to the individual movie. I have my own personal tastes as to where I'd like to not see things go, but sometimes this isn't what is best for the movie. I don't watch *Scrapbook* very much. As an individual movie watcher, the level of violence in *Scrapbook* is beyond what I want to see. But it is extremely appropriate for that movie, so I wouldn't change a bit of it."

TERRY M. WEST GETS FLESHY

For writer-turned-actor-turned-filmmaker Terry M. West, underground horror is the place to be. "I think that the independently-produced horror film market is stronger than it has ever been," he says. "With the advent of affordable technology, filmmakers are able to create and the limitations of the media make them strive harder to create the best that they can."

Yet West confides that underground horror filmmakers working in Europe and Asia sometimes seem to have it somewhat easier. "I don't think they have to worry so much about being commercial," he adds. "Here in America, the main consensus is tone it down. Filmmakers are encouraged to push the envelope overseas. Here, studios and producers want a certain Gen X (aren't we up to Z yet?) hip and cool horror lite. EVERYTHING has to have a happy ending (or a redeeming ending). I actually enjoy a lot of European and Asian horror for the fact that the movies are truly horrific and graphic. Horror should be extreme, not safe and comfortable."

There is nothing safe or comfortable in West's films, but there is plenty of style and more than a few good scares. After gaining notice as the author of young adult novels and horror short stories (most notably the "Confessions of a Teenage Vampire" series published by Scholastic), he made his first film in 2000 by adapting his comic series *Blood for the Muse* for the screen.

Shot in an appropriately creepy black-and-white (a tribute to George Romero's debut film *Night of the Living Dead* — West jokingly claims to "pray at the altar of George Romero"), *Blood for the Muse* follows a video store clerk who is also a serial killer preying on prostitutes. His crime spree has a bit of a pagan tinge to it: the murders are actually sacrificial killings designed to summon Melpomene, the ancient muse of tragedy also known as the "Dark Muse." Things get a bit complicated when he finally meets a pretty young lady and begins to question whether his actions have been appropriate — or whether this fine young lass is the ultimate sacrifice for his elusive muse.

Joe Kane, the syndicated columnist known (and loved) as the Phantom of the Movies and publisher of *Videoscope Magazine*, hailed *Blood for the Muse* as "better than *The Blair Witch Project!*" Strong reviews from online horror review sites followed. Yet West, curiously, opted away from straight horror in favor of a burst of features that mixed horror with parody and the faintest suggestions of erotica. In a two-year period he directed five features — *Sexy 6th Sense* and *Witchbabe*, both in 2001, and *Vampire Queen, Satan's School for Lust* and *Lord of the G-Strings*, all in 2002. The films are amusing for those with a taste for camp, and the sultry presence of B-Movie goddess Misty Mundae as West's leading lady helps to detract attention from inadequacies in scripting and production. Yet the promise of *Blood for the Muse* was not being well-served with these quickie jobs.

West, thankfully, has rebounded with the stunning 2003 release *Flesh for the Beast*. In this film, a team of parapsychologists (five men and a woman) investigate a haunted manor that was allegedly once a bordello where flesh-eating demons took the form of sensual prostitutes to prey on unsuspecting men. During their investigations, the male parapsychologists are visited by and fatally seduced by the seductive siren-demons of years gone by. The sole woman on the team discovers (not to her benefit) a mystical medallion which was first used a century earlier to conjure the demons.

Blessed with superb camerawork, a strikingly off-beat music score by Buckethead and colorful appearances by B-Movie veterans Caroline Munro and Aldo Sanbrell, *Flesh for the Beast* was (pardon the expression) a cut above your typical horror film. The resulting production was so strong that Media Blasters Releasing, which originally produced the film with the intention of taking it straight to video, instead secured a theatrical release. Even the *New York Times* got in on the act, with critic Dave Kehr cheering: "Fans of the genre — or 'gore hounds' as they are

A jocular ocular creature runs amok in Eric Stanze's *Ice from the Sun*.

Gals and ghouls congregate in Terry M. West's *Flesh for the Beast*.

known in fandom — will find plenty to enjoy in Mr. West's enthusiastic approach to his work."

Since the male characters are doomed from their encounters with the demonic seductresses, West needed to avoid the obvious in serving up the chills and scares. "Because most of the deaths occur after a seduction, it's rather like shooting fish in a barrel," he says. "What I attempted to do was present this dark fantasy that these researchers were finding suddenly personified. Then, when these guys are at their weakest (i.e. pants down around ankles) they are subjected to the most hideous death they can imagine. It was taking these universal fantasies men have and turning them on a dime. It was like having an audience teased and, yes, possibly turned on and then throwing a bucket of cold water on them."

As with Eric Stanze, West does not have a set limit for going easy on his audience in regards to violence levels. "It depends on the film I'm making, on what kind of feel I am going for," he continues. "For example, *Blood for the Muse* had very little gore, but people still refer to it as extremely gory. With *Flesh*, the plan was always to be as extreme as possible. I don't know if extreme gore will always be a staple of my work. If it is necessary to the type of film I am doing, then there will be a lot of crimson flowing. But, sometimes, the suggestion of it can be just as, if not more, powerful."

Audiences are not complaining, West adds. "By and large, the feedback has been tremendous. Of course, there are those who feel it goes too far. Horror is such a subjective genre. People have so many different tastes. There are those who hold *Flesh* up as one of the new spearheads of old school horror, and there are others who accuse it of being soft core porn. *Flesh* has benefitted from coming out at a time when excessive horror seems to be becoming more and more acceptable."

TIM RITTER: GOLD WITH THE COPPERMASK

True addicts of underground horror will genuflect at the mention of Tim Ritter's name. As the creative force behind contemporary cult classics including the *Truth or Dare?* trilogy or the grisly features *Creep* and

Killing Spree, Ritter has been terrifying and entertaining audiences with his intense, envelope-pushing approach to filmmaking that liberally mixes pulse-banging suspense with unapologetic violence. If Alfred Hitchcock and Herschell Gordon Lewis had their genes spliced together, the result would easily be Tim Ritter.

Born on a Friday the 13th back in 1967, Ritter was still in high school when he scripted, directed and edited his first feature, a 1984 Super 8mm production called *Day of the Reaper*. Shrewdly recognizing the potential of the then-nascent direct-to-video market, Ritter self-distributed his production to video wholesalers and, in the process, helped lay the groundwork for a new generation of underground filmmakers to reach a wide audience.

Ritter then co-directed the video anthology *Twisted Illusions* (1985) and in 1986 wrote and directed *Truth or Dare? A Critical Madness*. This uncommonly disturbing and powerful production is about a man who comes home ahead of schedule one night and discovers his wife in bed with his best friend. Unable to cope with the shame, the betrayed husband mutilates himself and is committed to a mental hospital. After extensive psychotherapy sessions, he is declared sane and released — but this diagnosis soon proves to be acutely premature. The mainstream media later discovered the film because it included an early acting gig for A. J. McLean of The Backstreet Boys in a small role (McLean would never take credit for the film, although he is clearly identifiable and is listed in the credits). Genre fans have embraced this film as a classic and have made the film's bete noir, the Coppermasked Madman, something of an icon.

Ritter followed *Truth or Dare?* with *Killing Spree* (1987), a gruesome tale of a young newlywed who becomes obsessed with the notion his beautiful bride is having sexual encounters with their suburban neighbors and even with strangers. He retaliates by launching a methodical and highly inventive campaign to eliminate the alleged lovers, using weapons ranging from a screwdriver to a large ceiling fan, and then buries their bodies in his backyard. However, his victims don't intend to rest in peace!

Throughout the 1980s and 1990s, Ritter helmed his own productions and also served a variety of function on other works including stints as writer, editor, second unit director, narrator, and even "creative consultant." In 1995, he directed *Creep*, a horrifying adventure following the crime trail of sibling serial killers. Even in the no-holds-barred world of B-Movie filmmaking, *Creep* struck more than a few nerves and 25 minutes of footage was excised before the film could hit the video stores; a restored version was subsequently released a few years later.

In 1999, Ritter achieved a personal best with his wicked *Dirty Cop, No Donut*. This wild, sicko parody of police-reality TV shows focused its cinema verite camera on a lunatic cop (named Officer Friendly!) barreling through an all-night rampage of bullying and brutality. The film earned Ritter his best reviews, including praise from the influential *Amazing World of Cult Movies* which cited the film as "everything an indie cult film should be." A sequel, *Dirty Cop, No Donut 2: I am a Pig* rolled out a year later with Officer Friendly on the loose for more miscreant shenanigans.

"I think the key to making a successful horror film is having people behind it that are passionate about the genre and the project they are making," says Ritter. "If someone is doing it just to make money or as just a 'job for hire,' they are less likely to come up with something that connects with the hardcore fan and delivers the goods. And even if you have all of that behind a given project, sometimes things just don't come out as you might have liked because of monetary restrictions or other extraneous factors. But examples where the synergy of the creative people behind it really worked and paid off include *Henry: Portrait of a Serial Killer, Last House on the Left, The Night of the Living Dead, The Texas Chainsaw Massacre* and, more recently, *Scream*. Those are some of my personal favorites. Most of these are independent films that were made outside the studio system and due to everyone's inexperience, passion, and desire to work together, the movies paid off. *Scream* is an example of a passionate script that was written by a fan and starring TV actors really wanting to branch out, with Wes Craven putting one hundred percent into the production. You could tell he was really inspired to make that movie, unlike *Scream 3*, where everything seemed tired, worn out, and strictly done for the cash. That's why most mainstream horror films fall short in the chills and thrills area and only occasionally do something really smart and wicked get through the pipeline. They are being made by people who don't necessarily love the genre."

Ritter himself is not immune to sequels — *Truth or Dare? A Critical Madness* had two additional adventures. However, Ritter feels the series needs to take a long rest. "At this time, there's no plans for a fourth installment," he claims. "But you never know if the right story hits me! So I wouldn't ever completely rule it out because I'm such a fan of Jason and those *Friday the 13th* flicks. The creative energies behind the Coppermasked Madman were my enthusiasm for those Jason flicks and wanting to emulate those classics. There were a lot of kids that rented *Truth or Dare?* to watch at slumber parties late at night when it first came out! It's very cool to meet them now and hear the great memories they had being scared by that movie when they were very young. It's like a campfire tale!"

Ritter's forced editing of 25 minutes from *Creep* is a very rare of example of somehow holding up a stop sign in the path of underground horror. "There were a lot of scenes cut because we were trying to appease mainstream video stores and not have a movie that was relegated to the back room, if we were lucky," he recalls. "If you mix extreme sex and violence, you limit your sales and we were obligated to the investors to try and deliver something that would make back a decent return. We ended up getting ripped off by a lot of dishonest wholesalers and after Sub Rosa took control of *Creep*, it was decided to add in a lot of the scenes that were trimmed. There's some flashbacks with the killers' abusive parents that were put back in. There's an extended sequence or two with Kathy Willets in the strip club and when she kills the photographer, it's much longer. And there's a big video montage that leads up to the ending which was put back in that better explains how the female cop hunted the creep down. There's also a lot more blood, sex, and skin as well. Audiences have really enjoyed the additions from what I've heard and a lot of people that bought the movie the first time are evidently buying it again to see the new stuff. They know exactly what they are getting and there's been no complaints. A lot of reviewers have said it is a much stronger, cutting edge movie now because of all this. Critic Allen Richards of *B-Independent.com* said the film 'wears its sleaziness like a badge of honor' and that he had trouble shaking some of the images from his mind, so that's a good accomplishment for any movie these days!"

Of all Ritter's horror films, *Dirty Cop, No Donut* is clearly his most unusual. An outrageous goof on police-reality shows like *COPS*, the film provides graphic violence with a maniac cop taking the law into his own hand

and excessively punishing miscreants while a stunned video camera crew follows him on his twilight patrol. While presenting an opportunity for supremely bad taste (in one scene, an accused rapist is forced by the rogue cop to castrate himself), it is saved in large part through Joel D. Wynkoop's over-the-top performance as the demented policeman and Ritter's gift for making the most extreme situation seem absurd.

Fortunately, *Dirty Cop, No Donut* did not create enemies within law enforcement. "Most officers realize it's an exaggerated comedy, like a *Saturday Night Live* skit on acid, and they laugh their heads off at it!" exclaims Ritter. "Most police officers really have a great sense of humor about things like *Dirty Cop* because they see so many bad things day in and day out. The officers I've talked to have really vented with *Dirty Cop* and had a good time with it. But if you don't like this type of movie or have a really sick sense of humor, nothing is going to change that. Yet *Dirty Cop* was never made as a statement against police; it just shows what could happen if someone let that kind of power get to their head for a night. And stuff like we portrayed in the movie has happened, unfortunately. But what good cop can honestly say that he wouldn't love to destroy a drunk driver's car? With all the lives that have been wrecked by drunk drivers, this is the very least I would think they would like to do in a fantasy context! And that's what a movie like *Dirty Cop* is all about — harmless fantasies and frustrations being released when you watch the piece."

Ritter has cut back on his horror filmmaking. His last horror film to date has been a 40-minute segment for the anthology feature *Twisted Illusions 2*, which has not been released yet. He has also published two novels and is working on a non-horror feature film with a religious theme called *Reconciled*. Yet he is also working on several horror screenplays and it is not difficult to assume that he will be directing more underground horror soon.

DEBBIE ROCHON: B-QUEEN GETS AN A+

One of the most celebrated icons in today's underground horror and sci-fi orbit is actress Debbie Rochon. She has appeared in more than 100 films to date and can be found in anywhere from five to 12 releases per year. Born in Vancouver and now based in New York, Rochon has developed into one of the most versatile and beloved stars of this genre. Her star power is so strong that she was asked to host the inaugural B-Movie Film Festival in 1999.

In films such as *Hellblock 13* (1999), *In the Hood* (1998), the Troma self-parody *Tromeo and Juliet* (1996), *Santa Claws* (1996), and *Black Easter* (1994), Rochon reigns with a consistent stream of entertaining, on-target performances which helps keep the genre alive and thriving. It is fairly easy to see why she rose to the top of this genre. Her beauty is more than apparent, but she is hardly just another pretty face. When she is on-screen, Rochon commands attention with her poise, diction, and sense of focus in her performance.

With training at three of New York City's most prestigious acting academies (the Lee Strasberg Institute, the Michael Chekov Studio, and the Herbert Berghof Studio), she did extensive work in New York's off-Broadway theater and in theatrical workshops before embarking on a full-time movie career. Whether her films bubble over the top or get a bit tawdry in their plotlines, Rochon's performance moors the production with a sense of professionalism that keeps the viewer enraptured by her true star presence.

Rochon's first film was as a preteen: the 1981 punk rock feature *Ladies and Gentlemen, The Fabulous Stains!* starring two unknowns named Laura Dern and Diane Lane. The film is now regarded as a cult classic, but originally its theatrical release was delayed for several years and then it was barely shown. "It was amazing because it was a Paramount Pictures film and the budget was very high," recalls Rochon. "It was a great experience because I spent three months on the set and really got to experience what making a movie was like. The food, the money and the positive attention was great for me at that time. I never interacted with Laura Dern, but Diane Lane was interesting. She was very much into the 'lead actress' thing but suffered a lot of independence issues with her mother being present all the time. She felt like she wanted to get away from her, but who doesn't at that age?"

To date, Rochon has not appeared in another Hollywood production — a fact she is hardly complaining about, given her excessively heavy work schedule. Yet even though many of her films can cause shivers

Actress
Debbie Rochon

Debbie Rochon

The occupants of a stately mansion discover a serial killer's handiwork in Andrew Repasky McElhinney's *A Chronicle of Corpses*.

just mentioning their titles (try *Rage of the Werewolf* or *Sandy Hook Lingerie Party Massacre* or *Dr. Horror's Erotic House of Idiots*), she enjoys the genre immensely and the unique dramatic challenges it presents.

"Some movies you do for the love of the craft and some for the money," she admits. "I'm a big fan of the horror/sci-fi/fantasy genre, ever since I was a little girl, and I enjoy working with 'creatures'! You just simply do the best job possible under the circumstances that are presented to you. If a movie is very rushed and doesn't have the script to showcase your talents or range, then you just go with the flow and do your best and that's it. I always try and enjoy myself regardless."

During the 1990s, Rochon was the reigning goddess of the beloved goof-factory called Troma Pictures. "I know it may not be a well-known fact, but all three of the movies I have made with Troma (*Tromeo and Juliet, Terror Firmer* and *Citizen Toxie: The Toxic Avenger Part 4*) each had a half-million dollar budget," she notes. "In the low budget world that's not so incredibly low. To Hollywood it is, but not compared to a lot of independent flicks. I met (Troma co-founder) Lloyd Kaufman in 1993 and started shooting movie posters and appearing at promotional functions with Troma. Then in 1995 we made *Tromeo and Juliet*, which was the first film Lloyd had directed in four or five years. *Tromeo and Juliet* was my first Troma movie so I didn't know what would happen. I loved the script from the moment I read it, but had no idea if it would be taken well or not. I was thrilled to find out that not just the Troma fans loved it, but some really mainstream folks too. We shot a four-hour movie and it was cut down to 90-ish minutes, so everybody had a lot of their scenes cut... including me!"

Some critics dismiss contemporary B-Movies as excessively violent and misogynistic in their depiction of women. Does Rochon feel there is any worth in such criticism? "Sure! Absolutely. But, I have always said film is a reflection of us, and an expression of us. If we were not allowed to make whatever movie we wanted to then it wouldn't be nearly as expressive a medium. If we could only use subject matter that depicted everyone in a nice correct way then all you would see is Disney films. I think there's a place for strong women in cinema and a place for 'fantasy' women in cinema and the same goes for men too. Men are stereotyped just as often as we are."

Rochon, on more than a few occasions, found herself in a position that is not uncommon for low-budget and no-budget filmmaking: the production shuts down due to lack of funds, leaving the film unfinished. Rochon's work in *Negatives* starring Duane Jones (of *Night of the Living Dead* fame) and the haunted asylum thriller *Strawberry Estates* (which was completed after a hiatus of a few years, albeit without Rochon), were among her aborted efforts. The actress admits it is difficult to keep her faith in the profession when she arrives at the set and discovers the film is canceled.

"Yeah, it's always a bummer!" she exclaims. "But that's the way it goes. It can be very depressing. I just started a film a couple of months ago in Las Vegas and it had to shut down because the director got very ill. I would have worked with Michael Berryman in that flick! I was sad about that."

Rochon's versatility has recently manifested itself in other pursuits, including the writing of a column in Joe Bob Briggs' newsletter/zine The Joe Bob Report and authoring a book on working in B-Movies. She tried her hand at co-producing with the 2000 feature *Split* and has been involved in other aspects of behind-the-camera work. She recently completed a non-underground feature, the dark comedy *Nowhere Man* for art-house favorite Tim McCann (*Desolation Angels, Revolution #9*), which is slated for a 2005 release.

A Gallery of Ghouls

For those with the courage to dive into the world of underground horror and sci-fi, here are some of the best films that you may wish to consider:

Absolution (2003): John Specht's theological horror-thriller about a fallen angel whose desire to experience life among the mortals involves the disappearance of discs that are key to the most devastating weapon on the face of the planet. The angel has to make the choice of interfering with the flow of mankind or watch mankind destroy itself with this new weapon. Web site: http://www.b-movie.com

American Nightmare (2000): Psychological thriller set on Halloween. Seven friends are stalked by a killer as the pirate radio show "American Nightmare" is broadcasting. Web site: http://www.american-nightmare.com

Aquanoids (2003): A Florida beach town is plagued by political and corporate corruption, but that soon pales when deep sea creatures with a taste for bikini-clad gals start hitting the beach. Web site: http://www.cinemacabre.com

Blood Feast 2 (2002): Sequel to cult director Herschell Gordon Lewis' 1963 horror classic. Features a cameo from John Waters (as a priest!). Web site: http://www.bloodfeast2.net

Cheerleader Ninjas (2001): Played with both tongue-in-cheek and sword-at-throat, this woolly mix of several B-Movie genres goes for both the laughs and the gore. But there is more in the way of gore than laughs, hence its appearance here rather than in the previous comedy chapter. Web site: http://www.cheerleaderninjas.com

A Chronicle of Corpses (2001): Imagine someone mixing the scripts of *Dementia 13* and *Barry Lyndon* and you have this film: a serial killer with a considerable axe to grind haunts the grounds of a very stately 18th-century manor. Dave Kehr of the *New York Times* actually named this as one of his Top 10 films of 2001. Web site: http://www.armcinema25.com

The Collingswood Story (2003): A pair of young lovers, separated by long distance, stay in touch via webcam transmissions. But the appearance of a creepy psychic on their webcam connection brings more to their online connection than they ever anticipated. Web site: http://www.collingswoodstory.com

Come Get Some! (2003): An army of flesh-eating zombies go on a rampage, while four hot chicks go on a mission and an Elvis-worshipping half-wit hero goes around and around. Web site: http://www.comegetsomethefilm.com

Cradle of Fear (2001): A gruesome mix of four stories all linked by the tale of Kemper, a child killer and cannibal who, despite being incarcerated, uses his ally in the outside world, a deranged dark spectral character named "The Man," to reap revenge on those who imprisoned him. Web site: http://www.cradleoffear.com

Dark Night of the Soul (1998): Four naive college kids find their way into the "Unknown Cemetery," which is ruled by skeleton freak philosopher Shawn and his drug induced zombie henchmen. Forced opium smoking, sexual deviancy, hypnotic anti-religious dialog, and the Tarot ensue. Web site: http://www.cutthroatvideo.com

5 Dark Souls (1996): Three high school students, eager to be accepted with the "in crowd," venture into the woods at the urging of a quintet of super-popular classmates who want to feature them in a film... a snuff film. Web site: http://moorevideoandmusic.tripod.com

The Glasshead (1997): A group of young campers are visited at their site by a mysterious man who relates the tale of a farmer in the 1860s who was attacked and left for dead by a group of ruffians, but was brought back to life as the subject of a bizarre and brutal medical experiment. Web site: http://www.trakkpro.com/glasshead.html

Goregoyles (2001): Working in a dark and murky office, Uncle Dodo (who?) selects a pair of "psycho-twisted original horror movies" and presents them to a somewhat surprised audience. Way to go, Uncle Dodo! Web site: http://www.braindamagefilms.com

Grey Skies: The Alien Conspiracy (2001): Three short films about the mishaps and confrontations that are typical for the always-uneasy union between those darn creatures from up there and us poor creatures from this part of the galaxy. Web site: http://www.lindenmuth.com

The Human Beeing (2002): An homage to 1950s B-horror movies, *The Human Beeing* is the story of an evil boss and a mad scientist who plan to get rich by turning all their employees at a typing company into worker bees. Web site: http://www.piefightfilms.com

The Jekyll and Hyde Rock and Roll Musical (2002): A musical retelling of the classic Robert Louis Stevenson novel. Cast includes famed L.A. session drummer Hal Blaine as a homeless street wino. Web site: http://www.jekyllandhyderock.com/

Jesus Christ Vampire Hunter (2001): Musical horror happening about the return of Jesus to earth in order to contend with an army of vampires that can walk in the daylight. Web site: http://www.odessafilmworks.com/jcvh/

Kettle Cadaver: A Taste of Blood (2002): The rock band Kettle Cadaver appear in this 20-minute exercise that mixes music with self-mutilation of the more sensitive parts of the body. Not for the squeamish. Web site: http://www.kettlecadaver.com

Killer Me (2001): Joseph Sturgeon awakes one morning with blood-covered hands, a badly infected wound on his ribcage, and very little memory of the previous evening. Web site: http://www.killerme.com

Mayhem Motel (2001): Bizarre and horrific events take place in an average motel throughout the course of one night, ranging from shooting to stabbing to vomiting to spanking. Web site: http://www.disturbancefilms.com

The Mutilation Man (2001): This feature gives a new twist to the old adage "there's no business like show business"! A strange guy tours the country with an act involving brutal feats of self-mutilation. While these performances have no problem in finding appreciative audiences, he is nonetheless haunted by a deeper secret and intensive depravity which brings an unexpected wave of horror across the country. Web site: http://www.b-movie.com

Nikos the Impaler (2002): A 12th-century Romanian barbarian is brought back to life in (where else?) modern-day Manhattan. B-Movie sirens Debbie Rochon and Tina Krause decorate the film. Web site: http://www.cinemaimages.net

Puphedz: The Tattle-Tale Heart (2002): A bloody puppet version of Edgar Allen Poe's "The Tell-tale Heart," performed by the Puphedz, a troupe of wooden puppets. A young man is driven to madness by an unnatural, torturous obsession with the deformed eye of the old man with whom he lives. Web site: http://www.puphedz.com

Rage of the Werewolf (1999): There's a full moon and guess who (or what) is out howling at it? Web site: http://www.lindenmuth.com

Sadomannequin (2001): Sadomasochistic black-and-white horror film about a security man working the night shift and what he finds in a trunk he's supposed to be guarding. Web site: http://www.popgunprod uctions.com

Science Bastard (2002): Blood, gore, electric drills used for non-home repair purposes, fights, evil aliens, and nice-looking women wearing very little clothing. The horror, the horror! Web site: http://www.exhil arateddespair.com/

Serial Killer (2002): Can you guess what this movie is about? Web site: http://www.angelfire.com/pa2/4thFloorPictures/2page.html

Shatter Dead (1995): Scooter McCrae's feature reimagines the zombie film genre with a startling premise: the dead return to life and try to become a part of society, only to be rejected in a bloody war between the living and the living dead. Amid the chaos, a lone woman (played by Stark Raven) tries to get through the madness, and her skill with firearms makes it clear that no one, either living or undead, will get in her way. Web site: http://www.b-movie.com

Sinyster (1996): Ronnie Sortor's feature finds a young criminal on the run after a simple hold-up is badly botched. Taking refuge in an abandoned house to await the arrival of his accomplice, the hood-in-hiding soon realizes he is not alone and is soon pursued by an axe-wielding butcher and his undying horde of mutilated victims. Web site: http://www.b-movie.com

Skinned Alive (1989): A somewhat unusual family who make "leather" jackets from an unlikely source (three guesses) stops in a small rural town and begins to create havoc. Web site: http://www.tempevideo.com

Skunk Ape!? (2003): Punk band Screamin' Scab and the Herpes disturbs the peaceful home of Skunk Ape (the "pussy version of Bigfoot"), who hitches a ride on the back of their van and stalks and slaughters each band member one by one before returning back home to masturbate in peace and quiet. Web site: http://www.zabbazabba.com

Terror House (1996): Filmmaking siblings Mark and John Polonia teamed with Jon McBride to direct this jolting tale of greed gone awry. Three college students falsely seek a $25,000 reward and arrive at a lonely house to claim the sum, but find themselves trapped within the house and become the prisoners of the ghost of a mysterious woman and a half-human creature with a taste for blood. Web site: http://www.b-movie.com

13 Seconds (2003): A rock band goes to their one-time boarding school (now abandoned) to record a new album. But supernatural forces try to get into the act. Web site: http://www.rainstorm-pictures.com

Timmy's Wish (2001): Timmy gets his wish — a violent death for his parents because they committed such misdeeds as making him eat brussels sprouts — but he later finds a glowing Jesus surrounded by the dismembered body parts of his parental unit. Web site: http://www.filmthreat.com/Reviews.asp?File=ReviewsOne.inc&Id=2838

Totem (1999): An old totem causes six teenagers, who were brought together by mysterious circumstances, to kill or be killed. Web site: http://www.filmthreat.com/Reviews.asp?Id=4694

The Vampire Hunter's Club (2001): The story of what happens to vampire hunters 50 years after they miss out on capturing Dracula in 1952. Web site: http://www.bloodbyte.com

Vampire Vermont (2000): A group of young people staying in a rural Vermont cabin make the lethal mistake of having the neighborhood vampire come over for dinner. Web site: http://www.lindenmuth.com

A Visit from the Incubus (2001): A young woman struggles with an incubus in the Old West while trying to become a singing star in the local saloon. Web site: http://www.lifeofastar.com/incubus.html

INTERVIEW

RON BONK AND THE B-STING

When it comes to film capitals, Syracuse, New York is where the fun is! Sundance may have the insiders, Cannes the flash and Hollywood the star power, but Syracuse has the buzz of the B's... as in the B-Movie Film

Festival, the B-Movie Hall of Fame, and *B-Movie.com*, the online home of Sub Rosa Studios.

Syracuse's unlikely designation as the B-Movie capital is because of the dedicated work of Ron Bonk, founder and president of Sub Rosa Studios. A talented filmmaker himself (with the creepy psychodrama *The Vicious Sweet* and the found-footage thriller *Strawberry Estates* to his credit), Bonk is keeping alive the B-Movie tradition which stretches back to the Golden Era of B's (the 1930s-50s) when Poverty Row studios like Monogram, PRC, Mascot and Republic, American International and the B-units of the top studios ground out hundreds of no-budget quickies — and often created classics like *Cat People*, *Detour*, and *Leopard Man* and launched careers of megastars like John Wayne, Roy Rogers, and Jack Nicholson.

While the Sub Rosa release slate includes a variety of different genres, it is best known and loved for its splatter-platter of underground horror and sci-fi. Widely regarded as the top distributor in underground horror and sci-fi, Sub Rosa has used the power of the Internet and the force of personality of founder-director Ron Bonk to keep horror and sci-fi addicts happy with the best of this genre's current output.

Q. You get to see an awful lot of horror/sci-fi movies during the course of the year. From your experience, what are the critical ingredients necessary for making a great horror/sci-fi film?

RON BONK: I would say a good story certainly helps — a lot of filmmakers just retread material from *Halloween* and *Friday the 13th* and all the movies those movies inspired. Starting with a good, original story is the main key, then making sure you have strong actors, good direction, and professional lighting and photography would help round out the film.

Q. At the flip side of the first question, what are the most common mistakes you see that doom the unsatisfactory films of this genre?

BONK: A lot of filmmakers fail to take their movie seriously. It doesn't matter if it is a comedy or a cheesy horror movie — take it seriously. I think because of the level of committment and work required to make a good movie, a lot of filmmakers bail early and just "crap" the movie out. It then has the feel of a backyard film a bunch of drunk buddies got together and made. Or the movie starts to slip away a few days into production — they start with the best intentions but then when it starts coming out less than desired, they stop trying. I see a lot of sloppy filmmaking, and it doesn't matter how good the script is, the movie won't overcome this. I know this is low-budget and all and you'll have every excuse in the book as to why the movie didn't come out right, but putting in 100% throughout the whole process of making the movie will result in a much better final product and a film fans will respond to that much better.

Q. Who is the audience for today's underground horror/sci-fi films? Do they fit a specific demographic or geographic pattern?

BONK: Male 15-35 seems to be the core, though we have seen more and more female customers in recent years.

Q. Tell us a little about the *B-Movie.com* web site and the goals it is trying to accomplish.

BONK: Well, the web site was first designed as a place to promote and sell the movies we were making. But right away we started adding movies from other filmmakers. As the site grew and traffic increased, we started getting more and more submissions to be added to the site.

Q. How did the filmmakers become interested in the site?

BONK: All of these filmmakers had been reading about the Net and wanted on, but there weren't many alternatives available to them. And for awhile we were the only company on the web promoting and marketing movies made at this level. So through us they had a chance to reach customers who never would have heard about their movies. We also wanted to educate the "average" movie fan about these movies — to show them what they were missing, so we started carrying articles and interviews on these filmmakers. This way, if someone came along who never heard the title of the movie and knew nothing about it, they could get the "inside" scoop through these articles.

Q. How did this information help the filmmakers promoted there?

BONK: It helped sales — especially on films that were less marketable — those with limited artwork, those that lacked the usually saleable elements (like a name star, nudity, action, gore). We have always tried to treat the filmmakers with a respect that they couldn't get elsewhere — we approached them with the attitude that these were productions on the same respect level as Hollywood movies, even if they didn't equal a hundredth of their production costs.

Q. Today's low-cost digital technology allows most anyone to make their own movie. Is this a good thing in terms of giving aspiring filmmakers a chance to shine, or a problem in terms of film quantity outpacing quality?

BONK: Well, it's actually both. Some talented filmmakers were held back in the past because of technical problems when making their movie - for example, shooting on S-VHS or Hi-8mm with available lighting would kill many movies. It looked great thru the viewfinder, but once it was knocked down a few generations via editing, it got very dark and grainy — unwatchable. So shooting and editing today on digital allows them to overcome this obstacle, and do it on little to no money as well! But yes, it also means we're getting even more film-makers who either don't take the art of directing seriously or just lack the talent completely, and this really muddles the market. Distributors have too many films to screen, and in some cases, believe it or not (and knowing my opinion is just my opinion of course), some of these really bad movies actually get out into the marketplace. And this just upsets the customers which upsets the buyers who end up buying less and less indie/cult product.

Q. You are also the driving force behind the B-Movie Film Festival. Where did that come from?

BONK: As I mentioned earlier, we have always tried to treat B-Movies, cult movies, and independent movies with a respect that was usually reserved specifically for "A" movies. I've always wished someone would create an "Academy Awards" type ceremony for the low-budget mov-ies - the films and videos that get ignored by Hollywood. So this was our answer. We have awards for Best B-Movie, Best B-Movie Director, Best B-Movie Actor, et cetera. It's a lot of fun and the filmmakers really appreciate the honors. They really take it serious. I could tell by the response from them that they basically felt the same way I did.

Anyway, the ceremony runs over two days, and we show the nominees for Best B-movie, Best B-Movie short and a show reel of all nominations. We try to bring in a few B-Movie celebrities, such as Debbie Rochon and Roxanne Michaels, and we set things up so everyone (filmmakers and fans) can sit around and network and chat and laugh in a casual atmosphere.

We also help lure in local folks by showing some production work from our own company. The fest is relatively small and simple right now, but we are still in a testing phase with it. Gradually we want to make it quite the event in Syracuse — on par with Sundance or Telluride. And the response has been great. We really think it will become the festival of choice for cult movies, B-Movies, and the ultra low-budget independent movies in the years to come.

Q. What films and filmmakers should fans of underground horror (the crux of the B-Movie.com output) be on the lookout for and why?

BONK: Eric Stanze — his movies are very raw, very powerful. He's not afraid to attack any subject matter nor his afraid to try anything new and different with the camera. Ronnie Sortor — he just knows how to make a kick-ass movie. He has fun scripts and a shooting style that keeps a movie rolling. Tim Ritter — some of the work from the middle of his career was hurt by bad production values and too many slasher-style scripts, but with his recent work on the *Dirty Cop No Donut* movies, I think he is starting to prove himself skilled at political and social satire. Those are three immediate filmmakers that come to mind.

Q. In your own work as a filmmaker, you helped a disturbing horror film called *Strawberry Estates*. That has a peculiar history behind it, yes?

BONK: Yes. I actually originally shot the movie back in January of 1997, but was unhappy with the original version. The story deals with a small group from a local college who are doing research on paranormal activity in a closed-down insane asylum nicknamed "Strawberry Estates." They hire a videographer to photograph everything they see. After three days, the group disappears without a trace. The tapes are all that remains and all the authorities have to go by in determining what happened them.

Q. Hmmm… sounds similar to *The Blair Witch Project*!

BONK: Yes, it is very much like *Blair Witch*. The thing is, I never heard of *Blair Witch* when I wrote the original script and made the original version. My idea came from a film book I had read (skimmed actually) that analyzed this movie from the 1940s called *The Lady in the Lake* that told the whole story from the lead actor's POV. The only time you saw him was in mirrors and things like that. I was experimenting around with different ways of shooting movies and telling the stories, and thought "How could I update this concept?" And then I thought "video camera!" And that was it — there was never any plans for the movie to be anything but the raw footage from this expedition — all played like it was completely real.

Strawberry Estates is actually a part of a series of ideas about F.B.I. cases I have called "Red Files" — my own sort of X-Files. This film is just one story. I was going to market them in the backs of UFO magazines like they were bootlegs — stolen from F.B.I. headquarters and packaged in black boxes. I wanted people to pick this movie up and right away feel like they were suddenly treading into forbidden waters — they were going to see something they were never meant to see, they weren't allowed to see. The problem with the original movie version was it was way too polished — the acting was too good, the lighting too good, the shots too well timed. No one was going to believe it was real. So I shelved it rather than ruin the idea. I had planned to reshoot it one day, but further on down the line.

Then *Blair Witch* came out and I figured that I'd better do it now. If I waited any longer, I knew that the host of imitators that *Blair Witch* would spawn would drive that idea deep into the ground. *The St. Francisville Experiment* came out after that and it's like they read my idea for *Strawberry Estates* on my site or in Fangoria (they covered it along with my last movie, *The Vicious Sweet*, in October of 1997) because it sounds like the same exact idea — it's in a haunted house, they have a ghost expert, a psychic, et cetera.

Q. In which direction do you see this genre heading?

BONK: Hard to say. I think the filmmakers continue to get better and better and more exciting, and the productions stronger and stronger.

New digital editing and effects software is also helping these movies. But the market is quickly getting saturated. DVD was a great option for these movies, but now with so many releases (on every level) out there, shelf space is running out. I sincerely believe that if you make a quality movie, the fans will find it. But a lot of times getting it on the shelves of major retailers and rental stores will be more a case of "luck" and "who you know" (or even "who you bribe") than whether or not it's truly a quality cult movie production.

5: The Digital Underground

O n May 22, 1993, motion picture and technological history was made. As with most historic events, very few people were aware it was happening.

The event was the first broadcast of a feature-length film across the Internet. The film in question was, not surprisingly, an underground movie: *Wax: Or the Discovery of Television Among the Bees*, an 85-minute avant-garde production by David Blair about a weapons designer and part-time beekeeper whose mind is taken over by his favorite buzzing insects. The film was rich with surreal humor, bizarre visuals, and appearances by such diverse and unlikely figures as Beat poetry icon William Burroughs and Clyde Tombaugh, the astronomer who discovered the planet Pluto. Blair's film had a brief theatrical release in 1992, where it gained some strong reviews and a small cult following by audiences in search of something truly original and weird.

When *Wax: Or the Discovery of Television Among the Bees* was chosen to be shown on the Internet, there was a slight problem: the concept of showing films on the Internet came before the technology was ready for such a broadcast. Remember that 1993 was literally the dawn of the cyber age, and at that time 9600 baud was considered to be a supersonic digital transmission speed. The Internet was a text-driven network, primarily used by research labs, academic centers, and government agencies for the transmission of documents. Sending a still photograph across the early online channels was a major event; broadcasting a feature film was the equivalent of asking the Wright Brothers to build a space shuttle after their Kitty Hawk glide.

The primitive technology of the 1993 Internet required the visual inventiveness of Blair's film to be severely compromised. The film, which was shot in color, had to be broadcast in black and white at a speed of two frames per second. Considering that the standard motion picture projection speed is 24 frames per second, the loss of 22 frames per second created obvious visual problems. This was compounded by audio problems: the soundtrack to the film never found a synchronicity with the slowed-down visuals and often disappeared completely during the broadcast.

Even more frustrating was locating the film online. Engineers at Sun Microsystems, who were among the exclusive few to experience this introduction in entertainment, never got to see the first half of the film — they were unable to locate the film's transmission within their Internet data stream. Considering relatively few people were online when *Wax: Or the Discovery of Television Among the Bees* was playing, this was a fairly embarrassing situation.

Perhaps more troubling than the woefully inadequate audiovisual presentation of this one-time-only broadcast was the fact it was an effort that had virtually no audience. Attempts to bring the online world to the general public were not experiencing anything even vaguely resembling a success rate. In fact, it would not be until the following year that America Online began mailing out start-up disks in voluminous rates, which many people consider to be the shot that the cyber world needed for expansion. But even that came with limits: the nascent online providers like Prodigy, CompuServe and America Online were only offering connectivity to their own digital bailiwicks, with only email and highly restricted Internet access capacity. Even if the broadcast of *Wax: Or the Discovery of Television Among the Bees* happened a year later, it would still have failed to reach a significant audience.

Enter the Features

Fast-forward through the decade and suddenly the Internet is no longer the private domain of scientists and academics. By the tail end of the

1990s, consumer and business use of cyberspace has taken off dramatically and the potential for the Internet had developed far and beyond the text-driven exchanges of several years earlier. Yet the notion of presenting films via the Internet was lagging. Problems with the speed of Internet connectivity (at this time, they were mostly dial-up connections and a 56k modem was considered a digital hot rod on the information superhighway) challenged the visual aspect of showing movies in cyberspace. Anything that played online usually resulted in a pixelated image with tinny sound.

Even more challenging was getting films to run online. No Hollywood studio in the late 1990s would allow their films, either current or classic, to be shown across cyberspace. Primarily the absence of these titles was pegged to a lack of consumer interest, but in truth fears of hacking and copyright infringement bothered the Hollywood bigwigs, who feared the Internet would become a video pirate's treasure chest.

The few films that showed up online were either hoary old films whose copyrights had expired into the public domain, thus allowing them to be duplicated and shown in any manner possible, or shorts made by amateur filmmakers which often displayed more enthusiasm than professional filmmaking prowess. Needless to say, no one was going out of their way to find these films. What the Internet needed, but lacked, was a film that would bring attention to the medium and bring eyes to the computer monitor.

In March 1998, a webcasting site called The Sync became the first Internet channel to present a contemporary feature film for real-time cyber viewing. The film was *Walls of Sand*, a 110-minute drama by San Francisco filmmaker Erica Jordan about an Iranian girl whose student visa expired and who struggles to remain in America and obtain a green card by working as an au pair for an agoraphobic mother locked in a nasty child custody case with her ex-husband. This small, independently produced film debuted in 1994 and played in numerous festivals around the world, winning fine reviews and several awards. But while it enjoyed much respect, *Walls of Sand* was unable to gain an acquisition deal to bring it into theatrical release — the common complaint among potential distributors was that it lacked commercial appeal and potential.

Yet the qualities that kept *Walls of Sand* out of theatrical release — black and white cinematography, a low-budget that kept the action limited to conversation-driven situation — made the film ideal for the still-primitive webcasting format. Since the film was not a slam-bang extravaganza, it could work well within the limits of 1998 Internet technology.

Furthermore, the pairing of *Walls of Sand* and The Sync was mutually beneficial (author's note: I should add that I was the person responsible for bringing the two parties together for this project). Since the film was not in circulation, Jordan saw the opportunity to reach a wide audience through the new format. "When *Walls of Sand* was invited to be the first contemporary feature film to be shown in its entirety on the Internet, I was very excited," recalls Jordan. "It took Shirin Etessam (the film's producer and star) and I several years to make *Walls of Sand* and we were interested in having as many people as possible see the film. At the time I knew very little about cyberspace, but I was very enthusiastic about its possibilities for organizing political ideas and sharing new creative work."

Likewise, The Sync needed a hit. Run by Carla Cole and Tom Edwards, a young couple in suburban Washington, The Sync began operations in 1997 and initially made money by doing web audio simulcasts of speeches by then-Vice President Al Gore and in rebroadcasting Senate hearings. The Sync's video programming at the time was limited to fairly silly short films (including home movies of a friend's "singing" poodle), a public access-style panel talk show called *CyberLove* starring Cole and her friends (Cole later admitted the initial broadcast had more people on the show than in its cyber audience!), and two silent features which had long fallen into the public domain, *Nosferatu* and *The Cabinet of Dr. Caligari*. The start-up webcaster was hungry to get a title that would raise awareness of its operations.

The debut of *Walls of Sand* on The Sync brought the concept of webcasting movies front and center. A large feature article in the *New York Times* Arts & Leisure (the first ever for a Net-based entertainment story in that publication) drove The Sync's web traffic up dramatically. In a short time, The Sync was a media darling with coverage in such diverse publications as the *Wall Street Journal*, the *Washington Post* and *Entertainment Weekly*.

As for the four-year-old *Walls of Sand*, the Internet gave it a new lease on life. "When *Walls of Sand* was first broadcast on the Internet, we received good press and positive reviews," says Jordan, noting she received additional invitations to film festivals around the world and later an offer for a home video release. "It definitely introduced a new audience to our work and careers as filmmakers."

The Sync followed the presentation of *Walls of Sand* with more feature films by entering deals with independent video distributors Sub Rosa Studios and Moore Video, which specialized in underground-style cult classics like *Reefer Madness* and *Lemora, Lady Dracula* and contemporary no-budget chillers like *The Glasshead* and *5 Lost Souls*. When The Sync began receiving complaints that its film programming was getting too dark and sinister (yes, it actually did field such accusations), it wittily responded by arranging the webcast premiere of Pasolini's *The Gospel According to Saint Matthew*.

While putting films online gained The Sync its initial volley of press and public notice, the network kept its internal focus on original programming produced at its studios. This included the comedy show *Snack Boy*, starring funnyman Terry Crummitt giving a five-minute rant each weekday, and *The Jenni Show*, a forerunner of reality TV with webcam pin-up Jennifer Ringely of the notorious JenniCam site as the center of attention. The Sync's reputation grew quickly enough to attract the cooperation of MSNBC tech reporter Brock Meeks, who hosted his own weekly program devoted to the latest happenings in the computer world.

As The Sync's original programming operations became more hectic, its cinematic slate quickly became a lesser focal point. "I hate to say it, but we don't really watch long-form films online," admits Carla Cole, the co-founder of The Sync. "In fact, we never really did watch them. We were much more into the shorter form content. In truth, we were always more content being producers than consumers."

Ironically, this view was shared by *Walls of Sand* director Erica Jordan. "My personal experience with watching films on the Internet has been quite frustrating," she says. "To tell you the truth, I've never made it through much more than a couple of minutes of any given film."

Walls of Sand found a wider audience than *Wax: Or the Discovery of Television Among the Bees*, but its time online was finite. Roughly a year after its Net debut, the film was taken offline by mutual agreement between Erica Jordan and The Sync. Within two years, the collapse of the dot-com industry and the failure to maintain adequate financial revenue streams forced The Sync to cease the cyber presentation of both its film line-up and its original made-for-Internet programming. Today, The Sync exists primarily as a webcam/blog for Cole and a gallery for the digital art of co-founder Tom Edwards; anyone stumbling on the site will have no clue of its importance in the development of putting movies online.

In retrospect, Cole is uncertain whether The Sync's pioneering role in putting films online was too far ahead of the curve. "This is hard to say," he comments. "The Sync really captured something in terms of using video to increase the bonds between niche personalities and their devoted fans. This was especially true at a time when the Internet was more mysterious and distant from the general public. We were able to connect people and concepts that the mainstream media could not."

Cole adds that their breakthrough presentation seems more relevant today than previously considered. "*Walls of Sand* was a very interesting look into Iranian-American culture, and post-9/11 I still think about that movie and the clash between Western and Islamic culture," she says.

THE CHANGING NET

Within four years of the premiere of *Walls of Sand* and ten years after *Wax: Or the Discovery of Television Among the Bees*, Internet connectivity made stunning technological progress. Broadband connectivity has taken the discomfort and awkwardness out of watching films across the Internet. Downloading films is even easier and is usually more desirable. Hollywood eventually got into the act, offering its newer flicks available for download via encryptable files over such services as CinemaNow and Movielink. Hollywood's fears of piracy across cyberspace proved to be prophetic as bootleg versions of major releases appeared online for instant downloading, sometimes before they even hit the theaters. But we'll leave that issue for another book.

As the Internet grew up technologically, it also grew up in terms of business savvy. Underground films were used to a certain extent to speed this maturing process, but once a money flow and corporate stability was ensured, these films were no longer the priority.

Despite the ballyhoo and potential that *Walls of Sand* offered on The Sync, it became obvious that the future (or at least the immediate future) of films online was not in the realm of feature-length productions. Short films, which had long been segregated to festivals and to Oscar categories that no one paid much mind, suddenly became in demand. As these films were the exclusive bailiwick of independent filmmakers rather than the studio system, it signaled a new venue for aspiring filmmakers eager to get that proverbial foot in the door.

"Short films had to be the prevailing genre to thrive for two main reasons," explains Erik Childress, editor of the review site *eFilmCritic.com*. "They are very hard to find in any other venue and they are short. Watching a 90-120 minute film on a small monitor in your work chair can be a chore, but a five-to-ten minute piece can offer a quick pleasure and open your eyes to the work of a new artist. Industry officials can use this outlet to discover the next new voice or visualist."

Two online resources were key in bringing new shorts to online audiences. The first was AtomFilms, founded in 1998. Unlike The Sync, which relied on its own production of original programming, AtomFilms established partnerships with many important companies. Within a year of its launch, its partner base included a virtual who's who of entertainment, online, and corporate players: HBO, @Home, Go Network/Infoseek, Sundance Channel, Warner Bros. Online, Continental Airlines, Air Canada, RealNetworks, Reel.com, Mr. Showbiz, Broadcast DVD, Film.com, College Broadcast Network, Air New Zealand and SonicNet, the American Film Institute, the Australian Film Commission, and the Norwegian Film Institute (the latter two entities finance many original short films).

Although many of its shorts qualified as underground movies, AtomFilms quickly sought to distance itself from the underground realm by aiming for higher-end prestige shorts. Its first major coup came with the exclusive online license for the 1999 Academy Award nominee *Holiday Romance*. It also went after higher-end financial sources. By the end of 1999, it secured $20 million in strategic financing, which more than impressive given that the dot-com world was beginning to crumble. In 2000 it merged with Shockwave.com, offering a diverse mix of more than 1,500 online titles with Shockwave.com's roster of online shows and series, interactive games, music, and creativity applications. Filmmakers including George Lucas, Tim Burton, and Spike Jonze climbed aboard the AtomFilms bandwagon. AtomFilms made history again in October 2002 when the new series of *Wallace & Gromit* cartoons premiered at its site. Whatever role underground films played in its establishment, AtomFilms forgot its past as it sped ahead with its corporate growth.

AtomFilms had spirited competition from iFilm. Launched in February 1999, iFilm never bothered with dial-up technology and kept focused on the possibilities of broadband. This slowed its progress at first, but soon it became obvious this strategy was prescient, as partnerships with Microsoft's MSN online channel, Real Networks, and even Miramax came about once broadband became more commonplace.

As with AtomFilms, iFilm's initial focus was on edgy and often wacky short films. Today, iFilm's programming mix still includes shorts (with all of the expected categories plus underground-worthy surprises including "spoof" and "underwater"), but it is hardly an underground venue for Net surfers. A visit to iFilm can present a selection of new music videos from the hottest recording stars, interviews with A-list movie personalities, and trailers for current and upcoming Hollywood films. The company went AtomFilms one better by branching into offline activities. In a wise move, iFilm diversified into subsidiaries including a market research agency, OTX: The Online Testing Exchange, and a book company called iFilmpublishing.

As with AtomFilms, iFilm was blessed to find and secure funding when the dot-com world collapsed. The privately-held company's investors include Axiom Ventures, Inc., Eastman Kodak Company, Liberty Digital, Rainbow Media, Sony Pictures Entertainment, Vulcan Ventures, Inc., and Yahoo!. Nothing underground here.

So what happened to the underground cinema in the online world? It never went away. While AtomFilms and iFilm snagged the corporate funding and the bulk of the media attention, the underground cinema quietly thrived in a high-tech sphere of its own. In many ways, the underground film sites mirror their cinematic inspirations by mixing low-budget ingenuity with a sense of humor, style, and focus.

THE KIDS ARE ALRIGHT

Typical of today's underground film resources is StudentFilms.com (*www.studentfilms.com*). As its name suggests, it is a Net resource which gives college and even high school filmmakers a chance to present their works to a global digital audience. StudentFilms.com was launched, appropriately enough, by a student named Chris Wright in the summer of 1998 while he was a senior in Boston University's College of Communication. "I had dabbled in some web design, mainly focused on bands that I liked and even did a bit of video streaming in the early days of the RealPlayer's RealVideo," recalls Wright. "It dawned on me that the Internet would be a great way to showcase student films on the web. The way I looked at it... the only way that people were going to see my films were if I showed them a tape... only my family or friends would be able to see it. When the site started in 1998 it was definitely the only site that dedicated itself to student filmmakers. iFilm was around but the student films they had got lost in the shuffle on such a big site."

Unlike AtomFilms and iFilm, StudentFilms.com does not have multi-million-dollar financing or Fortune 500 partners. In fact, its approach to marketing would make the average MBA student gasp.

"I actually don't market the site at all," says Wright, whose site receives an average of 40,000 hits per month. "All of the advertising is through word of mouth and/or web searches. When someone submits a film to the site I send them flyers that they can post around their campus to promote the site as well as their film."

There are currently more than 500 films on the site, and getting on the site is relatively easy. "The submitter has to be in some form of school; it doesn't have to be film school," explains Wright. "Practically all films are accepted. The only reason a film wouldn't be accepted is if the tape is bad or if it contained truly offensive content above what would be an R rating."

To date, a few alumni graduated from StudentFilms.com to wider acclaim. The most notable is Josh Koury, co-founder of the Brooklyn Underground Film Festival, who had three shorts on StudentFilms.com before his *Standing by Yourself* documentary feature received theatrical release in 2001. "I know that Dan Ryckert (*Furious George*) and JP Saalfield (*Breathe*) have gotten a lot of media exposure from having their films on my site," adds Wright, who is working full-time as a music video editor in Los Angeles.

Even more niche focused is SaS Films (*www.sasfilms.com*), an online film site devoted entirely to videos of people engaged in extreme winter sports (the SaS acronym stands for Skiing and Snowboarding). It was founded in early 2000 by then-19-year-old Neil Sotirakopoulous, a student at Rensselaer Polytechnic Institute in upstate New York who was studying Electronic Media Arts and Computer Science.

"SaS Films basically started up when my parents got me a video camera for Christmas," says Sotirakopoulous. "At the time I didn't really know what I wanted to film, so I shot what I loved most: skiing. Every weekend my friends and I would build jumps in my yard or head out to whatever ski areas we could afford and ride the park all day. Our tricks weren't really that great and the videos we made weren't very impressive, but being out on the mountain with the camera made us realize how many local kids were into jumping and how much talent was floating around New England."

Sotirakopoulous began SaS Films with five video clips and by the end of the winter season he was up to 300 video clips submitted by more than 75 ski and snowboard addicts. Today, SaS Films averages 300 hits daily during the peak winter sports season, which is admittedly on the smallish side but it is actually rather admirable considering the effort is aimed at a specific niche audience and it is being promoted primarily through word-of-mouth among diehard ski and snowboard fanatics. Summertime, obviously, witnesses a slowdown in web traffic and in the summer of 2001 the SaS Films traffic disappeared completely when the site's Internet service provider abruptly pulled the plug.

"Since the site doesn't have any kind of budget, over the summer the server was running off my cable modem from my house in New

Hampshire," says Sotirakopoulous. "Without any kind of warning AT&T / Road Runner (my Internet provider at the time) decided to block outgoing traffic on port 80. Without getting into details, this prevents you from hosting your own web site. Since the site uses up over 3 gig of space, it would cost a fortune to have our site hosted by another company, so we continued to run the site off of our own computer. AT&T blamed the sudden change on 'code red,' saying that running web servers was disrupting the service to others. It took about a week for us to figure out why the site suddenly stopped working. We decided it was in our best interest to just keep the site down until I went back to school. The server came back to school with me that fall and was relocated to run out of someone's dorm room."

But ultimately, can the Internet truly become a viable channel for viewing films? A key stumbling block to watching films off a computer can be traced to the computer itself. "Part of the fun of the moviegoing experience is not only watching a movie with a big crowd but also watching a movie the way it was meant to be seen: projected onto an enormous screen with Dolby Surround Sound," says MaryAnn Johanson, critic with *The Flick Filosopher* online magazine. "Online movies can't even compare with renting a video or DVD to watch in your living room, because that experience at least involves getting comfy on the couch. Most people don't have comfy couches in front of their PCs. I doubt that online films will be very popular until our toys converge more, until our TVs and PCs and Tivos and DVD players are all the same machine, or all connected to one another, and everything's hooked up to the Net with a super-fast connection, faster than anything we have today."

Carla Cole of The Sync is also dubious about the Net as a means to launching a filmmaking career. "I think that putting your movie on the Net in the hopes that it will get you into Sundance is a little nuts," she says. "Seeking professional success in filmmaking on the Net is a lost cause. Take the money you'd spend on a high-end DV camera and computer and throw a party in Hollywood."

And yet, for filmmakers who don't have access to audiences sitting in a crowded theater and who are not able to get DVD copies of their films into living rooms around the world, the Internet is at least a stepping stone to gain attention. And on occasion, it has proven to be success-ful. After Jonathan Liebesman's student thesis *Genesis and Catastrophe* was spotted on iFilm in 2000, he was recruited by Revolution Studios to direct their theatrical feature *Darkness Falls* while David Garrett and Jason Ward, who wrote another iFilm short called *Sunday's Game*, were signed by Buena Vista to create their 2001 Chris Kattan comedy *Corky Romano*. Admittedly, these are the exceptions to the story. But this story is still unfolding!

Top Sites for Underground Film Viewing

The Internet is not lacking online sites that present underground films, primarily live action and animated shorts. The list of underground film sites here is the most current to date. It is not uncommon for online sites to abruptly disappear, so don't be surprised if you click on one of the URLs below and find the site has gone.

Bijou Cafe (www.bijoucafe.com) — Primarily a treasure chest of vintage such as Larry Buchanan's egregious *The Eye Creatures* and the Hammer anti-classic *Horror Express* with Christopher Lee, Peter Cushing, and Telly Savalas (Telly Savalas?!?), this is among the relatively few online film sites offering recent feature-length underground flicks including the Texas-based monster spoofs *Barn of the Blood Llama* and *Die Hard Dracula*.

The Bit Screen (www.thebitscreen.com) — The novelty to this hand-somely produced site is the Random Shuffles feature that programs films to reconfigure with each successive site visitor. Four works are highlighted weekly and can be seen in either Shockwave or RealPlayer. One drawback: there is no archive on the site, so there's a good chance that a film you see once will not be seen again.

Camp Chaos (www.campchaos.com) — From animator Bob Cesca, with weekly updates of his latest cartoons plus MST3K-style "Public Domain Theater" that mixes cheap old movies with sassy new running commentary.

D.Film (www.dfilm.com) — Founded in 1997, the pioneering digital filmmaking resource is unique in that it highlights a single film each month. Each film can either be viewed directly online or downloaded for viewing later.

Director Unknown (www.directorunknown.com) — Dogme '95 influences this odd site, in which six filmmakers took turns shooting an episode for a 12-episode movie. The effect is often disconcerting and the shifts in style and substance require prompt attention.

Get Out There (www1.getoutthere.bt.com/index2.cfm) — This British-based site has more than 100 live-action and animated shorts which are graded in a Top 10 chart via points determined by the number of viewers for each film.

HotWired: Animation Express (http://www.wired.com/animation/) — A collection of outrageous animated shorts that make the South Park gang look as benign as Charlie Brown and Snoopy. The style is perverse and the subject matter gets mature, but anyone with a twisted sense of fun will have a blast. Viewing requires Flash, Shockwave, and QuickTime plug-ins.

Icebox (www.icebox.com) — More animation, albeit lacking the cutting edge of HotWired and giving a preference to episodic offerings that (more often than not) fail to keep the joke in flight. Still, many of the cartoons are amusing and provide bite-sized diversions that tickle the funny bone without taxing the mind.

Internet Film Network (www.inetfilm.com) — More short films, but the real charm here is the site's unabashed forwardness in asking for cash to keep its operations afloat. These folks remember that the word "business" is part of the expression "show business."

Mediatrip (www.mediatrip.com) — Best known as the online home for the truly hilarious *George Lucas in Love*, the site also has the spoofy *Meet Ed Testy* (about a redneck who is an alien and makes no attempt to hide his outer space heritage) and *Lil' Pimp*, (about a freckle-faced tot who is, well, a lil' pimp).

Microcinema (www.microcinema.com) — The Independent Exposure folks have cut back on the number of original short films that can be seen on their site (their focus has shifted to DVD sales and touring programs), but there are still plenty of online diversions to enjoy.

The New Venue (www.newvenue.com) — First conceived in 1996 but not launched until 1998 (the technology wasn't ready two years earlier), this digital short resource shines a light on one film per week. The most important part of the site, however, is the Flick Tips section for aspiring digital filmmakers.

Out of the Closet Television (www.outofthecloset.tv) — Made-for-the-Net offerings for the gay and lesbian set, this site tends to focus on gay-friendly shorts and TV-style episodic series such as a lesbian soap opera called *The Complex*. Several old public domain features, including *The Little Shop of Horrors* and *'Til the Clouds Roll By*, are included here, too.

The Quickie (www.thequickie.com/) — More gently off-the-wall animation inked in the style of the old UPA cartoons, including the mildly subversive *Star Wars - Episode 9* (with Han Solo finally cracking up) and takeoffs on overweight Americans, inane Klansmen, a none-too-frightening Osama Bin Laden, a blubbery Ariel Sharon, and a silly ass George W. Bush.

Random Foo Pictures (www.randomfoo.com) — Boston-based filmmakers C.C. Chapman and Dan Gorgone created more than 60 short films plus a feature called *After Midnight* (2001). They've been at it since 1996 and their films are mostly of a warped and skewered comic bent. Hey, it keeps them busy and they've already won several awards for their efforts.

Undergroundfilm.com (www.underground.com) — With roughly 200 shorts plus screenplays and MP3s, there is no shortage of goodies to pick from. The site's discussion boards also help to encourage contact and conversation among aspiring filmmakers and online film fans.

Urban Entertainment (www.urbanentertainment.com) — One of the relatively rare African American–themed online film sites, this offers episodic short film series including *Sistas 'n the City* (a sassy black spoof of *Sex in the City*) and *Joe Work* (a comedy character described as a mix between Chris Rock and Charlie Chaplin).

INTERVIEW

NATHAN BRAMBLE: NO DREAMS DEFERRED

In a famous poem, Langston Hughes once mused on the fate of a dream deferred by offering a variety of worst-case scenarios. Fortunately for Nathan Bramble, these scenarios are not plotlines to reflect his professional and artistic goals... for Nathan Bramble deferred his dream of being a filmmaker but then roared back into it with a vengeance.

Working from his home studio in Bensalem, Pennsylvania (just north of Philadelphia), Bramble is a one-man digital filmmaker and online theater operator. His Digital Video Documentaries (*www.dvdocumentarie s.com*) is home to his quirky nonfiction short films.

Bramble's films, which average 17 minutes in length and $100 for budget, offer unique visions of people living on the fringes of what might be considered normalcy. His first two films, *Centralia, PA – Modern Day Ghost Town* and *2001 Inauguration: Voice from the Street* offer a haunting and rueful examination of dreams that were deferred to the point of ruin: the former film examined the remains of a mining village whose residents were forced to flee thanks to an underground fire which has burned out of control for over two decades while the latter presented a montage of protesters and counter-protesters who populated the fringes of George W. Bush's inauguration, kept out of sight and ear from the main events by a fat blue line of police and an overwhelming sense of being shut out of the democratic process.

Bramble has since followed these films with *Ghost Hunters*, which follow a spirited group in search of elusive spooks; *EverQuest Players LFG*, which details how the popular Internet game has created an astonishing breed of addicted fanatics, many of whom attend conventions dressed like their beloved characters; and *Protest! The WEF in NYC*, in which a massive rally against an international trade conference somehow never quite makes its point despite the enthusiastic and sometimes buffoonish behavior of its protest marchers.

Bramble came to documentaries in a roundabout way. His art school education focused on computer and film animation, but the realities of daily existence and the pricetags that come attached dictated the pursuit of a financially lucrative job. Bramble put filmmaking aside and took a job as a webmaster for a software company; he currently holds a full-time position as a software developer, where he creates and tests computer networks for hospitals.

However, Bramble's filmmaking ambition never truly disappeared and a new inspiration came in the form of recent outside-inspired documentaries such as Crumb. Cashing in stock options, Bramble purchased a DV camera and a high-speed computer to enable editing and post-production work. Combining his techie skills with a natural eye for cinematic journalism, he began to create films and also present them online via his Digital Video Documentaries web site (which only cost $120 to set up and $18 per month to maintain).

Bramble's site is the rare online exhibitor to offer both low quality, high quality and download-ready versions of his streamed films, plus links to related sites that focus on his films' subjects and stills from the productions.

Q: What is your current web traffic on DVDocumentaries.com? Has it been rising or falling or remaining the same recently?

NATHAN BRAMBLE: On average I currently get about 1,500 visitors a week. With the release of each new short film I post to the site I'll get an increase in the average flow. Traffic spikes periodically and when it does it is usually somewhat dramatic. For example, my site was once briefly mentioned and linked to from an article that appeared on the BBC's web site. For about three days after that traffic went through the roof, I was getting thousands of hits an hour.

Q: Your college education focused on computer and film animation (one of the most hands-on controlled filmmaking genres around) yet your filmmaking work is focused on documentaries (which can be seat-of-the-pants and heavily improvised). How were you able to make the leap between these two wildly different schools of filmmaking?

BRAMBLE: When I got to college and I started to produce some projects in class I found that being an animator is a fairly solitary pursuit. Teams of people work on animated films, but when you're an animator doing your part for the film it's most often just you and your piles of paper for hours and hours alone. I suppose I had envisioned filmmaking as being much more lively. Also, the payoff of seeing my completed work left me a little unsatisfied. I would spend weeks in front of my drawing table, and days shooting the drawings on film one frame at a time and get only one minute of footage to show for all that work.

I know this may sound corny, but I got interested in documentary filmmaking after seeing *The Blair Witch Project*. Coming from my own experience in which I knew filmmaking to be an extremely long, arduous, and lonely process I thought that this film's spontaneous and frantic style of filmmaking was inspirational. The film was certainly fictional, but it really opened me up to the possibilities of documentary-style filmmaking. After watching *Blair Witch* I looked for more interesting documentaries and found films like *Crumb, American Movie*, and *Trekkies*. After seeing these films I learned to really love this genre.

Q: Your first two documentaries focus on fabulously lost causes: a virtually abandoned Appalachian town and a presidential election ultimately decided in the secrecy of the nine-person Supreme Court chambers. What attracted you to these victory-lacking tales?

BRAMBLE: I guess I'm just attracted to extreme topics. Centralia is literally on the verge of destruction in a slow, dramatic way. The protests in DC promised to be a very passionate and emotional environment. The idea of them both being lost causes never really occurred to me when I was considering them as topics for films, they just sounded like very lively, interesting stories to document.

Q: *Centralia, PA – Modern Day Ghost Town* is a curious production since none of the remaining residents would talk to you on-camera. How can someone make a film about a specific location when the residents of that location refuse to talk about their hometown?

BRAMBLE: Since I had never made a documentary film before I wanted to use this project to prove to myself that I'd be able to pursue this sort of thing with competence. I researched the town itself and its history in preparation for the two-day shoot I had planned. Being so inexperienced, I didn't really put enough thought into preproduction for acquiring interviews. Finding very few residents interested in talking to me was a big disappointment, but I got lucky when I arrived in the town and ran into several people who had come to the doomed place just to check it out — tourists of the destruction. They were willing to talk to me on camera, so my film changed direction on location. I got enough footage to put together a short interesting piece.

For my first try I was, for the most part, happy with it. But, I learned my lesson that preproduction in documentary filmmaking is of primary importance.

Q: What was the reaction to your first film?

BRAMBLE: When I first put the film up on my web site I was surprised at the almost immediate response I got. I was receiving email with positive feedback from people the same day I uploaded it. Since putting it up on the Web I've received comments from people running Centralia web sites, from students doing a geological report on Centralia, and from someone who runs a multimedia production company in Kansas encouraging me to keep making documentaries.

The most interesting reaction to the film was from a government official in Wyoming who was trying to get more federal funding to help put out several mine fires burning in his state. He wanted to use my film as an example of what could happen if they were left to burn.

Q: In *2001 Inauguration: Voice from the Street*, the anti-Bush protesters' signs and chants were ultimately in vain. What was the emotional climate on the streets of Washington that day? Was it one of bitterness, anger, or perhaps even hope that someone would hear the protests?

BRAMBLE: It was very clear that there were a lot of people and organizations that were extremely upset with George W. Bush's winning the presidency and a total dissatisfaction with this country's election process. There was a lot of anger and frustration being expressed, but there was no violence. I saw some arguments start up between protesters and Bush supporters that I thought might end in a fight, but there was so much police presence everywhere you looked that I think people were careful not to cross a certain line in their actions. It wasn't a happy place to be, but it was exciting.

Q: Your film *2001 Inauguration* runs only 13 minutes. How much footage was shot in total that day and what was the rule of thumb to decide who made the final print and who got cut?

BRAMBLE: I have about one and a half hour's worth of raw footage shot during the inauguration. It was freezing cold, raining, and very loud in the streets. So, after cutting out shots where my shivering caused the camera to shake too much, there was too much water on the lens, or where the crowds and music were too loud to hear the interview I had about 45 minutes of usable footage.

I started editing with a goal to get the final cut under 15 minutes. I spent a lot time watching films online at sites like *iFilm.com* and *UndergroundFilm.com* before I started making my own and I found that 15 minutes is a comfortable time for someone to invest watching a film over their computer. I cut out some interviews with some less coherent people whose agendas really weren't very clear and others where certain views were repetitive.

Q. How many of your films have played offline in festivals, microcinemas, etc?

BRAMBLE: So far I have only submitted my short film *Ghost Hunters* to play publicly off the Web. It's been in a few microcinema venues, which is such a great feeling. I've been to a few of them and sitting in a theater with a group of people watching my work is an intoxicating feeling.

I have received invitations from various festivals to submit both the EverQuest film and a short documentary I had shot during the World Economic Forum protests that took place in New York City, but I didn't want to send those. I was worried that Sony, the company that owns the online game EverQuest, might find some reason to sue me if I played the film publicly. The WEF protest documentary has a technical glitch in it that I'm pretty embarrassed by. It doesn't show on the Web, but I wouldn't want to see it on a bigger screen.

Q. How did you deal with the excessive reaction that came from the EverQuest film? Both in terms of web traffic and in terms of criticism from EverQuest fans who were angry at the *Film Threat* review (which many EverQuest players perceived as being hostile and insulting to those who were fascinated by the game)?

BRAMBLE: While making the film and poking around the various online communities that surround the game I knew that the EverQuest audience was huge. There are thousands of web sites out there devoted to the game and the players.

Soon after completing the film and posting it to my web site I sent out a few promotional emails to various game related sites and traffic to *DVDocumentaries.com* began to steadily increase. The reaction was very quick and I started to find a few conversations about the film on various computer game–related message boards. I thought it was pretty cool that I was getting some attention and some people had been watching my film. Then, once the review on *Film Threat* came out, traffic to my site spiked higher than I had ever seen it. Gaming communities on the Web that were devoted to EverQuest were insulted by the review and started linking to my site and *Film Threat*. Hundreds of thousands of people were hitting my site and watching the film.

By the end of the week after the review's release, and after the subsequent article on *Film Threat* that mentioned all the hate mail being received was posted, I was getting very worried that my monthly bandwidth allotment was going to go over its limit, which could get very expensive for me. I quickly designed an all-text version of the site without links to the videos to throw up on the Web, just in case I needed to stop the presses so to speak, and was watching the traffic numbers very closely. Luckily, I only came within a few megabytes of my bandwidth limit, but it was a close call.

My site is only a personal web site, I don't have much advertising or anything that would supplement the cost of running a big site. I was taken very much by surprise at the reaction the *Film Threat* review generated.

While I was initially worried about the sheer volume of hits to the site I was receiving, I was happy to see that the vast majority of the EverQuest player community liked the short film. While *Film Threat* was getting a flood of hate mail for the Trekkie comparison in its review, I was getting a lot of encouragement and praise. With very little effort in the way of distribution, the mention on *Film Threat* had handed me an audience on a level I had never even considered.

I remember one time months after the traffic and interest in the EverQuest film came back down to a more manageable flow I discovered that a co-worker in my office played the game quite regularly. When I told her about my site and the film I had made she said, "Oh my God, that was you? You're famous!" Does being famous in a virtual world really count? I guess all things are relative.

Q. How has your web site assisted you in your filmmaking career? This encompasses all aspects of your career goals: professional, artistic, financial, emotional, et cetera.

BRAMBLE: Well, the web site is my filmmaking career. The idea from the start was to use the Web and cheap new consumer-focused video technology to make filmmaking a hobby. With the site, I've shown people that anyone can not only make films, but also show and distribute them to a wide audience at very little cost.

I have gotten great reactions to this little experiment. Thanks to the site I was able to make the jump from shooting home movies to being taken somewhat seriously as an independent filmmaker and it hardly cost me a thing. So far, I consider it a huge success.

The limited amount of experience running this site and making these short films has given me a strong foundation upon which I might actually be able to build something bigger. I have a lot of confidence in myself now, I know I could make a bigger film.

Q. How did having your films and your interview on *Film Threat* help your web site and your career?

BRAMBLE: Being mentioned on *Film Threat* introduced me to a whole new audience of people interested in independent filmmaking in general. Up to that point all the visitors to my site that I heard from where interested in the individual topics my films covered. After the *Film Threat* mentions I was soon receiving email from people interested in filmmaking and the overall idea of my site and the boost in confidence that came with that sort of attention made the whole endeavor very much worth it.

Q. Have you received other press attention beyond *Film Threat?*

BRAMBLE: Yes actually. I've been mentioned, linked to, and interviewed by independent film and digital video-focused web sites. Mostly underground and small press, but occasionally my site will be linked to by other, larger sites. The BBC linking to one of my films is probably the biggest media mention I've ever gotten.

Q. What projects are you currently planning?

BRAMBLE: I've been collaborating with another filmmaker on a documentary he's directing about the culture surrounding video games in general and I've done some shooting for him on that project. I'm also working out two ideas I have for more short documentary films for the site that I want to shoot over the next year: one involving a group of caving enthusiasts who have contacted me through my site, and another film exploring the history behind a long ago shut down amusement attraction on the Jersey Shore.

I also have an idea for my first feature-length documentary film exploring the growing world of online comic strip artists. There are many great personalities in that world that I would love to explore, but I need to get funding for it somehow.

Q. What advice can you give to anyone planning to start their own web site similar to yours?

BRAMBLE: I would say if someone were to try showing their film work online they should try very hard not to lose sight of their goal. It's very easy to get lost in all the technical aspects of designing a web site. Always keep it simple and remember that the films are what is important.

Q. How do you view the Internet's potential for the presentation of original filmmaking? Is it being maximized to its fullest or is it not being used to its fullest?

BRAMBLE: I don't think enough creative people see the Internet as a viable venue for their work, which is too bad. It's such an open forum for pretty much anything you can think of, but the technical aspect of putting one's film up on the Web is just too intimidating to a lot of people. As it becomes easier to do, and I'm sure that it will, I think more people will be inspired by the idea of distributing to the Web.

Unfortunately, the overall concept of films on the Internet has been tainted by the ongoing controversy surrounding pirated films being downloaded. The professional film industry has, so far, seen the Web as a flat-out threat. Apart from streaming some movie previews, film studios in general have done very little to utilize the full potential the Internet can offer them.

The independent filmmaker stands to benefit most from using the Internet to their advantage. The comparably low cost of getting your work shown to an audience of untold thousands should be extremely enticing. With an ever increasing audience of people getting access to broadband Internet connections I think the idea of online distribution is growing, especially thanks to services and communities offering to serve as a venue for online films. Such services take away the worry of getting bogged down in the complex technicality of computer coding and online video hosting, but they also take away some measure of control over how and when the film is shown from the filmmaker, which really turns a lot of filmmakers off to the whole idea. I truly feel the full potential of world wide exposure that the Internet can offer independent filmmakers is limitless. But, as of yet, and apart from a handful of success stories, it is still mostly unexplored territory.

6: From "Collector-to-Collector"

I
n 1987, a young filmmaker named Todd Haynes arrived on the film scene with a fairly rude and highly original production. The film was *Superstar: The Karen Carpenter Story* and it created a major sensation through its facetious retelling of the life and death of the doomed pop star with a cast made up of Barbie dolls. For two straight years *Superstar: The Karen Carpenter Story* played in festivals, midnight movies, and a few theatrical engagements, entertaining those who experienced its wonderfully warped vision.

Well, almost everyone. Among the less-than-amused were the Carpenter family, especially Karen's brother and musical collaborator Richard, and A&M Records. It seemed that Haynes happily overlooked one teeny detail in creating *Superstar: The Karen Carpenter Story* — he never cleared the music rights to any of the Carpenters tunes featured on the soundtrack. Complicating matters was the arrival of lawyers for the Mattel Corp., which objected to the less-than-wholesome and thoroughly unauthorized use of their Barbie product line as the cast of this flick.

After building a nice collection of cease-and-desist orders, Haynes withdrew the film from circulation. Every now and then over the years, the filmmaker has attempted to get official approval for a re-release from the various parties blocking the film, but to date this has proved fruitless.

Over time, Todd Haynes' reputation as a filmmaker and the notoriety surrounding his debut film have grown substantially. In the ideal world, this would seem like a cinematic tragedy since *Superstar: The Karen Carpenter Story* cannot be shown in any release channel (theatrical, non-theatrical, television or home video) and it would thus be considered as a major missing piece to a highly regarded filmmaker's output. Yet contrary to the belligerent and fatalistic tone of the cease-and-desist notices served to Haynes, *Superstar: The Karen Carpenter Story* is very much alive and with us. In fact, the film wound up on Entertainment Weekly's 2003 survey of the Top 50 Cult Movies of All Time, which is no mean feat for a film that has not been publicly screened since 1989.

So how are we able to defy Richard Carpenter, A&M Records, and Mattel Corp. in order to sing along with "We've Only Just Begun" while poor Karen (or her Barbie doll alter-ego) wretches her bulimia-tortured way to an early grave? In order to experience this title and an extraordinary bounty of rarely-seen classics and curios, one has to tiptoe into the funky world of collector-to-collector video services. Most of this is quite fascinating, and a high percentage of these services involve business operations of which some people (especially those in the entertainment industry and law enforcement) may not approve. In this chapter you will be thoroughly prepared to know who is doing what, what you should expect and avoid, and where you can find the best hard-to-find films circulating surreptitiously on video. And don't fear — if you read this chapter, you will not run the risk of being dragged into any situation that will require the services of a lawyer or bail bondsman.

Sources of Rare Films on Underground Video

Even at this late date, a surprisingly high number of noteworthy films cannot be found in official video releases. Their absence can be attributed to any number of situations, ranging from problems in clearing rights for home video release to the need for the titles to undergo extensive restoration before they can be made available for sale to the plain fact that some of these films may not be considered commercially viable for video distribution.

In the world of collector-to-collector services, every film is worthy of release on video. In some circumstances, however, there is a slight problem: the person or persons offering these films on video does not have the legal capacity to make these titles available for retail audiences. Or, to be less polite, they are video bootleggers who are violating copyright laws through the unauthorized duplication and sale of films on video and, increasingly, on DVD.

Let's make one legal point clear and concise immediately: the production and sale of illegal videotaped versions of copyright-protected films and television shows is very much a federal offense and those found guilty of such shenanigans can face the prospect of jail time and fines as high as $100,000. The readers of this book are not encouraged to produce duped videos of copyright-protected material for sale or even trade, since that is a blatant violation of the law.

However, it is not illegal to purchase a bootlegged video or DVD. Whatever ethical or moral hang-ups may decorate the purchase of such material is something for each reader to live with. From the standpoint of American law, you're not doing anything wrong if you buy or own a bootlegged video.

In fairness, we need to stress that most people selling videos in the collector-to-collector services sector are not bootleggers. Indeed, many of the rare titles being sold in this manner can be made available because the laws allow it. How is this possible? Two reasons:

1. If a film's original copyright has lapsed without being renewed, thus making it a public domain property. Any film in the public domain can be duplicated and sold without the threat of prosecution. One of the most famous public domain titles is also one of the hardest to find: Stanley Kubrick's first feature, the 1953 war drama *Fear and Desire*. Kubrick was always embarrassed by this film and made a concentrated effort to round up all of its prints to prevent it from being screened. However, he failed and a few prints remained in circulation even after the film's copyright lapsed into the public domain. In 1994, the Film Forum theater in New York showed *Fear and Desire* and Kubrick unsuccessfully tried to halt the screening, which he could not do since he did not own the rights to it any more.

2. If a film falls under the "Berne Act" section of the United States copyright law, which states: films unreleased in the United States, including original versions of films altered and/or edited for release in the United States, are not protected by American copyright and are thus considered public domain. This provision allows a very high number of international films to be made available on video. Of course, if the film in question does become commercially available in the United States, then it becomes a copyright-protected title and is no longer in the public domain. All of the major collector-to-collector groups make the promise to cease selling titles which become commercially available (though, admittedly, a few entities are having a little trouble keeping that promise).

So where do the rare films in the collector-to-collector sector come from? There are actually five key areas which have been the sources for these flicks. Some of these sources are keeping with the letter of the copyright laws while others admittedly sail into piracy-infested waters.

1. Collectors' Prints. Prior to the videotape phenomenon, diehard cinephiles who wanted to own copies of their favorite films had to buy prints and movie projectors. Most serious collectors owned 16mm projectors and purchased prints from a number of catalog companies. Also, many film societies, schools, libraries, and even television stations relied on 16mm prints to fill their cinematic needs.

When video came along, something curious arose: many classic films that were available in the 16mm format were not being released on video. Enterprising collectors who wanted to share the glory of the old but absent films took it upon themselves to transfer their 16mm prints to video and sell videotape copies based on their private prints.

Is this legal? Of course not. But without this kind of operation, many noteworthy films would remain unseen. Otto Preminger's 1959 adaptation of *Porgy and Bess* can only be seen today this way. That film was shot in the widescreen Todd-AO process, but none of those prints survive any more. An extant 35mm print survives, but it has not been, as of this writing, restored or remastered for video. Thus the collector-to-collector video copies of *Porgy and Bess* can be traced to 16mm prints.

Surprisingly, many of the videos made from 16mm prints are very good in regards to their audio and visual quality. Color films tend to be a little faded, but this should not be a surprise given the circumstances (many of the original 16mm prints can be upwards of 40 or 50 years old).

2. Borrowing From Out-of-Print Labels. Over the years, a high number of video labels have gone out of business. In their journey to obsolescence, many noteworthy titles went along with them. One of the best-known defunct labels was Magnetic Video, which was a leading distributor in the late 1970s and offered such titles as the Beatles documentary *Let it Be*, the Sophia Loren–Marcello Mastroianni love story *Sunflower* and the titles in the American Film Theatre canon. When Magnetic disappeared, those films went along with them (although the American Film Theatre titles, once among the prime titles among collector-to-collector sellers, were recently brought back thanks to Kino on Video).

Those who were savvy enough to purchase videos in the late 1970s and the first part of the 1980s became owners of a great many rare films. And with the relatively easy process of hooking up video cassette recorders and popping in blank tapes, a duplication process was born that kept these out-of-print titles alive and in circulation.

As with the copying of films from 16mm to video, this is also not legal. But that has not stopped many film fanatics from selling these titles on video. The quality of these videos, however, usually suffers from two elements: the obvious degradation that comes in duping videos (especially from an older source) and the fact that films that were put on video in the late 1970s and early 1980s were often not of the highest visual quality in the first place. The concept of restoring and remastering films for video release is relatively new, and back then the prints that were used for home video release were often battered and worn theatrical prints that played endlessly in cinemas. In many cases, the visual quality of these videos are inferior to those taken from 16mm source material.

3. The Bounty of Foreign Sources. Some enterprising collector-to-collector services look into other countries to get their titles. But unlike the previously mentioned Berne Act in relation to the import of unreleased foreign films, these are actually American films which cannot be found on commercial U.S. video labels that have turned up in duplicated copies taken from foreign video labels. An easy search

through the collector-to-collector channels can locate Paul Morrisey's *Forty Deuce* (with French subtitles), Stanley Donen's *Staircase* and Paul Newman's *The Effect of Gamma Rays on Man-in-the-Moon Marigolds* (with Portuguese subtitles from a Brazilian source), the Olsen and Johnson comedy classic *Hellzapoppin'* (with Hebrew subtitles), and Irwin Allen's *The Story of Mankind* (with Spanish subtitles). These videos are best if one doesn't mind the distraction of watching an English-language film with foreign subtitles, let alone being perturbed by the tiny fact that this falls practice way outside the boundaries of the Berne Act.

4. Direct From TV. Even more audacious than bringing over American films with foreign subtitles is videotaping films from television broadcasts and then selling the videos (sometimes with the network's logo clearly visible on the screen). There is a well-known film historian and author who supplements his income by videotaping cable television broadcasts of rare films not currently on home video. Any questions regarding the legality of such practices shouldn't even be raised — if you think this is even vaguely legal, you're the one who should be arrested!

5. Pilfered Products. Last and certainly not least is the practice of making collector-to-collector titles available by "borrowing" from video screeners, video masters, and even workprints and then duplicating them for sale (sometimes with the time code still on the screen). The practice of pirating from video screeners (which are tapes designed specifically for preview purposes, mostly for critics, exhibitors and film industry award voters) and video masters (the main tape used for duplicating commercial video releases) is primarily aimed at contemporary titles rather than older films, and this has been a major source of concern for the entertainment industry and the law enforcement entities trying to bust video piracy operations. *Superstar: The Karen Carpenter Story*, which began our chapter, most likely came out in this channel by having the original video copies duplicated without Todd Haynes' permission.

The appearance of workprints in video channels is even more disturbing, considering these are elements that are created before the final stages of postproduction. The original five-and-a-half hour workprint for Apocalypse Now is among the most popular titles among the collector-to-collector set, and how that was ever spirited into this orbit is a mystery which has yet to be addressed.

THE BEST ONLINE COLLECTOR-TO-COLLECTOR SITES

The Internet has an awful lot of collector-to-collector sites, not to mention a lot of awful sites. Many sites have limited collections and more than a few seem to be duplicating titles found at other locations.

The following line-up are among the finest collector-to-collector sites online. All of these entities have strong reputations and are a pleasure to do business with.

Beatles Extravaganza Video List

http://hometown.aol.com/emailpsych/vhsbeatles2.html
The ultimate stop-and-shop for Beatles fanatics, with very rare TV appearances as a group (including the full uncut 1964 *Ed Sullivan Show* episode of their American debut) and as solo artists in the 1970s, plus assorted films and even the long-unseen cartoon series from the mid-1960s.

Bubonic Films

http://bubonicfilms.com/bubonic/BubonicFilms.htm
No need to fear the plague here. This site is the e-commerce heaven for fans of Lollywood, the Pakistani horror film industry's headquarters. If you've been looking for such Pakistani lollapaloozas as *Balaa: The Witch* or *Adam Khor: Man Eater*, this is the place to click into.

Darker Image Videos

(No web site; email darkerimagevid@webtv.net)
This collection primarily focuses on hard-to-find American films from the 1930s through the early 1960s, although some international titles and vintage TV broadcasts are also included. All business is conducted by a mail order catalog; the company does not operate an online business and has no plans to start one in the near future, though all email inquiries are promptly answered.

International Historic Films

http://www.ihffilm.com/
This company has generated much controversy over the years for their video sale of films produced by the Nazi Germany film industry. In recent years, however, their inventory has grown to accommodate

both the Allied side of the wartime cinema experience and they've also branched out offering films focusing on World War I, the Korean War, and the Vietnam War.

Lost Performances by Marilyn Monroe

http://web.lconn.com/mysterease/monroe.htm

The videos on this private archivist's web site traces the glorious MM from her early bit parts in films like *Scudda Hoo – Scudda Hay!* through her unfinished final movie *Something's Got to Give*. Rare newsreel and TV kinescope footage plus foreign documentaries never released in America are also included. This site encourages both direct purchasing and swapping rare titles.

Mexican Horror Video

http://www.geocities.com/videomexfilm/mexhorror_video.html

Well, the site's name pretty much sums it up: Mexican horror productions from theatrical and TV broadcasts. However, none of the videos are in English nor do they have English subtitles.

Pimpadelic Wonderland

http://www.pimpadelicwonderland.com/haves.html

Focusing exclusively on the 1960s through the early 1980s, with a heavy emphasis on the crazier edge of the cult movie universe. This is perhaps the only place online where you can find Serge Gainsbourg's French TV variety specials, Andy Kaufman's infamous 1981 disruption of the *Fridays* comedy show, and *Fuk Fuk, the Brazilian Wonder Midget* listed on the same page.

Shocking Videos

http://www.shockingvideos.com

Perhaps the finest company operating in the collector-to-collector sphere (see interview with company president Mark Johnston later in this chapter).

Subterranean Cinema

http://www.subcin.com

This site aims for more cult-oriented art-house fare, including experimental shorts and workprints. Also featured here are rare books, screenplays, and MP3 and WAV files with sounds from such favorites as *El Topo* and *Beyond the Valley of the Dolls*.

SuperHappyFun.com

http://www.superhappyfun.com

A fascinating, if somewhat bewildering mix of the typical Eurotrash and Asian madness typical of such sites, plus hard-to-find classics like the John Wayne cult fave *The High and the Mighty*, the 1943 B-Movie classic *The Leopard Man*, and Luchino Visconti's epic *The Leopard* (in the original Italian with English subtitles). A few nice curios listed here Quentin Tarantino's first film *My Best Friend's Birthday* and the original Disney shorts collection *Paul Bunyan & Pecos Bill* (including Bill's cigarettes, which have since been erased from the prints in circulation).

The Video Beat

http://www.thevideobeat.com

Music-related films, concert footage and rare TV broadcasts from the 1950s and 1960s are the focus here, covering everything from the 1950s J.D. flicks to European and Australian rock TV programs never broadcast in the U.S. (including an Aussie version of *American Bandstand*). There's plenty of rock, R&B, jazz, and blues to go around here — and even Pat Boone's appearance on *The Beverly Hillbillies* is included!

Video Screams

http://www.videoscreams.com

With such headings as "Bikers, Bitches and Babes" and "Cannibals," you know the emphasis is not on polite entertainment. The emphasis here is primarily on Eurotrash offerings, with some unexpected surprises including a kinescope of Boris Karloff's appearance on *This is Your Life* and *Pharaoh*, the 1966 Polish Oscar-nominated epic about ancient Egypt.

Video Search of Miami

http://www.vsom.com

This service requires a $10 membership fee for signing up, but this minor inconvenience is followed by uncommonly fast service (all orders are filled within two days of being placed). Be aware that unlike many companies and individuals in the collector-to-collector market, VSOM's catalog includes a large quantity of hard-core pornographic titles from Europe, Asia, and South America (most of these films don't have English subtitles — but then again, who watches XXX films for the dialogue?).

For more collector-to-collector sites, you can refer to the Rare Video Resources page at http://www.angelfire.com/movies/oc/vidlinks.com. While some of the sites listed there are not collectors-to-collectors outlets (including B-Movie Theater and Critic's Choice Video), the majority fall into this category.

THE BEST OF THE BUNCH

As of this writing, none of the following titles are commercially available on home video or DVD in the U.S. They can only be obtained through the collector-to-collector circuit.

Ace in the Hole (1951). Billy Wilder's biting drama about a ruthless reporter's exploitation of the victim of a mine cave-in was a resounding failure when it was first released and Wilder later dismissed it as one of his worst endeavors. Today the film is considered by some critics as a classic, but its heavy and frequently toxic cynicism makes it a very uncomfortable experience and Kirk Douglas' teeth-gnashing overacting often recalls Frank Gorshin's classic imitation of the no-holds-barred star at his scenery-chewing extreme. Audiences still seem turned off by the film: a highly-publicized 2002 revival of the film in New York was a conspicuous commercial failure. Available from: Darker Image Videos.

Apocalypse Now: The Workprint (1979). The horror! The horror! The original workprint for Francis Ford Coppola's Vietnam-themed updating of Joseph Conrad's *Heart of Darkness* runs an extraordinary five-and-a-half-hours (covering two videotapes) and includes all of the footage that was restored to the *Apocalypse Now Redux* edition from 2001 plus alternate takes, different music samplings and more Marlon Brando then you'll ever want to experience for the rest of your life. The workprint comes with a time code running at the bottom of the screen, though this is easy to ignore as the film progresses. Available from: Videoshack (http://members.tripod.com/videoshack/tapes.html)

Apocalypse Pooh (1987). Filmmaker T. Graham mixed Disney's "Winnie the Pooh" cartoons with the soundtrack of *Apocalypse Now* and thus transformed the Hundred Acre Woods into the Mekong Delta. Pooh's flight via a runaway kite is framed to the water skiing sequence with the Rolling Stones' "Satisfaction" blaring on the soundtrack. The "Fuckin' Tiger!" sequence has Tigger as the dreaded jungle feline. And who needs Dennis Hopper when Piglet is available to mouth his dialogue? And yes, that whirring noise you hear is A. A. Milne spinning in his grave. Available from: Subterranean Cinema. Also available for online viewing at iFilm.com.

Alyas Batman and Robin (1993). Holy copyright infringement, Batman! This no-budget, high-camp, unauthorized Philippine version makes a happy mess of the Bob Kane characters. A crime wave is sweeping Manila (which is alternately referred to as Gotham City, for no clear reason) as the Joker, Penguin, and Catwoman (supported by a brigade of women in evening gowns) stage elaborate bank robberies that include extended song and dance interludes. The Caped Crusaders (or unreasonable Tagalog-speaking facsimiles) try to save the day but only seem to add to the mayhem. The Philippine Batman engages in some highly un-Batmanlike behavior, which includes biting Catwoman on the neck and using a woman's bikini top as a disguise when his mask falls off. None of this makes much sense and the film illogically ends with a musical number where the cast sings "Let's Be Good, Not Bad" (to the tune of the 50s doo-wop classic "At the Hop") while people dressed like Spiderman and Peter Pan run around. Available from: Shocking Videos.

A Run for Money (Kac Para Kac) (1999). This excellent thriller was the Turkish entry for the Best Foreign-Language Film Oscar in 2000 and it is a shame it did not get nominated. A men's clothing store owner, who is struggling with financial problems and weak sales, unexpectedly finds himself in possession of a suitcase packed with cash. The money is clearly stolen and the suitcase's original carrier, who left it accidentally in a taxi, is in pursuit of its return. The clothier should be able to relieve much of his financial woes, but hiding the large sum of cash proves trickier than expected and circumstances spin out of his control as paranoia and fear of discover begin to weigh down on him. The film maintains a subtle, uneasy tone reminiscent of Hitchcock's finest dramas. *A Run for Money* only played in a few American film festivals and never had a commercial release. Available from: SuperHappyFun.com

The Barber of Siberia (1999). Russian director Nikita Mikhalkov, who won the 1994 Oscar for his searing *Burnt by the Sun*, helmed this mammoth wreck which deserves notice only as it is arguably the single worst film ever directed by a major international filmmaker. This ponderous tale of an American adventuress in 1885 Moscow (played by British actress Julia Ormond in a grating faux-American screech) who tries to assist her wacky inventor-father (Richard Harris at his hammy worst) in perfecting a Rube Goldberg–style tree-harvesting machine. In between chops of wood, she finds her way into the life of a Russian military cadet (Oleg Menshikov, at least a dozen years too old for the role) and promptly destroys his life. Mikhalkov himself turns up as the Tsar, as if to reign over the debacle. A mess, to be certain, but a fascinating one for any fan of contemporary Russian cinema. Available from: Video Search of Miami.

The Brasher Doubloon (1947). This vigorous little programmer was one of two films from 1947 based on Raymond Chandler's private eye novels (the other was the artsy *The Lady in the Lake* starring and directed by Robert Montgomery). George Montgomery (not related to Robert) was too young and too energetic to match Chandler's concept of world-weary seedy gumshoe Philip Marlowe, but the film's rush of madness, murder and double- and triple-crosses in the pursuit of a rare stolen coin more than compensated for the miscasting. In typical Chandler fashion, the plot makes very little sense up until the conclusion, and even then you need to think about why the characters bothered to go through the extremes they did. Director John Brahm, best known for his noirish thrillers *The Lodger* (1944) and *Hangover Square* (1945), keeps the action moving while stylishly using clever camera angles and lighting effects to hide the film's B-Movie production values and the silliness of the storyline. *The Brasher Doubloon* is no classic but it is an entertaining diversion. Available from: Darker Image Videos.

The Brazilian Wizard of Oz (The Tramps and the Wizard of Oroz) (1984). Ooooooooooooh, we're off to see the Wizard, the wonderful Wizard of... Rio de Janeiro? Toto knows we're not in Kansas, especially with the samba music and non-stop Portuguese chatter that filters through this bizarre movie that was designed to highlight the none-too-apparent talents of The Tramps, a Brazilian quartet who combined the worst elements of the Three Stooges and the Wiggles into a musically violent brand of kiddie entertainment. The film borrows the characters of the Scarecrow, the Tin Man, and the Cowardly Lion and plops them into a hodgepodge tale of the extreme measures taken by the Tramps to bring water to a drought-stricken village. After shenanigans involving a spell of shoplifting and a take-off on *2001: A Space Odyssey*, the Tramps ride on a giant flying bone to Rio, where they promptly engage a group of housewives in a knock-down brawl and then peddle racing bicycles head-first into a gas station. In an attempt to bring solemnity to the film, the Holy Family inexplicably shows up and a grin from the Virgin Mary brings the much-needed rain. Goodbye Yellow Brick Road, indeed! Available from: Video Search of Miami.

Calypso Heat Wave (1957). This B-Movie quickie about a jukebox tycoon's failed attempt to take over an artist-friendly record label was designed to cash in on the calypso music craze. The score here is so-so, but the film is worth checking out strictly for its very unlikely cast: Joel Grey, Maya Angelou, Darla Hood (of *Our Gang* fame, in a rare adult starring role), plus an obscure rock group called The Tarriers who included a young singer named Alan Arkin. Available from: The Video Beat.

Death of a Salesman (1951). Arthur Miller had nothing to do with the 1951 film adaptation of his classic play and has frequently denounced it for portraying Willie Loman as being merely insane. This is actually strange in itself, as the film is virtually slavish in following the letter of Miller's text and even recreating the stage directions to the point that many critics complained of the production's theatrical appearance. But in any event, Fredric March's harrowing interpretation of the ill-fated Loman was nothing short of stunning, and he was ably supported by Mildred Dunnock and Kevin McCarthy (all three earned Academy Award nominations for their performances). The film was a major commercial failure when it was first released, owing in large part to an obnoxious boycott orchestrated by McCarthyist elements who accused Miller of being a Communist — clearly forgetting his absence of involvement in the film. Available from: RareVideos.com (the title is not on the web site, but can be obtained by contacting the site's owner directly).

Don Quixote de Orson Welles (1992). Exploitation director Jess Franco, who worked as Orson Welles' assistant director on the 1966 classic *Chimes at Midnight*, coordinated this attempt to locate the far-flung footage from Welles' unfinished adaptation of the Cervantes landmark. Several problems arose during the restoration, including the refusal by

Welles' collaborator Oja Kodar to contribute the footage in her possession and the absence of an English-language soundtrack for most of the footage that Franco obtained (Welles shot the film silent and originally planned to dub all of the voices, but only recorded a few sequences). Franco opted to keep Welles' surviving dialogue track and fill the rest of the film with dialogue spoken by other actors, which created a peculiar aural sensation. Despite these obstacles, the resulting work was a fascinating study into a bizarre and overlong project (stretching 1955 through 1971) that poked fun at the Cervantes legend. During the course of the film, Don Quixote and Sancho Panza wander out of 16th-century La Mancha and into modern Madrid, where they encounter such oddities as the motor scooter, the radio, and even Orson Welles making a movie about their adventures. *Don Quixote de Orson Welles* had some U.S. festival playdates, but legal complications regarding the film rights and a lack of interest from American indie distributors in its commercial viability prevented any commercial release. Available from: Copies of the film can be found on occasion on eBay and a DVD with both the English and Spanish language versions can be obtained for international purchases through the Spanish e-commerce site DVDGO.com. No current American provider in the collector-to-collector circuit is offering this film as part of their regular inventory.

The Dragon Lives Again (1976). Bruce Lee (played by non-lookalike Bruce Leong, real name Hsiao Liang) dies and goes to the Underworld, a predominantly Chinese purgatory ruled by a king wearing a beaded lampshade who spends most of his time chasing concubines around a hot tub. The Underworld is facing a coup lead by James Bond (a bushy-haired white guy in a tuxedo), Clint Eastwood (a Chinese guy with a glued-on beard wearing a costume from the Leone films), the Exorcist (a Chinese guy in a Nehru jacket) and Emmanuelle (a white chick in '70s chic). Bruce Lee gets back-up support from the fabled One-Armed Boxer (whom he refers to as "One-Arm") and Popeye the Sailor (played by a Chinese man with a shaved head who is dressed in a floppy sailor suit and crunches a corncob pipe). All told, this is fairly coherent until a lengthy sequence when the concubines sit down to discuss Bruce Lee's penis. Probably the weirdest thing to come out of Hong Kong, this movie would be more at home in a surrealist film festival than in a martial arts round-up. Available from: Shocking Videos.

Fear and Desire (1953). No one would recall this talky one-hour meditation on war and survival had its creator been someone other than
Stanley Kubrick, who made his feature film directing debut here. In an
unspecified conflict during an uncertain time, four soldiers find themselves behind enemy lines and slowly make their way to safety, but
their unlikely encounters with a glamourous peasant girl and the headquarters of the dreaded enemy creates unexpected changes that lead to
glory and tragedy. Kubrick's attempts to secure all of the prints of Fear
and Desire failed, as at least one copy is still in circulation. While the
picture quality leaves a lot to be desired, there is no need to fear: this
curio is more than watchable and it offers irrefutable proof that even an
uber-perfectionist like Kubrick could make serious mistakes. Available
from: Subterranean Cinema.

Filming Othello (1978). Produced for West German television, Orson
Welles' last completed film as a director was the quiet, almost medi-
tative celebration of the raucous production history surrounding his
1951 version of *Othello*. Welles concentrates on the more colorful
aspects of the creation of *Othello*, most notably the decision to film
Cassio's murder in a Turkish bath because the costumes were not
delivered, but he also carefully avoids many of the thorny problems
surrounding the film including the horrible dialogue synchronization
(all of the footage presented is silent) and the problems in casting
Desdemona (Canadian actress Suzanne Cloutier's performance was
judged lacking and ultimately dubbed by another woman). But one can
overlook the evasiveness and enjoy Welles' deep gift for raconteur tale-
spinning, especially when he hosts a Boston Q&A session for the film
and engages in a hearty reunion with his co-stars Hilton Edwards and
Micheal MacLiammoir (who nearly out-talk and out-charm Welles over
a lengthy luncheon). *Filming Othello* was never released in the United
States due to a long-running conflict between the film's producers and
Beatrice Welles, the filmmaker's daughter and the owner of the rights
to Othello. Available from: Copies of the film occasionally surface on
eBay. No current American provider in the collector-to-collector circuit
is offering this film as part of their regular inventory.

FTA (1972). This documentary on the "political vaudeville" tour led
by Jane Fonda and Donald Sutherland in the areas surrounding U.S.
military bases in the Pacific Rim was the rare feature to openly question

American policies in Indochina during the height of the Vietnam War. The audiences for these shows were the men and women in the American military and they were overwhelmingly supportive of the entertainment, although in one scene a loud malcontent is ushered out after he disrupts the performances. The satirical sketches performed by the racially mixed ensemble rarely rise above the level of a Beetle Bailey comic strip, although the folk songs (including a few performed by military audience members) and the poetry slams are more reflective of the anger and hypocrisy of the time. *FTA* only played for a week's theatrical engagement before being abruptly withdrawn from release. The available video material is not of the best visual quality, but due to the rarity of the title it deserves to be seen anew. Available from: Shocking Videos.

The High and the Mighty (1954). William Wellman's airborne adventure about a jetliner facing serious problems was the forerunner of the various all-star disaster flicks, although the vehicle's fate can never truly be in doubt once John Wayne takes over the wheel. This is one of the most sought-after titles currently out of circulation thanks to an ongoing fight between the Wayne estate (which controls the rights to the film) and Warner Brothers (which originally released it) regarding who is going to pay for the much-needed restoration of this epic (the film's negative is reportedly badly deteriorated and the few surviving original prints are supposedly in an equally miserable state). Contrary to popular belief, *The High and the Mighty* was briefly released on home video in the early 1980s and the copies available for collector-to-collector purchase are traced to this source. Available from: SuperHappyFun.com.

His Majesty, the Scarecrow of Oz (1914). The father of the Oz stories, L. Frank Baum, wrote, produced and directed this early silent film, which is the only Oz adventure which he made directly for the screen. The familiar Yellow Brick Roadsters are here, but this time the Tin Woodsman decapitates the Wicked Witch with his axe while the Scarecrow engineers a coup d'etat against the vile King Kruel. Available from: Darker Image Videos.

The History of Racist Animation (1990). Some of our favorite cartoon characters traffic in a surprisingly high degree of racial, religious, and ethnic intolerance. African Americans carry the brunt of the abuse here (most egregiously with Bugs Bunny tormenting a dumb black version of Elmer Fudd in *All This and Rabbit Stew*), but there are plenty of nasty happenings aimed at Jews, Japanese, Chinese, Mexicans, American Indians, Arabs, and Italians. Most of these films cannot be shown on American television, though the cartoons involving American Indians and Arabs can still be found on the air. This is definitely not for kids. Available from: Shocking Videos.

Jamboree (1957). A '50s rock extravaganza starring Jerry Lee Lewis (doing an alternative take of "Great Balls of Fire"), Carl Perkins, Fats Domino, Lewis Lymon and the Teenchords, Frankie Avalon, Count Basie (Count Basie???), and Dick Clark. Go, cat, go! Available from: The Video Beat.

Jud Suss (1940). One of the most repugnant films ever made, this propaganda tract about a Jewish financier in 18th-century Germany who brings moral wreckage and economic ruin to a small duchy before receiving a violent comeuppance was designed to be shown in Nazi-occupied Europe as a means of justifying the anti-Semitic terror that ultimately led to the mass annihilations of the Holocaust. The film is rather extravagant in its production values but brutally harsh in its relentless presentation of Jews as being the enemy of the Germany people. Jud Suss is still banned in Germany, and today it serves as a sad reminder of what can occur when the power of cinema is placed in the wrong hands. Available from: International Historic Films.

Let it Be (1970). Six years after bursting on movie screens as the cheery and fresh-faced moptops of *A Hard Day's Night*, the Beatles were a bickering, hirsute, none-too-healthy-looking bunch in Let it Be. The film has always been difficult to endure, given that the group is literally breaking up before the camera by what they say to each other (especially George's confrontation with Paul) and by what is not said (most conspicuously in the way Yoko Ono is ignored by Paul, George and Ringo). But the peerless soundtrack (the winner of the Academy Award for Best Original Song Score, the only documentary to win this now-defunct honor) more than compensates for the film's uncomfortable human drama and the rooftop concert, complete with the wild mix of onlooker reactions, is the band's final masterwork. Available from: Beatles Extravaganza Video List.

Let it Be Outtakes (1970). Can't get enough of *Let it Be?* Then try two hours of outtakes consisting of alternate takes and deleted scenes, most notably a visit by Peter Sellers and his happy praise of "Acapulco Gold" (to the visible discomfort of the Fab Four, who pretend they are not being filmed). Most of the footage is in black-and-white and none of it is arranged in anything resembling a coherent stream of logic. But for diehard Beatles fans, this bounty is a video treasure chest. Available from: Beatles Extravaganza Video List.

1984 (1954 and 1956). Two rare versions of the George Orwell landmark can be found in the collectors-to-collectors circuit. The first and superior version is a kinescope of a live 1954 BBC telecast, starring a cadaverous Peter Cushing as the doomed rebel in a spirit-crushing dystopia. This production is unusually extravagant and ambitious for a live TV drama, and its use of sadistic violence created so much controversy that the production was debated furiously in the House of Commons. It is also noteworthy as being among the relatively few live dramatic presenta-tions of 1950s British television to survive extant. The second version is a British feature film, although much of its effectiveness was blunted by the severe miscasting of burly American character actor Edmond O'Brien as Winston and also by the antiseptic performance of American actress Jan Sterling as Julia (their casting was most likely designed to aid the film's chances of a U.S. theatrical run). While the 1984 version of the mate-rial starring John Hurt and Richard Burton was visually and emotionally closer to Orwell's version, the earlier versions deserve consideration for tackling what was clearly commercially risky and artistically challenging material. Available from: Copies of both versions can be found on eBay. No current American provider in the collector-to-collector circuit is offer-ing either version as part of their regular inventory.

The Optimists (1973). One of Peter Sellers' finest performances came in this small drama about two children from a poor family whose friend-ship with a melancholic busker helps bring them a sense of hope for a better life. Despite the twin challenges of sharing screen time with kids and a cute dog, Sellers gives a performance that is equally vibrant in its musical moments (with songs by Lionel Bart) and troubling in its melodramatic periods when the character's troubled life is brought into question. Sellers, whose career at this period was stalling after a stretch of box office flops, embedded himself so deeply into this role that many onlookers who saw the film being shot in London genuinely mistook him for a street performer and failed to recognize the star beneath the costume. Unfortunately, the film was incorrectly marketed as a jolly musical-comedy and audiences who were expecting a song and smile were puzzled and disappointed at what they found instead. After the commercial failing of *The Optimists*, Sellers returned to the safety of the Inspector Clouseau character and successfully resurrected the Pink Panther films and re-established his box office viability. Available from: Video Search of Miami.

Pharaoh (1966). Can the headstrong but hunky son of the Egyptian pharaoh find romance with a nice Jewish girl from the other side of the pyramids without the interference of the power-hungry ruling class of priests and the local warmonger rabble-rousers seeking to invade neighboring Assyria? This opulent and historically accurate Polish film received an Academy Award nomination as Best Foreign-Language Film. While it lacks the camp value found in most American epics involving ancient Egypt, the film's handsome production values and detailed recreation of this early civilization will please those who take their pharaohs seriously. Available from: Video Screams.

Population: 1 (1986). The world's first (and, to date, only) nuclear holocaust musical was designed as a vehicle for The Screamers, a Los Angeles punk rock group who supposedly enjoyed a considerable cult following even though they never recorded an album. *Population: 1* is basically a running commentary by the sole survivor of the world's demise, an off-kilter civil defense employee who recalls the rise and ruin of 20th-century America in a series of original songs and funky covers of old-time classics. Tomata DuPlenty brings a kooky charm as the film's singing survivor and Sheela Edwards provides a nice balance of chic and creepiness as his mind's elusive muse. Available from: Shocking Videos.

Porgy and Bess (1959). Long unavailable for re-release and never officially made available for home entertainment viewing, Otto Preminger's adaptation of the Gershwin classic is actually a strange and unsuccessful venture. The film is never certain whether it wants to be an opera or an old-style musical: the blatantly dubbed singing voices for leads Sidney Poitier and Dorothy Dandridge belong in an opera house, but Sammy Davis Jr. and Pearl Bailey belt out their numbers as if they were either on Broadway or in a Las Vegas revue. Preminger's direction is also fairly stagnant, with musical numbers and dance sequences that rarely come to life, and the cast clearly seems uncomfortable for most of the proceedings. However, the film's lack of availability has raised its reputation much higher than it would be had it been easily accessible, and *Porgy and Bess* is noteworthy as Hollywood's last all-black production before the civil rights movement permanently changed how the film world viewed the African American experience. Available from: RareVideos.com (the title is not on the web site, but can be obtained by contacting the site's owner directly).

Queen Kong (1976). This no-budget British parody was halted from getting a wide release by Dino De Laurentiis, who was producing his big-budget remake of the 1933 at the same time. Unavailable outside of England for many years, the film is a cheery little piece of slapdash and satire, with the roles reversed to have a giant female ape falling in love with the handsome Ray Fay. *Queen Kong* pokes a lot of fun at the feminist politics of the 1970s, and the argument goes that the ape is not being persecuted because she destroyed half of London but because she is a woman seeking her equal rights! You go, girl. Available from: Shocking Videos.

Rock Pretty Baby (1956). A rock combo consisting of Sal Mineo (on drums), Rod McKuen (on bass), and John Saxon (on guitar) try to hit the big time. Okaaaaaaaaaaaaaaaaaaaaaay! Edward C. Platt, better known as the Chief on *Get Smart*, is also on hand along with Henry Mancini and Jimmy Daley and the Dingalings. Available from: The Video Beat.

The Sandwich Man (1966). The sandwich in question is an advertising platter board for the clothiers Finkelbaum and O'Casey, and it is worn by a gregarious East Ender who walks across London (Michael Bentine, one of the original stars of BBC's legendary *Goon Show*) and encounters an endless mix of eccentrics from all levels of Britain's ossified class structure. The film is only moderately amusing, but rabid Anglophiles will enjoy its travelogue-worthy glimpses of celebrated London neighborhoods plus its all-star line-up of British stage and screen stars of the era (including Terry-Thomas, Diana Dors, Ron Moody, Norman Wisdom, Dora Bryan and Wilfrid Hyde-White). Available from: Video Search of Miami.

Sh! The Octopus (1937). Running less than an hour, this surreal B-Movie finds two numbskull detectives (Allen Jenkins and Hugh Herbert) in a lighthouse with a pack of suspicious characters who may be hiding a deadly criminal. Or maybe one of them is the criminal? Or maybe the criminal never existed? The film's wild mix of switched identities, vague jokes, surreal sight gags, and nonlinear storytelling predates the excesses of David Lynch by a half-century. How this Warner Brothers effort got approved for release is a minor mystery, perhaps worthy of a film unto itself. Available from: Darker Image Videos.

Skidoo! (1968). Otto Preminger's spoof on the drug culture of the late 1960s was a major bomb when it first came out, but today it plays like an endearingly square time capsule with more than a few camp laughs. Jackie Gleason plays a gangster who gets himself sent to Alcatraz to rub out a mob stoolie, but he is unable to achieve his goal and realizes he's been double-crossed and is stuck behind bars. To aid his escape, he spikes the prison's soup with LSD and builds an impromptu balloon to float to freedom. Carol Channing plays his zany wife, who gets carried away with the hippie happenings of their flower-power daughter and her drug-friendly friends. The film's all-star cast includes Groucho Marx as a crime boss named God, Frankie Avalon as a mobster, Cesar Romero as his father, Peter Lawford as a corrupt senator, Burgess Meredith as the Alcatraz warden, and George Raft standing around doing next to nothing. Available from: Video Search of Miami.

Song of the South (1946). Disney's politically incorrect film version of the Uncle Remus stories actually played in theatrical re-release through the early 1980s, but when it came time for a home video release the company would only put it out in Europe and Japan. Although no civil rights group has called for a boycott of the film and the sequence with the Oscar-winning tune "Zip-a-Dee-Doo-Dah" has been included on a sing-a-long video, *Song of the South* remains unseen to anyone in the United States and no plans have been announced to give it a release in the American market. Available from: This title is widely available on eBay, albeit from copies of the European and Japanese VHS and laser-disc releases. No current American provider of collector-to-collector titles lists this in their inventory.

Staircase (1969). Important as the first film to depict a gay mar-riage, Staircase is nonetheless an astonishing mess due to the wildly uncontrolled hamming of Rex Harrison and Richard Burton as the homosexual couple whose long relationship has hit a major downturn. Under Stanley Donen's direction, any genuine emotion or sincerity relevant to *Staircase* was chased away in favor of extravagant primping and fussing by the stars, who clearly were having too much fun. While more mature representations of the gay experience would come later, *Staircase* needs to be considered as the first step in cinema's acceptance of gay characters and situations — even if it is so bad it is funny. Available from: Subterranean Cinema.

Superstar: The Karen Carpenter Story (1987). Perhaps the most famous film in the collector-to-collector world, this retelling of the pop singer's life is equal parts hilarious, tasteless, brilliant and banal. Once you get over the novelty of the all-doll cast, the story itself is no better or worse than any typical TV movie or second-rate documentary. And the cruel depiction of the obnoxious Carpenter family's overbearing control of Karen seems strangely played for laughs, even though the results of their actions were tragic. Karen herself doesn't have any genuine personality here and she quickly becomes the butt of sick jokes as her Barbie alter ego becomes disfigured thanks to her fatal bulimia. But for the sheer audacity of the concept and execution (filmmaker Todd Haynes supposedly never publicly apologized for appropriating the Carpenters' music without permission), the film has no equals. Available from: Widely available for sale on eBay.

The T.A.M.I. Show (1965). Jan and Dean host this to-die-for musical line-up featuring Chuck Berry, James Brown, The Supremes, Gerry and the Pacemakers, Smokey Robinson and the Miracles, Marvin Gaye, Lesley Gore, The Barbarians, Billy J. Kramer and the Dakotas, and others. Look closely and you may spot a teenage Teri Garr among the go-go dancers. Available from: The Video Beat.

The Turkish Star Wars (1982). Probably the craziest film to come out of Turkey's subculture of Hollywood ripoffs, this intense adventure flick "borrowed" FX footage from the George Lucas landmark and taped it into a new tale about two middle-aged space jockeys who crash on a strange planet and help a foxy faux-blonde fight an army of razor-clawed mummies and zipper-backed furry monsters controlled by a giant blue robot with an ambulance light on its head. Music from *Raiders of the Lost Ark* is pilfered for dramatic effect and the film's lack of budget is second only to its lack of logic. There's plenty of sound and fury and it may signify nothing, but the film moves so fast and takes itself so seriously that any criticism is ultimately moot. Available from: Shocking Videos.

The Turkish Wizard of Oz (1971). A glamourous and big-breasted Dorothy goes over the Istanbul rainbow to meet an effeminate Scarecrow, a grouchy Tin Woodsman, and a Cowardly Lion with an excessively hairy groin. A group of magical midgets, a clan of dancing cavemen and a Wizard who looks like one of the ZZ Tops adds to the mayhem, and Toto gets into the act by jumping up Dorothy's dress. Compared to this, *The Brazilian Wizard of Oz* is a carbon copy of Judy and company! Available from: Shocking Videos.

Victory (1919). The first and still the best adaptation of the Joseph Conrad classic is this hyperactive version complete with exploding volcanoes, sultry sirens, depraved torture, double- and triple-crosses, and a wild hamming duel (complete with arched eyebrows and sneering lips) between Lon Chaney and Wallace Beery. It makes little sense, but who cares? Even those who loathe silent films will enjoy this madcap offering. Available from: LS Video (www.lsvideo.com).

THE TEN MOST WANTED FILMS NOT ON UNDERGROUND VIDEO

While the collector-to-collector scene is packed with a high number of fascinating and funky movies, there are still some titles which have eluded repeated and determined attempts at capture. Running the timeline from the silent era to today's heavy metal universe, these films are among the most sought-after by those duplicating and selling videos on a collector-to-collector basis. If anyone reading this has any leads on where to obtain either prints or clear video copies, please contact the author in care of the book's publisher.

1. *The Adventures of Robinson Crusoe* (1954). Luis Buñuel's first color film and first English-language production is a fairly straightforward and surprisingly un-Buñuel-like interpretation of the Defoe classic.

Bruce Leong (center) as a very unconvincing Bruce Lee gets upstaged by a Chinese version of Popeye the Sailor in the Hong Kong phooey *The Dragon Lives Again.*

The original Yellow Brick Roadsters join forces in L. Frank Baum's very rare 1914 feature *His Majesty, the Scarecrow of Oz.*

Original poster art for the masterpiece of rip-off Turkish cinema, the 1971 classic *The Turkish Wizard of Oz.*

Indeed, except for a dream sequence where Crusoe's father is bathing a pig, it would be almost impossible to guess this was directed by the same man who helmed *Los Olvidados* or *The Exterminating Angel*; the film's driving force is Dan O'Herlihy's vigorous performance as Crusoe, which earned him an Oscar nomination as Best Actor. *The Adventures of Robinson Crusoe* was widely seen up until the early 1970s and had been a programming staple for many local television stations, but prolonged legal complications regarding the ownership of the film (at least five parties are claiming it is theirs) has kept the film out of theatrical and home entertainment release. U.S. non-theatrical rights belonged to Kit Parker Films, which offered a faded 16mm print up until its corporate demise in 2000, and the film's last known public screening was a one-time exhibition as part of the weekly Light+Screen Film Festival series in New York in 1999. Other 16mm prints are known to exist, but to date none have been transferred to video for sale as a collector-to-collector title. If there any videos from international sources, they've not been made available in the American market.

2. *All This and World War II* (1976). This was probably the weirdest idea every brought to film: a history of the British experience in World War II using a combination of newsreel footage and Beatles songs. Yes, Beatles songs. But not the original recordings, but rather newly recorded covers by such diverse artists as Elton John (singing "Lucy in the Sky with Diamonds"), Helen Reddy ("The Fool on the Hill"), Leo Sayer ("I Am the Walrus"), Tina Turner ("Come Together") and The Bee Gees ("Golden Slumbers/Carry That Weight" and "Sun King"). The lack of coherence between the images on the screen and the soundtrack selections ("Get Back" is performed while footage of Nazi tanks is run in reverse) was a cause for confusion and frustration for the relatively few people who saw the film in its brief theatrical run. Problems regarding the music rights to the film has kept *All This and World War II* out of circulation in most markets (it is known to have played recently on New Zealand television), and to date there has never been a video release nor a CD soundtrack reissue. There is even a rumor that the film's distributor, 20th Century Fox, destroyed all prints and negatives. The only available elements connected to the film, the original two-record soundtrack album and poster art for the film, turn up occasionally on eBay.

3. *Catch My Soul* (1973). Actor Patrick McGoohan made his debut as a film director with this adaptation of Jack Good's rock opera based on Shakespeare's *Othello*. Also known as *The Santa Fe Satan* (the film's location was moved from Venice and Cyprus to the trendy New Mexico capital), *Catch My Soul* gave singer Richie Havens his first starring role as Othello (also making him the first black performer to essay the role in a film). Season Hubley was cast as Desdemona, Susan Tyrrell (fresh from an Oscar-nominated role in *Fat City*) played Emilia, and Lance LeGault was Iago (a role played by Jerry Lee Lewis in the London stage version!). Unlike two other rock-flavored musicals of the same year, *Godspell* and *Jesus Christ Superstar*, *Catch My Soul* was a resounding commercial debacle and its failure helped speed the doom of its distributor, Cinerama Releasing, which went out of business shortly after the film tanked. Whether this production was deserving of its fate cannot be determined today since it has not been seen in three decades. Despite an intense search, it seems that no one in the collector-to-collector orbit has a copy of the film. It is known that 20th Century Fox currently controls the rights to the film.

4. *The Day the Clown Cried* (1972). Perhaps the most famous film never released, *The Day the Clown Cried* was written and directed by Jerry Lewis and was intended as his first serious dramatic role. And what a role it was: a broken-down clown in 1940s Germany who is sent to be imprisoned in a concentration camp where he is assigned to entertain the children before they are sent to the gas chambers. The production disputes between Lewis and his business partners became the stuff of legend and a barrage of lawsuits kept the film from ever gaining a theatrical release. (Whether or not the film was actually completed is open to dispute, as several versions of its postproduction status are floating around.) According to Lewis biographer Jim Neibaur, the film currently exists in two parts: most of the film is in Sweden, while the final reel is in Lewis' collection, which means it never existed as a whole. Yet rumors persist of a video copy, but if it does it has yet to make its presence known. Drafts of the screenplay are online and can be downloaded, offering a tantalizing tease for this highly unusual venture.

5. *Dr. Strangelove: The Pie Fight Finale* (1964). The original ending to Stanley Kubrick's black comedy masterwork *Dr. Strangelove or: How I Learned to Stop Worrying and Love the Bomb* had the various military and

political leaders gathered in the War Room lose all sense of composure and maturity and engage in a massive pie fight reminiscent of a Three Stooges knockabout. For a film that builds its cynical satire on the foundations of Cold War paranoia, the notion of an abrupt shift into flying pastry slapstick could either seem like the proper conclusion to the film's tale of a world falling apart... or it would just be the wrong way draw the movie to a close. Kubrick decided the latter was the case and the pie fight was excised from the final print. While the footage of the pie fight sequence was preserved by Kubrick (writer Terry Southern saw it in 1996 at Kubrick's screening room), it was never made available to the public. Even the 2000 video documentary *Inside the Making of Dr. Strangelove* failed to include any of the surviving footage. The closest we can get to this sequence are grainy production stills found online at http://www.geocities.com/SunsetStrip/Underground/9798/ piefight.htm

6. *Forbidden Paradise* (1925). A brief consideration of this silent film's storyline and talent could make any serious film scholar's salivary glands work overtime: Ernst Lubitsch's extravagant epic retelling the rise-to-power and excessive love-life of the Russian Empress Catherine the Great, played by Pola Negri at the height of her Hollywood glory, with reigning 1920s matinee idol Rod La Rocque as her lover/adviser Captain Alexei Czerny and the always-dapper Adolphe Menjou as her wise Chancellor. Considered a "lost" film for many years, a single extant print of *Forbidden Paradise* survives and is safely stored in the UCLA film archives. And, unfortunately, that is the only place you can find it. Silent movies have been among the least successful titles for home video release, and with very few exceptions (most notably Kino on Video and Milestone Film & Video), no major label will take a chance on issuing these titles. The lack of commercial viability has helped to keep *Forbidden Paradise* off home video, and the sad fact that only a single print survives has kept it out of the hands of the collector-to-collector duplicators.

7. *Maidstone* (1969). During the late 1960s, Norman Mailer took it upon himself to create several improvised feature films which were widely regarded as the most horrible ego trips ever to snake their way through a movie projector. Taking credit as director, screenwriter, co-producer and co-editor, Mailer's most ambitious of these efforts was *Maidstone*, a

supposed political satire in which he plays an A-list Hollywood director whose disgust with the Washington power structure forces him to abandon Tinseltown to run for the White House as an independent candidate. Mailer actually ran for Mayor of New York City the same year, and his real-life political campaign was as feeble and unsuccessful as his reel-life endeavor. *Maidstone* included the unlikely presence of two real film talents: Isaac Hayes, who wrote the film's music score, and Rip Torn, who ironically turned down the *Easy Rider* role that Jack Nicholson snagged as his ticket to superstardom in order to make this! Torn and Mailer's relationship was supposedly so wretched that the men got into a brawl (captured on film and included in the final print) and Torn bit Mailer's ear with enough gusto that he drew blood. Mailer's then-wife Beverly Bentley inserted herself into the fight. Mailer retains the rights to *Maidstone* and his other films (*Beyond the Law* and *Wild 90*) and has kept them locked away from any possibility of video transfers.

8. *Mussolini Speaks* (1933). It is difficult to comprehend the fact today, but back in the late 1920s and early 1930s the Italian fascist dictator Benito Mussolini was widely admired by many influential people in the United States for bringing a sense of order and dignity to his once-troubled country. Among those impressed with Il Duce was Harry Cohn, the founder and president of Columbia Pictures (and himself a bit of a minor league dictator). Cohn's fondness was so strong that he commissioned a one-hour documentary singing the praises of Mussolini's accomplishments and featuring lavish footage of the dictator giving his famed operatic-style speeches (radio announcer Lowell Thomas gave a simultaneous English narration while Mussolini boomed in his native tongue). The 74-minute cinematic love letter to Mussolini grossed an astonishing $1 million during its 1933 release, which was phenomenal for a documentary, and the film would probably have been considered a classic had Mussolini not bothered to align himself with Hitler's Germany, provoke world outrage by invading Ethiopia in 1935, and join the Axis side of the World War II line-up. Harry Cohn had *Mussolini Speaks* completely removed from circulation and no copies are known to exist beyond the Columbia vaults.

9. *The Naked Ape* (1973). Playboy publisher Hugh Hefner's rare tiptoe into motion pictures was this PG-rated (yes, PG!) semi-documentary based on Desmond Morris' best-selling book. Intended to humorously chart man's

evolution from prehistoric times to the swinging '70s, *The Naked Ape* seemed terribly tame and almost anachronistic when it appeared, especially when compared to the racy and daring films being released at that time (this was the same year that X-rated *Last Tango in Paris* was playing to sold-out audiences in neighborhood theaters). This Florida-based production starred Johnny Crawford, best known as Chuck Conner's son on the long-running TV Western *The Rifleman*, and much of the hoopla surrounding *The Naked Ape* was Crawford's appearance in the nude (or as nude as a PG film would allow). Modern audiences would probably pay more attention to the film's leading lady, an unknown named Victoria Principal who had her first starring role here. Universal released *The Naked Ape* in theaters, but apparently Hefner retained the rights to the film and has chosen not put it out on home video. No errant prints are floating about, thus frustrating the collector-to-collector crowd who would love to get this into their VCRs.

10. *We Sold Our Souls for Rock 'n' Roll* (2001). Penelope Spheeris, arguably the finest director of rock-oriented documentaries, brought her camera to follow the touring heavy metal festival known as Ozzfest which centers around Ozzy Osbourne. This central feature of this Ozzfest was the reunion between Osbourne and his old band Black Sabbath. While the film captured high-octane performances by the likes of Godsmack, Primus, Slayer, System of a Down, Slipknot, and Rod Zombie, the human core of the film was the relationship between Osbourne and his wife/manager Sharon. And, yes, the Osbourne kids are here as well, usually being watched over by Rod Zombie, of all people. *We Sold Our Souls for Rock 'n' Roll* was clearly a forerunner of the MTV reality series *The Osbournes*, with Ozzy and Sharon's now-established public personalities clearly in place here. The film debuted at the 2001 Sundance festival to strong feedback and was supposed to go into national theatrical distribution that year, but a very unlikely snafu (Sharon Osbourne's failure to clear the music rights to the Black Sabbath songs) aborted its release. While one would imagine the popularity of *The Osbournes* would benefit the film, this is not the case. Outside of some festival screenings, *We Sold Our Souls for Rock 'n' Roll* never played on a big screen and no plans are in place for an official video release. While plenty of collector-to-collector Black Sabbath titles can easily be found, this one is still missing.

INTERVIEW

MARK JOHNSTON, PRESIDENT OF SHOCKING VIDEOS

In the realm of collector-to-collector videos, one of the most respected figures is Mark Johnston. A movie buff who turned his passion into a career as a film historian, Johnston presents a wild world of cinema through his Hinton, West Virginia–based company Shocking Videos.

A tour through the Shocking Videos catalog (found online at *www.r evengeismydestiny.com*) leads into a world of intensely insane productions from around the world. Dividing his extensive offerings into easy-to-follow genres (Women in Prison, Eurotrash, Mondo Macarbo), Johnston is constantly searching for the most extreme, eccentric, and exotic films imaginable.

Among Johnston's presentations are *W*, a Philippine thriller about a policeman who seeks revenge on a mob after he is castrated on his wedding night; *Legendary Panty Mask*, a Japanese action flick about a female crime-fighting superhero whose costume consists of an Indian sari and leather undies worn on her head; *Shame of the Jungle*, a Belgian animated Tarzan spoof where Jane is kidnapped by a tribe of bouncing penis monsters while Cheetah swings off Tarzan's manhood; *Bad Boy Bubby*, an Australian wonder about a 35-year-old retarded man who wanders through the world with his dead cat and becomes a rock star; and *Gran Bollito*, an Italian horror/revenge tale with Shelley Winters chopping up and boiling people in an oversized cauldron. Johnston is perhaps best known as the man who brought the insanity of Turkeywood into the VCRs of America (see earlier references to *The Turkish Star Wars* and *The Turkish Wizard of Oz*).

So what kind of person is involved in selling collector-to-collector titles? Funny you should ask...

Q: How and why did you first get involved in the film and video business? And what inspired you to aim for the more extreme and edgier titles versus, say, the classic and artistic offerings?

MARK JOHNSTON: There were a lot of factors and influences that led up to this, not the least of which being a life-long love of weird movies. As a kid growing up in the PC (Pre-Cable) era I cut my teeth on stuff like *Attack of the Mushroom People, Kitten With a Whip, The Frozen Dead, The Brain from Planet Arous, Planet of the Vampires* and *The House That Screamed*. Years later, books like Michael Weldon's seminal *Psychotronic Encyclopedia of Film* and Re/Search's *Incredibly Strange Films* helped bring things into even sharper focus (so to speak). The zine revolution of the '80s provided access to fan-made publications like Rick Sullivan's *Gore Gazette*, Steve Puchalski's *Slimetime* (later renamed as the still-excellent *Shock Cinema*), and Weldon's magazine offshoot from his book of the same name, *Psychotronic*. These were where I first discovered the DIY world of "collectors videos." I ordered all of the early catalogs from all of the various "companies" most of which have long since gone by the wayside.

Many crappy multi-generation tapes later it started to dawn on me that if I had a 12th generation copy of Jackie Chan's *Armour of God* someone else must have the 11th and someone else the 10th and so on back down the line. Yeah, I know. I'm a little slow. The bottom line is, that after a lot of unintentional market research, I looked at what was available and said, "I can do this. And I can do it a lot better than most of these bozos." So I did.

Why do I aim for the "more extreme and edgier titles"? Well, as Manfred Mann said, "That's where the fun is." It's not all perversion and debauchery though. In fact, if you take a look through my catalog you'll see that I cast a pretty wide net. I've got everything from biker and women in prison flicks to naughty nuns, spaghetti westerns, martial arts, film noir, British sex comedies, documentaries, you name it. If its overlooked, out of reach, or currently unavailable and it's weird, wild or wonderful, I'm all over it like a cheap suit. I think it's pretty safe to say that mine is the only site on the Net where you can buy the Turkish version of *The Wizard of Oz*, the necrophilia soap opera *Love Me Deadly*, and Luis Buñuel's *The Criminal Life of Archibaldo de la Cruz*.

Q: From a geographic standpoint, which countries put out the strangest and most peculiar films? Can you provide some examples?

JOHNSTON: It's all relative, isn't it? I'm sure *Die Hard* or *End of Days* must seem just as strange and peculiar to someone in Jakarta as anything that's come this way from there might be to us. But speaking as your typical arrogant, white, ethnocentric American, I'd say Turkey and Indonesia are definitely at the top of the list. Japan and Mexico are no slouches either.

Thanks mostly to word of mouth, in the past few years Turkey has become known as the "go to" country for crazed knock-offs of Hollywood product, giving us bizarre, no-budget variations on everything from *Star Wars*, *Star Trek*, *E.T.*, *The Wizard of Oz*, and *Superman* to *Conan the Barbarian*, *The Exorcist*, and even *Young Frankenstein* and *The Sting*. They also have put out some of the most wildly over-the-top kung fu, action, and crime films to ever see the light of day. Take for example one of my current faves, *The Biggest Fist* (original title *En Buyuk Yumruk*). It stars my main man, Cuneyt Arkin, a chain-smoking karate expert and human dynamo who's sort of a Turkish Jackie Chan, Errol Flynn, and Ed Wood all rolled into one. In *The Biggest Fist* you get: A man set on fire and thrown out of a high rise window, a car bombing, a high speed chase, and *five* fiery car crashes. And that's just during the opening credits!

Meanwhile, Indonesia with its rich tradition of sorcery and superstition continues to startle and amaze with masterpieces like *Mystic in Bali* which features a flying head (with spinal cord and internal organs still attached) that swoops between pregnant women's legs and sucks out their fetuses; and Barry Primas' *The Warrior*, a mind-boggling hodgepodge of martial arts and black magic where during the final climactic duel the villain gets his arms, legs, and even his head lopped off and the various body parts just hop right back onto the guy and he keeps on fighting.

As for Japan and Mexico, well, with countless generations of brutality, cruelty, and bloodlust to draw from, lets just say these folks know how to party.

Q: How did you first learn of Turkeywood, the Turkish genre of Hollywood rip-offs? And when you finally got to see these films, did they live up to your expectations? And... do you know why the Turks, of all people, create such weird films?

JOHNSTON: I have to give credit where credit is due. The whole weird Third World cinema thing was inspired by the book *Mondo Macabro* written by UK author and authority Pete Tombs. Thank God for that guy because I, for one, was getting pretty burned out on Lucio Fulci, Dario Argento, and Hong Kong pistol operas. Did the Turkish stuff live up to my expectations? Yes! Yes! A thousand times yes! I can honestly say that anyone who sits down and watches something like *The Turkish Star Wars* will have their concepts of what a "movie" is and should be forever changed. And that, as Martha Stewart would say, is a *good* thing.

Why do the Turks make such weird movies? I don't think it's necessarily intentional. I think they're just some vibrant "can do" motherfuckers who don't let little things like lack of budget or ability (much less copyrights) slow them down.

Q: How do you go about tracking down the films in the Shocking Videos collection? And how do you determine what makes the cut and what doesn't?

JOHNSTON: I don't think you want me to answer that first question because if I did I'd have to kill ya. Seriously though, aside from my own excavation efforts I've got scouts around the world who keep an eye out for stuff for me and let me know when things turn up. These are the people that make me look good and I'd love to be able to give them public recognition, but it just wouldn't be good business. So I'll just have to say "Thanks, guys! You know who you are!" and leave it at that.

One thing I *don't* do is buy from my competitors and then turn around and resell copies of their copies. I *hate* that!

What makes the cut? Whatever I feel is amazing, wonderful, bizarre, shocking, insane, jaw-dropping, mind-bending, and/or too stupid to ignore. What doesn't make the cut? Everything else.

Q: Which films are your personal favorites in the Shocking Videos collection?

JOHNSTON: Wow. So many to choose from. Okay, here are a few that I think truly embody the spirit of what Shocking Videos is all about. I won't try to describe them all. I'll just list the titles and the categories they can be found in and your readers can go and check em out for themselves:

The Boxer's Omen (Asian Invasion)
Darktown Strutters (Blaxploitation)

Death Warrior (Mondo Macabro Turkey)
Enter the Seven Virgins (Women In Prison)
Forty Deuce (American Trash)
Ghosts of the Civil Dead (Aussie Trash)
If Footmen Tire You, What Will Horses Do? (Hicksploitation)
Insan Avcisi (Mondo Macabro Turkey)
Killers on Wheels (Asian Invasion)
Lady Exterminator (Mondo Macabro Indonesia)
Mad Foxes (Bikers)
Metal Skin (Aussie Trash)
The Telephone Book (American Trash)
The Turkish Star Wars (Mondo Macabro Turkey)
Virgins From Hell (Women in Prison)
The Zebra Killer (Blaxploitation)

And that's just the tip of the proverbial snow cone. I could go on all day about movies like *They Call Her Cleopatra Wong, Dynamite Johnson, The First Bionic Boy, Alex Joseph and His Wives, The Stabilizer, Joe Caligula, Katharina and Her Wild Stallions*, etc., etc., etc.

Q: On the flip side, have there been films which sound too good to be true... and turn out to be simply terrible?

JOHNSTON: Just about anything from Jerry Bruckheimer.

Q: What comes next for Shocking Videos? Are you moving into DVD versions of your titles? And would you consider trying theatrical release?

JOHNSTON: More, more, more. More rarities uncovered. More value for your dollar. More fun in the new world. Over 100 of our rarest, most collectible and most popular titles are currently available on DVD-R, with more on the way. Theatrical releases? Not unless drive-ins or grindhouses come back in a big way.

7. Festivals of Their Own

The first stand-alone film festival was held in Venice, Italy, in 1938. Benito Mussolini, who was not exactly celebrated for his good taste in cultural pursuits, shrewdly saw the universal language of film appreciation as a means to bolster his standing in the eyes of the world. The festival concluded on something of a controversial note, with top honors going to the Leni Riefenstahl documentary *Olympia* when the audience favorite seemed to be Walt Disney's *Snow White and the Seven Dwarfs*. *Olympia*, of course, was a product of the Nazi German film industry and while Mussolini loved Uncle Walt, he had to answer to Uncle Adolf.

The French naturally felt they could do better and planned to host their first film festival at the Mediterranean resort village of Cannes the following year. Unfortunately, the festival's opening day was September 1... and as anyone who stayed awake in high school history classes can recall, September 1 in the year 1939 was just not the right day to start a film festival in Europe.

The festival at Cannes eventually came about in 1946 and immediately gained a spot as the pre-eminent international film event of the year. The Germans, apparently still eager to one-up their Gallic foes, launched their own festival in West Berlin in 1951. The post-Mussolini Italians revived the Venice Film Festival as well. The Americans were a bit late in getting on board the film festival express, with the first U.S. event coming in San Francisco in 1957.

In the beginning, film festivals were open to underground productions (which were usually dubbed "experimental films"). In fact, the first major exposure that New York underground filmmaker Maya Deren ever received was not in New York or elsewhere in America, but at Cannes when her landmark surreal production *Meshes of an Afternoon* won a prize and international media attention.

Yet over time, the concept of festivals as prestige gatherings began to take root. The global media swarmed to these events, often for reasons that had little to do with cinematic art (especially at Cannes, where bikini-clad starlets romping on the beach helped more than a few photographers use up their inventory of film). For international events, politics began to spill into the equation. Sometimes the politics could have a positive effect, such as when Akira Kurosawa's *Rashomon* won top honors in Venice in 1951 (many film scholars credit this as being a key step for reintegrating post-war Japan into the community of nations). But sometimes the politics got nasty, most notoriously in 1955 when the American delegation at Cannes lobbied furiously but unsuccessfully to deny an award to *Rififi*, a crime thriller directed by the blacklisted American filmmaker Jules Dassin, who was then living in self-exile in France — Dassin's presence was an embarrassment to an American film industry which was trying to convince the world there was no blacklist in Hollywood.

Lost in the shift were the underground films, which were considered to be too scruffy and non-commercial to warrant serious attention. By the 1970s, very few major festivals bothered to give a screen to these films.

In 1978, a new film festival debuted. The idea for the festival was to give a home and a screen to smaller films and new filmmakers that were being ignored by the prestige-hungry festivals that only wanted A-list productions and glamour names in attendance. The event was billed as the United States Film Festival and in its first year it attracted very little interest from the media, the public, and the motion picture industry. Underground cinema, it seemed, had a new friend.

Do you have any idea what became of that festival? Here's a hint: It was held in Salt Lake City during its first two years, but then moved across Utah to a place called Park City in 1981. Here's another hint: festival operations were taken over by Robert Redford's Sundance Institute in

1984. Okay, it is fairly obvious what happened to the United States Film Festival, which officially changed its name to Sundance in 1989.

The year 1989 was also significant for Sundance for another reason: The premiere of Steven Soderbergh's *sex, lies & videotape* occurred at the festival that year. As any indie cinema lover knows, the arrival of *sex, lies & videotape* was a significant event in the rebirth of independent filmmaking; its critical and commercial success helped to put Steven Soderbergh on the proverbial map and it helped to boost Sundance's reputation as a festival of value.

In a way, 1989 was a bad year since the rise of *sex, lies & videotape* also served to destroy what Sundance and its United States Film Festival roots were all about. This was probably the last time unheralded films made outside of the mainstream were able to shine on the Park City screens. Within less than a decade, Sundance was as bloated with big shot deal-makers, publicity-seeking actors and filmmakers, and tons of media as the festivals in Cannes or Venice. Many films turned up at Sundance with distributors and theatrical and/or television playdates already scheduled. The smaller films made by unknowns that were being submitted with the hope of rising higher via a Sundance premiere were barely getting accepted for competition, yet the films that had power and glamour names attached to them had no problems getting accepted. Even films that were being marketed as being old-school Sundance, like *The Blair Witch Project*, were not the overnight sensations of *sex, lies & videotape* but actually came into Sundance with high-powered and high-financed support (*The Blair Witch Project* had already been featured twice on John Pierson's *Split Screen* cable television show, had several test screenings in Florida and New York, and was being hyped to death by a New York PR flack before the first screening at Sundance).

Sundance's gradual shift to become Cannes-in-the-snow was mirrored by a new explosion of interest in low-budget independent filmmaking that was primarily inspired by the wild success of Quentin Tarantino's *Pulp Fiction*, and was further fueled by the introduction of affordable digital video film-making equipment on the consumer market. A flux of filmmakers were finding their way behind the camera and were eager to get their work shown. But Sundance, which had been the beacon of home for the outsiders, was slowly shutting its doors to the outsiders; in fact, Sundance would not project films in the digital format until 2000. But as that hackneyed expression confirmed, as one door closed another opened. But in this case, there was more than one new door opening up on the festival circuit.

In 1995, a festival that was also based in Park City, Utah, and was running parallel to Sundance's schedule debuted under the name of Slamdance. Its purpose was to pick up where Sundance stumbled: as the launch pad for smaller films which were no longer being sought out for the Sundance schedule. The Sundance organizers did not try to stop Slamdance — they were too busy getting rich to care and they assumed that Slamdance would not cannibalize the lucrative territory they had staked out for themselves. Quite frankly, their assertion was correct. Slamdance's initial lack of star power kept the most of the media and the Hollywood movers and shakers away from its events. Whereas the Sundance awards ceremony was major entertainment news, very few people knew who won an award at Slamdance outside of a few film industry trade journals and the immediate families of the award winners. As for acquisition deals being made at Slamdance — well, anyone expecting a heavy torrent of six- or seven-digit contracts was waiting in vain.

But Slamdance eventually found its footing. Within five years of its debut, it was fielding over 2,050 submissions and was presenting films that gained wide attention, including the cult favorite *Six-String Samurai* and the documentary *Ayn Rand: A Sense of Life*. Even Chris Gore, the *Film Threat* editor and author of the definitive festival text *The Ultimate Film Festival Survival Guide*, gave Slamdance a body-praise that surpasses the notion of thumbs-up: "This festival kicks serious ass," says Gore, who is not one to drop praise lightly!

Success breeds imitation, at least in the film world, and Slamdance soon begat other parallel festivals that sought out the little films: Slamdunk, No Dance, and Tromadance (the latter created by the zany folks behind the legendary Troma Pictures). All of these smaller festivals appeared on parallel schedules with Slamdance and Sundance within the Park City vicinity. These little festivals received the films that did not make it into Slamdance — which, of course, received the films that did not make it into Sundance.

To date, these festivals are still trying to find their footing. Several films that played at Slamdunk eventually snagged theatrical and home video distribution deals, though the majority of these deals came after the fact rather than on the ground at Park City. In time, it is not hard to imagine Slamdunk and the other festivals gaining in importance, and most likely there will probably be more festivals to challenge to play in Utah's annual film festival frenzy.

Of course, the story doesn't end there. Actually, from a sense of the annual cinema calendar, it is the beginning. All of these Utah festivals take place in January, kicking off a year's worth of festivals both on a national and global forum. Almost every major city on the planet has at least one film festival and many cities have dozens of festivals relating to a variety of genre-specific categories (usually serving specific communities, such as Jewish films or gay/lesbian films or Asian films). There is even one city that doesn't have any movie theaters but has an annual film festival: Atlantic City, New Jersey, a cinema-bare resort that gives its name to an annual independent film festival which is actually held at the theaters in neighboring towns!

For the aspiring filmmaker and the die-hard movie lover, this should be celluloid/digital video heaven. Sadly, it is not. The majority of these events do not exist to encourage a love and appreciation of films. Nor do they function as viable industry "meet markets" where filmmakers can connect with potential distributors or investors. Instead, in many cases the festivals provide a happy union that exists only between the festival organizers and their bottomline.

"Most festivals are a waste of time," comments Peter M. Hargrove, president of the film and video distribution company Hargrove Entertainment. "They are set up to make money for the organizers and to bring tourism to their communities."

Hargrove adds that in many cases, filmmakers who show their work in some festivals run into economic hiccups, especially if the film is being angled for theatrical release. This has been a problem for Hargrove, whose key focus is to ensure his films get commercial engagements rather than one-time festival screenings.

"In most cases, if the festival charges admission we will insist upon a rental fee," says Hargrove. "We're not in the business of ruining our theatrical markets by giving a film away. In New York, one theater straight out tells you if the film plays in 'X' festivals they won't book the film."

ALTERNATES TO THE ALTERNATE

Yet for underground filmmakers who are eager to present their work in a theatrical setting, the festival route is often the only chance they have to surface and get noticed by the mainstream. Underground film festivals have multiplied rapidly over the past half-dozen years. Many of these have taken the route of traditional film festival organization: a single location, solid schedule and post-festival award event. Yet other underground events have reconfigured the concept of festivals, seeking a looser concept that adapts easier to the genre's intolerance for the conventional.

Atlanta-area filmmaker Michael Williams has been a key force in what he calls the BYOF festival: the acronym standing for Bring Your Own Film. In the mid-1990s, Williams launched what might be the first BYOF event, Light+Screen Film Festival in Atlanta, which encouraged local filmmakers to show up to a weekly event and present their short films either in 16mm or on video. The films were not screened in advance, so neither Williams nor the audience knew what to expect. Williams held his free Light+Screen shows in several Atlanta venues before bringing it to New York in 1999, where he found an unlikely home for his happening at the Siberia Bar, a grunge-dive bar located (believe it or not) inside a subway station a few blocks north of Times Square. The Siberia Bar had a party room that accommodated both video projections and live entertainment and the establishment's fun-loving crowd seemed like the right audience for the Light+Screen events.

As with most transplants, the BYOF concept didn't quite work when it arrived in New York. Most weeks, only one or two people showed up with films to share. Light+Screen quickly changed its format to include feature films along with the shorts. Some of the features were rare classics, such as Luis Buñuel's *The Adventures of Robinson Crusoe*, while others were underground productions that were finding New York audiences for the first time. Two of these features, the romantic comedy *Cupid's Mistake* and the comedy/horror escapade *Zombie! Vs.*

Mardi Gras, would later find theatrical playdates in New York following their Light+Screen debut.

Light+Screen's New York incarnation eventually turned into a cult feature film showcase, mixing both rare classics with contemporary flicks. Another film, *The Art of Amalia*, was acquired based on the successful screening at Light+Screen (the late Robin Lim, founder and president of Avatar Films, was present when this documentary on Portuguese fado singer Amalia Rodrigues played to an ecstatic SRO audience who packed the Siberia Bar and began negotiating with filmmaker Bruno de Almeida to acquire the film, which opened theatrically seven months later). Sadly, the Siberia Bar was evicted from its subterranean home in the fall of 2000 and Light+Screen was extinguished. Williams had since returned to Atlanta to launch the Downstream International Film Festival, a conventional annual event. In 2002, the BYOF concept returned to New York with Monday Night Shorts @ Freight Film Salon, held at the Freight Restaurant in the city's trendy Chelsea section.

"I met co-producer, Erni Vales, who designed the Freight restaurant in the Chelsea Market building, and we started brainstorming about things to do to attract customers and the film salon idea came out of that," says Victoria Clark, producer and curator of the weekly event. "They have a huge plasma screen in the restaurant and there's a huge network of emerging independent filmmakers in New York, so we thought, why not create a showcase for them? Our first meeting was in September 2002, the series launched November 4, 2002."

Before any film was projected, Clark did her homework and came up with a solution to keep the Monday Night Shorts @ Freight Film Salon screening schedule packed. "Over the past year, I've done outreach to film organizations, groups, and web sites promoting the series as an option for emerging filmmakers to showcase their films," she says. "By building a strong word of mouth, grassroots campaign with zero funds — the independent film community in New York, Los Angeles, Philadelphia, Cincinnati, Miami has responded by consistently submitting films and supporting the series. Hopefully in year two there will be sponsors who can offer postproduction grants and/or donations to our filmmakers."

Alternative festival audiences first noticed Nicole Severine as a newly-broke heiress in Mark L. Feinsod's *A Sense of Entitlement.*

Calvin Robertson goe in for the kill in Be Coccio's Columbine inspired *Zero Da*

The living dead live it up on Bourbon Street in *Zombie! vs. Mardi Gras.*

Clark's audience has been, she says, "ranging from 50-100 people. I don't have concrete demographics but attendees work (or are trying to work) in film or television, whether they are composers, directors, make-up artists, writers, actors, et cetera."

Mark L. Feinsod has shown his short films at Clark's Freight Film Salon and other alternative venues and he has been highly satisfied with both the exposure and the feedback. "I think any chance to show your work to an audience is a valuable opportunity, whether it be to film professionals in California or to dairy farmers in Wisconsin," he says. "I find alternative film venues to be immensely valuable. I mean, my work has never screened in a major festival — not Berlin or Rotterdam or Sundance or anyplace like — and yet I've still managed to be reasonably successful for someone of my age at my state of the game. Venues like Freight Film Salon are fantastic because they're in New York and draw regular audiences comprised of industry professionals, other creative people, and film fans. I think that as the film industry continues to become more and more corporation-focused not only on the Hollywood level, but on the so-called independent level, that alternative exhibition venues are going to become more and more important in terms of being able to see 'cinema with a capital C' and films that demand a lot from a viewer."

Filmmaker John T. Ryan has also shown his features at unlikely non-theatrical venues and has no problems with the settings. "The places where my work has been shown vary from the Light+Screen Film Festival at the Siberia Bar in New York to a shop owner's work space out in East Hampton, Long Island," he says. "The best way to show your work is to be proud of it — excitement about your own project is more important than the location of the screening. I hate to think of the places where my work has been shown as 'alternative.' I had a screening in the East Village of New York at a place called '13' and all different types of people came: Whites, Blacks, Hispanics, Asians, straight, gay, drag queens, conservative people, hookers, you name it! To me, this is really who we are as people and for all of us to get together in one place is how life should be. This is not 'underground' or 'alternative' to me."

Even more intriguing than showing up in an unlikely but intriguing venue for a film festival is having the festival itself pick up its roots and travel from city to city. Berkeley-based filmmaker Antero Alli spear-headed the traveling festival notion when he put together the first Nomad VideoFilm Festival in 1992.

"The NVF started out in Seattle of 1992 as Nomad Video, organized by me and four friends (Camille Hildebrandt, Gavin Greene, Richard Bradshaw, and Troy Skeels) to screen experimental short films and videos at a different venue every other month," recalls Alli. "For a couple of years, we booked a different nightclub, sports bar, cafe, restaurant, and whatever hole in the wall or dive that had enough chairs and space for us to set up our giant video monitor and PA system. For awhile we created this illusion of numerous microcinemas popping up all over town until eventually we burnt out on the bi-monthly format. I was the only one who wanted to continue the festival and so, I changed the name to Nomad VideoFilm Festival and restructured it as an annual West Coast touring event which continued every year until the fall of 2002.

"In the early Seattle days, Nomad Video appeared at The Weathered Wall, The Dog House, Still Life Cafe, The Gravity Bar, and other venues that have since gone out of business. Between 1995-2002, the West Coast circuit was Port Townsend, Washington (Max Grover Studio, PT Community Center, The Oracle Arts Center), Seattle (911 Media Arts Center), Portland (Hollywood Theatre, Clinton St. Theater, NW Film Center), Mendocino, California (Helen Schoeni Theatre), Sacramento (MatrixArts Space), Petaluma, California (Cinnabar Theatre), San Francisco (Venue 9, CELLspace, ATA, Gallerie Luscombe), and Berkeley (Fine Arts Cinema)."

Alli marketed the Nomad events through word of mouth, web site announcements and in the "call for entries" section of film trade publications such as the Independent Film & Video Monthly and MovieMaker Magazine. "What made Nomad unique and why we attracted so many innovative mediamakers to us was the prize we offered," he add. "Winning entries received hand-written responses from audience members from each city we toured through, which meant that artists could be reading anywhere from 200-500 index cards praising and condemning their work in terms as honest as they were anonymous. I don't know of any other festival that does this. It was a lot of work compiling all those remarks but well worth it in the end."

Audience attendance and demographics were somewhat trickier to pinpoint, given the nature of the traveling festival. Alli estimated attendance for Nomad screenings ranging anywhere from a dozen to more than 200. "Because we toured numerous cities and venues, the demographics also shifted," he notes. "I can say that most of the people who showed up were actively seeking entertainment and art that was obviously subversive to mainstream values, partly because that's how we represented ourselves in our press kits and posters, and partly because I think that's a legitimate demographic."

So what kind of filmmakers submitted work to the Nomad festivals? "All types and mostly by amateurs," says Alli. "Amateurs in the absolute best and absolute worst sense of what that means and everything between. Out of the 150 submissions received each year, about 10% were selected for that year's tour. We occasionally had themes such as 'real & fake documentaries' and 'videopoems.' In terms of overall quality, we received the gamut of extremes from cutting edge to utter dredge. This wide cross section of work also gave us a sense of being a kind of antennae for what was going on out there every year, what people were pointing their cameras at and investing time, energy, and money to produce."

While Alli closed down Nomad to concentrate on his filmmaking and publishing work, other touring festivals have followed in his path and have gone further. Microcinema International's Independent Exposure and the Resfest Digital Film Festival, both launched in 1996, have taken the traveling festival concept beyond America into different countries around the world. Independent Exposure has focused exclusively on short films while Resfest showcases film plus music, art, design, and technology. Both have also launched into non-festival opportunities that capitalize on their far-flung screenings: Microcinema International offers DVDs of the films from its exhibitions while Resfest also offers DVDs and publishes *RES Magazine*, a bi-monthly chronicling the union of popular culture and digital technology.

A variation of this set-up is the Substream Film Festival, which presents a single festival running simultaneously in multiple cities. The third annual event for 2004 was booked for five cities: three in Florida (Fort Myers, Gainesville, and Orlando) plus Atlanta and Memphis. To date, no other festival has attempted this type of opening.

THE UNDERGROUND FILM FESTIVAL SCENE

For underground filmmakers seeking out venues to screen their work and for audiences who are looking for these films, the following list offers the finest of the current underground-friendly film festival circuit. The list does not include genre-specific festivals that are often open to presenting underground films, such as gay and lesbian festivals (which could fill a chapter unto themselves).

Festival playdates are frequently highly flexible, and the following listings include the average month or months when the events are held. It is not uncommon for smaller festivals to suddenly disappear or newer festivals to appear with equal speed, but as of this writing this is the most comprehensive underground film festival listing available.

Bare Bones International Film Festival, Muskogee, Oklahoma (http://www.barebonesfilmfestivals.org) — March/April. Accepting entries in all genres, as long as the films came in under one million dollars. The festival honors its finest with the "Bonehead Award," although the excess of categories (including for poster art, both in large and small formats) may dilute the effectiveness of the honors.

Black Point Film Festival, Lake Geneva, Wisconsin (www.blackpoint filmfestival.com) — April. Located at the crossroads from Chicago (90 minutes away) and Milwaukee (45 minutes driving), this five-day celebration focuses on independent film while running simultaneous live music and art gallery presentations.

B-Movie Film Festival, Syracuse, New York (www.b-movie.com) — Summer/Fall. The world of low-budget/high-entertainment filmmaking is honored in this festival, which features the Killer-B's award presentation and the annual announcement of inductions into the B-Movie Hall of Fame (as voted online by B-lovers). The festival's annual dates have floated between summer and fall and the event was twice canceled since it launched in 1998 (once in 2001 following the 9/11 attacks and again in 2003 due to financial considerations which were later solved).

Boston Underground Film Festival, Boston (www.bostonundergroun dfilmfestival.com) — September/October. The primary focus is on New England talent, ranging from features to shorts to documentaries.

Brooklyn Underground Film Festival, Brooklyn, New York (www.br ooklynunderground.org) — October. The focus here is primarily short films, organized by a group of New York film and media artists who see their mission as "an outlet for emerging and radical new voices from around the globe." (See interview with festival director Josh Koury).

Chicago Underground Film Festival, Chicago (www.cuff.org) — August. Founded in 1993, this festival has such boosters as John Waters and Roger Ebert and since expanded its operations to include to include a postproduction grant and year-round screenings and events.

Cucalorus Film Festival, Wilmington, North Carolina (www .cucalorus.org) — March. Founded in 1994 by a group of filmmakers calling themselves Twinkle Doon, the festival was originally conceived to celebrate local filmmakers but soon expanded to offer international productions and revive classic titles. Yet underground film is still the main thrust of its programming.

Dahlonega International Film Festival, Dahlonega, Georgia (www.diff.tv) — June. Located in the town which was home to the first American gold rush, this event is designed to showcase "the undiscov-ered artists whose vision demands to be seen and heard and the DIFF will strive to be at the forefront in exhibiting works from emerging artisans who have been ignored by the more conventional exhibiting venues."

DancesWithFilms, West Hollywood, California (www.danceswithfil ms.com) — June. This festival got off to a litigious start when Orion Pictures served a cease-and-desist letter regarding the event's name, which they saw as ripping off the Kevin Costner movie *Dances with Wolves*. Orion went out of business, but the festival has thrived thanks to brilliantly focused publicity and a convenient location that attracts industry scouts on the hunt for a new hit.

DC Underground Film Festival, Washington, DC (www.dcuff.org) — May. The festival seeks out low-budget filmmakers who "are not afraid to confront economic, political, and artistic issues that main-stream moviemakers ignore." The festival organizers have also begun the Underground Filmmakers Fund, a grant program that literally puts money where their mouths are.

DIY Film Festival, Los Angeles (www.diyconvention.com) — February. The festival is held in conjunction with the annual DIY Convention, which teaches filmmakers, musicians, authors, and entrepreneurs how to create, promote, protect, and distribute independent film, music, and books. During the course of the year the festival presents select entries submitted for consideration at venues in Los Angeles and other cities under the heading of the Club DIY series.

Downstream International Film Festival, Atlanta (www.downstreamfest .com) — Late Fall. Initially planned to celebrate Southeastern film talent, this festival is now accepting applications from across the country. In a curious decision, the festival acceptance ratio is demographically evenly split by gender: half of the entries are by male directors and half are by women directors.

Hi Mom! Film Festival, Chapel Hill, North Carolina (www.himomfilm festival.org) — March/April. Perhaps the only festival named in honor of a film (in this case, an early Martin Scorsese effort), the event was the child of University of North Carolina students who felt their region needed its own short film festival complete with "prizes and revelry." The festival has kept its eye on short and "shortish" films and has even taken to touring the country with the best of its annual selections.

Johns Hopkins Film Festival, Baltimore (www.jhu.edu/~jhufilm/fest) — March/April. Organized by the Johns Hopkins Film Society, who facetiously claim that "eight months of work lead up to the ultimate anticlimax that is the four days of JHFF." This is among the rare film festivals associated with a university (and one without a filmmaking curriculum, to boot!).

Microcinefest, Baltimore (www.microcinefest.org) — November. Unlike its academic-inspired rivals across town at Johns Hopkins, this rowdy underground fest bills itself as "the film festival equivalent of a DIY (Do It Yourself) punk show, except we're very concerned with things like presentation, organization and doing things for the right reasons (that way our festival can still be enjoyed by people who would normally have a lousy time at a DIY punk show)."

New York International Independent Film & Video Festival, New York City (www.nyfilmvideo.com) — April. Billing itself somewhat grandly as

Thank you for supporting the 2nd annual Brooklyn Underground Film Festival this past October 8-14. It was an amazing week of rare films, art, and great music. A full festival update will come shortly.

FESTIVAL PREPARATION PHOTOS - frenzy of pre-fest preparations, late nights, lots of beer.

MAP and DIRECTIONS
All screenings, unless otherwise indicated, are held at BUFF's home, and the shared mainspace for The Nest arts collective:
85 Front St. @ Washington St
DUMBO, Brooklyn
info@brooklynunderground.org

STILLS 0 1 0 2 0

SCHEDULE   PRESS   EVENTS   SPONSORS   MERCHANDISE   LINKS   WEEKLY CINEMA   ABOUT   JOIN

Downstream International Film Festival

Screening of the
Best of Downstream 2003
Date & Venue: TBA

Next Entry Deadline: June 30, 2005

Click **Here** To Receive Festival Announcements via Email

slamdunk

Festivals
Films
Events

Transmitting the Art of Independent Film and Video

Films
Current Projects
Who We Are
Contact

Slamdunk Films LLC

Slamdunk Films LLC is a partnership created to distribute and produce feature length motion pictures. The company acquires finished films for worldwide distribution and completed screenplays for production and distribution.

The distribution company specializes in gaining the widest possible exposure through traditional and non-traditional distribution for completed films world wide. Channels exploited for distribution by Slamdunk Films LLC include domestic theatrical, pay television, broadcast television, home video, DVD, and Video-On-Demand. Slamdunk acquires up to seven films per calendar year.

Slamdunk Films LLC also serves as producer's representative for films throughout the acquisition process. Films represented by Slamdunk are not potential acquisition titles of Slamdunk Films LLC. The company may get involved as producer's representative at any stage of pre-production, production or exhibition.

The production arm of Slamdunk Films LLC specializes in packaging, finance and production of completed screenplays for film and television. The company also acquires and brokers, intellectual property. Slamdunk combines equity, incentive based structures, international co-financing, and domestic and international distribution agreements, to finance independent production and co-productions.

Slamdunk Films LLC is managed by Justin W. Henry and John Peterson in association with Slamdunk Europe managed by Christoph Servell and Michel Culang. The company's legal representation is shared by Mendelsohn Law Office, Inc. and Pierce / Gorman.

"the largest film festival in the world" and "one of the leading film events of the festival season." Many people will beg to differ, though the festival does earn points for enabling free admission to its screenings.

New York Underground Film Festival, New York City (www.nyuff.com) — March. Launched in 1992 and programmed by film critic Ed Halter, the festival has seen a few of its recent titles jump into theatrical release (including the documentaries *Standing by Yourself* and *Horns and Halos*). Although well-regarded on the festival circuit, the event itself has not received satisfactory review coverage by the New York media in recent years and, admittedly, its programming as of late has seen more than a few productions from the wrong side of amateurish.

No Dance Film Festival, Park City, Utah (www.nodance.com) — January. Billed as the world's first DVD-projected film festival, No Dance runs parallel to Sundance. While the films in competition have, for the most part, not captured much attention, the festival itself has attracted A-list talent to its panel discussion, including actor/director Forest Whittaker, director Mike Figgis, and *Film Threat* editor Chris Gore.

Ohio Independent Film Festival, Cleveland (www.ohiofilms.com) — November. Midwest regionalism rules here with a festival that credits itself for being the only independent film and video festival primarily dedicated to Ohio filmmakers and the "only awards ceremony in Northeast Ohio dedicated to independent filmmakers, (the) Annual Off-Hollywood Oscarz."

San Antonio Underground Film Festival, San Antonio, Texas (www.safilm.com) — June. Begun in 1993, this festival openly claims its titles are "best unified by the do-it-yourself punk ethic." Entries are accepted from across the country, although an uncommonly high number of Texas films are included in the schedule.

Slamdance International Film Festival, Park City, Utah (www.slamdance .com) — January. The first of the Sundance spinoffs, this festival attracts a high caliber of competition from around the world yet maintains its original focus on bringing the best of outsider cinema to the forefront.

Slamdunk Film Festival, Park City, Utah (www.slamdunk.cc) - January. Founded in 1998 and running parallel to Sundance, Slamdunk has established itself as a source for high-quality low-budget filmmaking.

Several of its films have found their way into mainstream release, including Ben Coccio's *Zero Day* (released by Avatar Films), John Henry Davis' *Ordinary Sinner* (released by Jour de Fete), and Nick Broomfield's *Kurt & Courtney* (distributed by Roxie Releasing). Slamdunk has also taken its prize-winning films on tour, including a stop at Cannes.

Tromadance, Park City, Utah (www.tromadance.com) — January. Another festival running parallel to Sundance, but the wacky Troma team have made this one different on several levels: no entry fees for films seeking a screen, no entry fees for audiences coming to the screenings, and "no VIP reservations or preferential treatment regarding films, panels, or parties of any kind given."

Worldfest-Houston International Film Festival, Houston (www .worldfest.org) — March/April. America's third oldest film festival (after San Francisco and New York), this Texas event prides itself as "Fiercely Independent!" and features worthwhile seminars including the Eastman Kodak Seminar series on cinematography and an indie film distribution conducted by Stuart Strutin of Panorama Distribution, which has picked up several titles for release at this festival including the award-winning drama *The Bread, My Sweet*.

INTERVIEW

JOSH KOURY: FROM FESTIVAL STAR TO FESTIVAL STARTER

The year 2001 was a tumultuous one for Josh Koury. The young filmmaker's feature-length documentary *Standing by Yourself* debuted to rapturous critical and audience reaction at the Slamdance and New York Underground Film Festivals and gained a theatrical playdate in New York, where it earned more praise from reviewers. The film played at additional festivals through the year, but while *Standing by Yourself* was in motion Koury was anything but inactive. He became a driving force in the November 2001 launch of the Brooklyn Underground Film Festival, a celebration of cinematic and new media art.

Needless to say, very few people start the year as a star of the festival circuit and close it by creating their own event. Koury reflected on the dramatic journey which his career took thanks to the film festival world.

Q. When you were readying *Standing by Yourself* for the festival circuit, how did you go about determining which festivals to pursue and which to avoid?

JOSH KOURY: It's important to select the right festivals or you're really just wasting money. U.S. fests are usually expensive and it becomes impossible to submit to everything. I generally concentrated on festivals that I felt would be interested in a film like mine — often those were ones that also showed work I admired. Mostly, I submitted to anything alluding to underground cinema and those that were receptive to non-traditional docs. Video festivals were also on the top of the list.

I also pursued some good international fests — a lot of times, they're free, and it's a good opportunity to get involved with other interesting international filmmakers. It's good to gain a bit of international recognition, while still maintaining the "U.S. premiere" status that many film festivals look for.

When I considered a festival, I also looked at the type of films screened in previous years. Film festival programs tend to look somewhat consistent year after year. *Standing by Yourself* really didn't play at that many festivals, it just was played at the right ones.

Q. How many festivals did you apply for, and how many accepted your film? And which ones declined to show your film?

KOURY: I seem to have lost total count. Shadowfestival in the Netherlands (one of the finest doc festivals I've ever been to) was the world premiere of the film. Next came Vancouver Underground, followed by the U.S. Premiere at Slamdance. Some other notable fests are Cinematexas, NYUFF, Chicago Underground, and a handful of others. I think Seattle Underground was the first to reject the film. I may have been rejected by more than I've been to, I sort of lose track.

Filmmakers shouldn't take it too hard if their film is rejected. It may have been due to the type of program the festival puts together or who was on the committee at that particular time — this is why I pre-screen everything that comes into the Brooklyn Underground Film Festival (BUFF). Some festivals are looking for a specific type of film. For instance, I submitted two films to the Brooklyn International FF in 2001 and 2002.

Both years they rejected my work. Looking at their program now, I can understand that it was an inappropriate fit for their festival.

It's also important to not let a rejection letter turn you away from that type of festival. Every underground film festival is different, and showcases different types of work. I would have never made it past Seattle if I let a rejection letter get to me. Also avoid only submitting to only one type of festival. A much more diverse audience will see your film if you screen at a variety of venues.

Q. What criteria do you recommend to filmmakers who are looking to bring their films on the festival circuit?

KOURY: It's important to understand the film you've made. Understand how people will take it, and what their reactions may be. Show it to as many test audiences as you can during the editing process. I'm a firm believer in a good critique, especially when dealing with questionable material. I was aware that my film could be offensive to some viewers, I was also aware that it could seem a bit scattered or chaotic in the beginning. It's important to entice a viewer. Keep them interested in the film as it unfolds so they will keep watching. During a normal screening, it's not as much of an issue, but I've met many programmers with very little patience. This can be done by accenting the elements within your film that may spark someone's interests. For instance, in *Standing By Yourself* the main themes I accented were adolescence, rebellion (punk), and the film's setting (upstate New York). It would be more appropriate to talk about family life and isolation, but that just doesn't sound as interesting on paper. Catch the programmer's attention, and if the film is good, it will do the rest.

Festival screening committees go through hundreds of films. Keep your press kits sharp and concise. Programmers won't read through twenty pages of a press kit. Keep it simple; understand what your film is, and who you're submitting it to.

Q. How did you come away from the festival circuit experience? Were you able to make the contacts you wanted?

KOURY: I met many people that made for an incredible experience. Some festivals are better than others. Shadow Festival introduced me to a new world of international filmmakers, Slamdance had a really strong sense of community — something I took for granted until visiting some other festivals. Cinematexas I couldn't attend, but I still met some brilliant and supportive people from the festival, many of whom I'm still in contact with today. These are the most important experiences for me, the festivals that not only accept and showcase your work, but also inspire you to create more, connect with filmmakers, and come back again.

Q. What was the decision behind bringing a new underground film festival to Brooklyn?

KOURY: It just felt like something was missing from the New York festival scene. I had just gotten back from traveling all over the world with my film, seeing festival after festival. After experiencing a few in New York, I was a little disappointed. I guess I expected to meet more people and have a more rewarding experience from festivals in New York. The fests were just not as inviting and inspiring as I had hoped they would be. It was really this that made us feel justified by bringing a new festival to the city.

We wanted to develop a festival that represented other aspects of underground art, urban and street art, graphic design, that kind of edge that is used in underground cinema. It was very important for us to not just rent a theater for the screenings. This is a big part of the BUFF, the atmosphere and environment that is created around the festival. The films showcased are incredible, but if nothing is there to maintain your interest after the screening, then people will just leave. This was the idea behind our lounge area, and the murals and art showcased around the space — we converted a warehouse into an underground film fest and arts gallery, and the people who came to the festival stayed at the festival. The filmmakers came for their programs, but then came back to see the other work as well.

This is a rarity for many film festivals that I've been to. This sense of community, which I mentioned with some of the other fests that acted as inspiration for us, is what BUFF is really pushing to create. We want the public to feel like if they miss the festival, they're really missing something besides films. The solution isn't just seeing that film at its next festival stop. People should want to come to a festival to experience something different.

And of course Brooklyn is also home to so many cinematic (and otherwise) artists. It's good to know that we now have a film festival showcasing truly experimental and underground work.

Q. Were you concerned that the surplus number of New York festivals (including the New York Underground Film Festival) would detract from the interest in BUFF?

KOURY: When we started BUFF, it seemed like everyone was telling us there were already too many festivals in New York. Everywhere we turned someone was questioning our judgment about opening this new venue for filmmakers. Our mission was, and still is, to provide an alternate venue for underground and experimental artists from all over the globe. We're not a pretentious or starstruck film festival. Most of the staff are filmmakers, or artists struggling to make our own work as well as put on the festival. We're doing this because we believe underground cinema needs this new venue. It's very important for us to have a truly original program.

One of my biggest complaints coming off of the film festival circuit is how much exposure some of the poorest films can receive, while some of the most creative and original ones often get pushed to the side, or often not screened at all. The idea that once a film gets played at a major film festival, it's instantly passed on from one fest to another is very discouraging. I feel it should be the festival's priority to find and explore other avenues of cinema. Digging up what may have been lost or rejected by others.

Programming a film festival shouldn't be as easy as bringing a notepad to Sundance. The same goes for Underground film festivals. We really do try to create an alternative to the major underground fests out there. In that sense, there's plenty of room for the BUFF. There's always room for quality alternative film festivals. It's always been our intention to create an outstanding program consisting of mostly unseen cinema. There are a lot of film festivals, but not enough original fests to go around.

Q. How much time, money and manpower went into creating the first BUFF? Can you provide a rough schedule of how the festival progressed from planning to opening night?

KOURY: The first BUFF was developed in just under six months. I think it was late April when we decided to start BUFF. Our last call for submissions happened just three-and-a-half months later in mid July. In that time we collected over 600 submissions from all over the world. What started as a small idea slowly grew into something much larger in scale. The permanent staff was developed over the first four months of the fest. People were excited to be a part of something like this. Filmmakers were excited to have another venue for their work. It was really a crash course in film festival production for us. Every month that went by it seemed we had stepped a little deeper into things, and we had to catch up with ourselves or things wouldn't work out.

We also had a lot of guidance from other film festivals. Many we knew from traveling with our work, some we just called at random or met somewhere along the way.

The program was assembled by mid August. The design, art and lay-out for the festival were completed sometime around this date as well. We were really fortunate to be given the 4,200 square foot warehouse in DUMBO, one of the most up-and-coming areas of Brooklyn. But a major caveat was that we were given only six days to assemble the festival, and six days to tear it down. The space itself was beautiful — it was a corner storefront lined with windows, which is perfect for a lounge, but a pain because we had to lightproof the screening area. So in six days, we had constructed 30-foot walls around massive cement columns to create the screening room, installed the art, and created an unusual cinema salon.

It's one of the many reasons that BUFF differs from so many others in New York. We wanted to create a film festival with the heart of an underground arts gallery. Street art, graffiti, design, paintings, and mixed media were all used to accompany the outstanding film program. Overall, I think it was a really different and positive experience for filmmakers.

BUFF is a totally volunteer run, not-for-profit organization. I can't tell you how much time was spent because it was very scattered throughout the first six months. At times it was a full-time job for some of us. It still tends to be. We've definitely come a long way since its birth just over a year ago. The thing that makes BUFF unique is that all of our staff are the same people building the enormous cinema constructions, drilling in chairs, wheat-pasting posters in the street. When filmmakers come and see this, it really brings people to a different level. This festival is happening because of everyone involved. It's a showcase, but it's also a community that's being designed. By the end everyone knew each other, and hopefully left with a slightly new outlook on underground cinema and the festival circuit.

Q. How did you market your festival? And what kind of filmmakers responded to your call for entries?

KOURY: A great variety of filmmakers submit each year. It's amazing how small the world of film fests can actually be. I'm always recognizing previous submitters at other festivals and screenings. I even saw one of our rejected films on the new release rack at Blockbuster. Seeing all of these films and seeing which fest is programming them is an important way to gauge what work a film festival is interested in and what that festival is all about.

It's very important to market in the right places. Our mission has very much to do with new filmmakers and rarely seen cinema. The web is the most important tool for cheap marketing. We spend a ridiculous amount of time posting our call for entries, contacting filmmakers, spreading the general word of the fest. This is how we manage to get so many films each year, 600-800 films is actually an incredible number for such a new festival. The variety of films we receive is astounding. Each year we get work from all over the world, our festival usually consists film from 10-15 countries.

Word of mouth is very important for us at this point. Since most of our filmmakers came out of our festival having had a great experience, it's more than likely that they will tell their own filmmaking peers to get involved, or submit the following year. We are still in contact with many of our 2002 filmmakers and we're always seeing them at our various BUFF events. Some have even joined our part-time staff. These are important relations and really help out in the long run.

Q. What mistakes (if any) were made in the first year of the festival?

KOURY: I've been told by some filmmakers that we are one of the most organized film festivals they've ever been to. I really don't see it. Working from within the festival is a much different experience. Many of us are artists and filmmakers with little business experience. We do have to remember that aside from being a film festival and art movement, it also needs to be treated as a business--as awful as that sounds. It seems that we're always scraping by. Luckily, coming from poor artist backgrounds, most of us can be very resourceful when given the chance.

Things are changing, though. We're currently in the process of attaining our official 501(c)3 non-profit status, as well as assembling a board of directors. The staff has also become much more diverse this past year. We are taking on many young professionals familiar with art-based organizations such as ourselves. It's all a long process, but we're getting better at it.

Q. What do you see as your goals for the BUFF in the years to come?

KOURY: BUFF's growing at a somewhat scary rate. A little over a year ago it began as an idea, a small movement made to expose unseen underground cinema from the roots of the city. Today we're a permanent venue in one of the most up-and-coming sections of Brooklyn. We're opening a permanent cinema in the area and the festival itself is growing and being recognized all over the world. We've showcased over 80 films from 15 countries, most of them premieres. A strong community is being built and developed, a few years down the line and we can only imagine where we will be.

Plans have started for a community-based traveling film festival. The idea is to bring appropriate BUFF cinema to areas of Brooklyn and New York that may not have to chance to come to an underground festival like ours — like high schools, community colleges, anywhere that we can showcase. We're trying to change the way people perceive independent cinema. This type of filmmaking shouldn't be an experience exclusive to just those familiar with art-houses and alternative film venues.

Another community-based project BUFF is working on is a tech hub for Brooklyn-based artists. Being artists, we understand how difficult and restrictive it can be to not have certain filmmaking equipment. BUFF is hoping to create facilities in the near future for underground filmmakers, photographers, and artists who want to create new work but lack certain essential materials.

8: When Underground Films Surface

Film distributor Peter M. Hargrove has a succinct way of classifying movies: "I put films into four categories: award-winning, good, sellable and burn-the-negative. Most, alas, fall in the last category."

Hargrove's view may seem harsh, but he recognizes the film business is, after all, a business. The economics of film distribution has changed dramatically in recent years, and this has not worked to the advantage of underground films that try to break into the mainstream. At a time when theaters are flooded with expensive, CGI-packed features backed by zillion-dollar marketing budgets, the challenge for the low-to-no budget underground films to secure their place before the public has become more and more of a challenge.

GETTING INKED

During the course of the year, it is not uncommon to see the films of the underground cinema pop up into mainstream exhibition. Usually these presentations are limited in scope (limited to engagements in a handful of cities, usually one at a time). Their commercial runs are generally not well promoted, do not last very long, and barely register a blip on the proverbial radar.

On some occasions, their emergence even brings hostile results from critics unwilling to cut these films any slack.

Case in point: In 2002, a no-budget comedy about a struggling actress with a disastrous love life called *Being Claudine* appeared. This feature film was originally created as a student thesis project by I-fan Quirk and went on to play at several second-tier film festivals. But unlike many underground comedies, *Being Claudine* opened in a theatrical engagement at The Screening Room, a now-defunct New York venue that was primarily a second-run house but which occasionally gave a screen to first-run offerings.

On the surface, it would seem like the set up for a perfect cinematic Cinderella story: a tiny film made for next-to-nothing manages to snag a theatrical engagement in the nation's top media market, with a filmmaker poised for the proverbial bigger-and-better. Everything seemed to be in place, but there was one problem: The critics hated the film.

Dave Kehr of the *New York Times* was the kindest, dubbing *Being Claudine* a "good-natured but amateurish film." Noel Murray, writing for *The Onion*, called the movie's student film roots to task: "When a novice graduates from showcase screenings and regional festivals to theatrical bookings, it's not unreasonable to expect an original cinematic talent, or at least gifted craftsmanship. Quirk provides nothing to get excited about." Megan Lehmann of the *New York Post* echoed Murray's sentiments, stating that "each frame shrieks 'student film'."

But perhaps the deepest cut to *Being Claudine* came from Michael Atkinson, the *Village Voice* film critic: "Savaging wooden, graceless, derivative student films is, admitted, like punting a three-legged puppy, but that's what Quirk and his breed get for so stupidly undervaluing filmgoers' time. I hope Mr. and Mrs. Quirk are proud, at least."

Mr. and Mrs. Quirk were unavailable for comment on the level of support they maintain for their filmmaker son, but Michael Atkinson was in regards to his review. As one of the *Village Voice's* most respected critics, Atkinson's command of the language is vigorous and he is not afraid to voice his opinions on unsuccessful films (or, for that matter, offer intelligent and gush-free praise for successful projects). In the case of this review, he was not apologetic for his sharp take on *Being Claudine*.

"It may seem harsh, but I rarely if ever give any notice to how a film was made, how experienced the filmmaker is, how much it costs, et cetera," he says. "When it is a repeat offender — an Ed Burns, say — then it's pertinent. But first-timers don't get slack just because they're first-timers. There have been too many good-to-great indie debuts, so there's no grading curve. Certainly Quirk shouldn't get points for going to an expensive film school and spending a bundle of cash on a movie he was too inept to pull off. Ideally, we would know little or nothing about a film's production before we see it or evaluate it. I often wish I didn't even know the filmmaker's gender. Of course, usually we end up knowing far too much. So was it justified? Sure. Or not, depending on what you think of the film. Amateurishness can sometimes seem endearing to some people (Burns's debut, say), but I'm not one of them, normally."

Burdened by horrible reviews, *Being Claudine* was a box-office loser and was removed from the theater after a week's anemic run. The film had no further commercial engagements and, as of this writing, it has not been seen on home video or DVD.

But was this a defeat for *Being Claudine*? From a commercial standpoint, most certainly. But in terms of being seen and appreciated, the fact that *Being Claudine* was able to get a theatrical engagement was an achievement that the majority of underground films don't enjoy. A pyrrhic victory, perhaps, but a victory nonetheless.

Thomas Edward Seymour, whose 2001 comedy *Everything Moves Alone* enjoyed a brief New York commercial run of its own, was also on the receiving end of several harsh reviews from the demanding New York critics. "Stephen King once said that in the end it doesn't matter what the critics say because in 20 years either people will be reading your work or they won't," he comments. "I think that applies to film, too. In Elvis Mitchell's review in the *New York Times* I actually remember him getting angry at the main character because he was written with naive qualities. Never did he realize that the point of the entire story was about inexperience. That made me laugh — months after the initial sting, that is."

Of course, the critics do not dwell in an endless state of sour grimacing when viewing underground cinema. Even the battered *Being Claudine* received a few glowing reviews in its festival travels.

Doug Miles, whose zany *Don't Ask Don't Tell* (a rehash of a 1950s B-level sci-fi flick with a gay-friendly new soundtrack) was reviewed on both the festival circuit and its New York theatrical engagement, is pragmatic regarding the critics and how to deal with their commentary. "The commercial reviews were probably about half and half," he says. "We had some people who really loved it, like the *Boston Globe*, and some who thought we should never be allowed near a camera again, like the *Village Voice*. I think I've heard that you're not allowed to believe the good reviews unless you also believe the bad ones. Well, the hell with that!!! So we paid attention and used the blurbs that worked and pretended the bad ones never happened."

And sometimes, the critics are not the ones to blame if they don't voice their appreciation of a film. Robert Firsching, former editor of the *Amazing World of Cult Movies*, had been a prime Internet media review source for underground movies during the late 1990s and early part of this decade. But many filmmakers didn't quite get the thrust of Firsching's focus.

"My web site dealt primarily with horror and exploitation films," says Firsching. "And I would get loads of art films about Greek shepherds or shoot-'em-up sci-fi/action films in the mail. While I might have enjoying watching them for free, I didn't put them on the web site, so the filmmakers just wasted their postage and the cost of a DVD, not to mention the associated glossy photos and press kits."

Greg Hatanaka, president of the now-defunct distribution company Phaedra Cinema, is among those willing to cut the critics slack — albeit to a point. "By and large, the critical press have their own select brand of taste," he concedes. "To be a critic is to be one of the most overworked people in the world. You screen six-to-ten films a week in very desolate screening rooms. You're always in the dark, pressured by editorial deadlines to deliver reviews. You lose the fun of moviegoing, I would think. Given these circumstances, it's very hard to be objective when you're under these sort of pressures and I think the smaller films fall through the cracks when it comes to getting press. Ironically, it's these films that need the press the most given they've no real advertising budget to speak of, no star actors, et cetera. I would think, though, that the studios do impose some kind of pressure on critics to give their

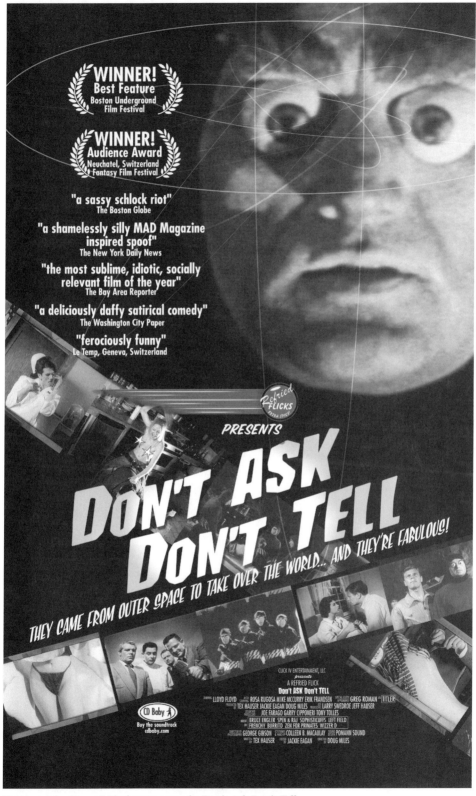

Poster art for Doug Miles' zany comedy *Don't Ask Don't Tell*.

films major coverage. Studios such as Miramax, and the majors (i.e. Sony, Paramount, etc.) will routinely fly in critics to luxurious press junkets and parties for their latest releases. It's hard to be objective when all that is lavished on you."

But not everyone has a dark cloud in their sky. When Ben Coccio's *Zero Day* was presented for critical approval, the feedback stunned its creator with its positive force.

"I was amazed to see my movie reviewed in large circulation papers and forums — the *New York Times* calling me 'Mr. Coccio' — it was very surreal and bizarre," he says. "And no matter what critics said, it was just a fascinating experience. I was on a Metro-North train and I watched some business dude read the *Times* review of *Zero Day*, and then leave the paper on the seat. The still from the film was facing upwards, and there it was in black and white — I had made a movie and people could go see it at a theater. I went to film school — an art school (Rhode Island School of Design) with a film program — and we would have intense critiques where other students would watch your rough cuts and give you the benefit of their college-student's worth life-experience. It was actually really useful, and after that I started to rely on honest critiques of my work at the editing stage from people I respected or trusted. Critics writing reviews of movies is not the same thing, and I can't learn too much from it other than how to make that particular critic happy or unhappy."

PRESENTED BY...

Relatively few major distributors are willing to take a chance on giving full theatrical release to underground movies. One that did was the late, great Phaedra Cinema. During its relatively brief time (1996 through 2001), Phaedra offered an eccentric line-up of films that included high-brow art house class such as the French drama *La Separation* starring Isabelle Huppert and the Japanese revenge thriller *Gonin* starring Takeshi Kitano as well as no-budget shenanigans such as *The Underground Comedy Movie* and *Men Cry Bullets*. Phaedra helped lower one significant bar in cinema: its final release, Young Man Kang's romantic comedy *Cupid's Mistake*, had a budget of $980, which was confirmed by the Guinness Book of World Records as being the lowest-budgeted film ever to have a theatrical release.

"I'm a rabid fan of anything film, which means that I love all types of films running the gamut from typical arthouse fare to the more experimental and cultish," says Greg Hatanaka, Phaedra's founder and president. "I think that the films I distributed at Phaedra were a reflection of this taste. I think that a 'Phaedra' film could not be immediately identifiable or categorized because you (the audience) never knew what to expect be it, the intense French drama *La Separation* or the very commercial comedy *Just A Little Harmless Sex*, the offensive *Underground Comedy Movie* or the classy but shockingly revolting Japanese film *Wife To Be Sacrificed*. During Phaedra's peak, roughly 1999/2000, it was still a very tiny operation and we were able to take chances on theatrically releasing these challenging and financial risky titles, without having to suffer the wrath or backlash from a more corporate environment. It was a real sense of freedom to be able to acquire the films, market and sell them myself, put the advertising charges on my credit cards, count the heads in the theaters and collect the box office receipts (or lack thereof). Of course, it was also disheartening to live through the failures, of which there were many."

So why did Phaedra Cinema go boldly where other distributors feared to tread? "Well, for one thing, these films were hardly commercial in any sense and if you refer to their theatrical reviews you will see that none had any sort of critical support either," states Hatanaka. "But for every film that I distributed through Phaedra, there was something of each that intrigued me whether it be the subtle Cassavetes-like quality of *Cupid's Mistake*, the intensity of Zack Winstine's *States of Control*, the glossiness of *Ratchet*, the over-the-top excitement of *Gonin*, the complete incomprehensibility of *Soft Toilet Seats*, the Frankenheimer feel of *The Taxman* or the simple romance told in *Love Etc.* From the start, I had modeled Phaedra Cinema after World Northal Films, an independent distributor from the 1970s known for distributing martial arts classics from the Shaw Bros. but who also made a name for releasing such art house hits as Peter Weir's *The Last Wave*, and Nicolas Roeg's *Bad Timing*.

"But getting back to the question: I think that the other distributors simply weren't interested in the challenging films we released. They had to be financially responsible to their corporate parents and simply could not take these sort of risks. Remember, this was all before the DVD boom, the cable market was relatively static but the theatrical market was, as it still is, non-existent for marginal fare."

Hatanaka enjoyed more commercial success with Phaedra's global titles than its underground titles, which should not come as much of a surprise. "I think it's easier to release a foreign-language film from an unknown director versus an American independent film from an unknown director," he says. "Foreign films have always had an audience ever since the 1950s when the U.S. started importing Kurosawa, Bergman, and Fellini films into art houses across the country. Whereas Cassavetes was really the only major independent filmmaker throughout the '60s and then you had people like John Sayles and Joan Micklin Silver in the '70s. But the 'American Indie' boom didn't really occur until the '80s with Spike Lee and Steven Soderbergh changing the face of indie cinema as we know it.

"I also think that your average art-house-goer is typically in their 40s-60s and someone who probably started going to foreign films in their college days twenty, thirty years ago, whereas the audience for American indie films tends to be in the 24-34 age range. It's a tough crowd to get into a theater unless you hit them over the head constantly with rave critical reviews and a large advertising campaign."

Ultimately, Hatanaka notes the financial burden facing distributors today has scared more than a few of them from even considering the release of underground films, let alone acquiring and distributing them. "Well, the deck has always been stacked against the smaller companies because there's never enough capitalization, it's always a hand to mouth existence, and so anything you do as the owner of these companies, you've got to be doing for the true passion of it. It's getting harder and harder to find a niche. Gay films have crossed over into mainstream cinema and now television and the major studios and networks are jumping in, taking over the market. The Hollywood studios are now buying the rights to Asian films and remaking them. It seems that everyone now wants to or is making a Latino or urban-themed film. Simply put, the theatrical marketplace is too crowded. Ticket prices are ridiculously high, the audiences have become very demanding and selective and there are just too many films to choose from. Add to that the recent development of films having their theatrical release and then debuting on DVD and video a mere three months later means that if you have a film that is an 'unknown quantity' to an audience, they're probably going to wait the few months and then rent the DVD. I think that DVD has created more of an audience for these films and that filmmakers shouldn't be disappointed if their film is not released theatrically.

"Launching a film theatrically easily costs around $100,000 and if the film fails, you will find your video and television profits eaten away by this loss. I know it can be a hard reality to accept given that you, the filmmaker, shot the film to be seen on some theatrical screen somewhere but a debut on DVD or television can give you exposure to a much larger audience than a small arthouse theatrical release."

With Phaedra Cinema gone (and with Hatanaka currently working at Pathfinder Pictures, which focuses primarily on the straight-to-video market), few distributors have stepped into their shoes. Artistic License is among the brave distributors that is willing to release edgy and offbeat underground-worthy titles, such as the lesbian crime comedy *By Hook or By Crook*, the raucous documentary on the backwoods Florida music scene *Mule Skinner Blues* and the campy cult-ready musical *The American Astronaut*. But due to the challenges in presenting these titles, the company prefers to have a stronger sense of participation from the filmmakers in the distribution process.

"When working with Artistic License, filmmakers often take an active role in the publicity and promotion of the film," says Sande Zeig, president of Artistic License. "I recommend that filmmakers add a contingency to their production budget for distribution in case the film is not picked up by a company that offers a minimum guarantee and purchases all rights (or if the filmmakers prefer to have a first hand involvement in the distribution of their film.) If this is the case, filmmakers come to companies like Artistic License Films. Artistic distributes the majority of our films on a 'service deal' basis. In our case this means we handle the theatrical distribution of the film exclusively and the P&A (print and advertising) is paid by the filmmaker or by outside investors. The filmmaker retains all the other rights, which include non-theatrical, video/DVD, Internet, and television."

Zeig is pragmatic about the market and the commercial chances for smaller films surfacing from the underground. "Releasing independent films has never been easy," she says. "I don't find it more difficult now than ten years ago. Since independent films never have the amount of P&A that studio films have, distributors usually work harder doing what used to be called 'grass roots outreach' (now called promotion). The target audience is located and an enormous effort is put into making them aware of the film and getting them into the theater the first weekend. The Internet has made this process much easier and the results are much more immediate."

The Syracuse, NY-based Sub Rosa Studios tried its hand at theatrical release, but found no solid market and focused instead on DVD and home video titles. The company enjoyed uncommon success in bringing its underground titles (primarily horror, sci-fi, urban action, and thrillers) to major channels which rarely offer underground titles — retailers and wholesalers including Ingram, Baker & Taylor, Pro-Active, Tapeworm, VPD, Norwalk, DVD Empire, Best Buy, and Tower. In the summer of 2003, Sub Rosa expanded its operations by creating the Global Independent Media Force, a united coalition designed to assist smaller companies enhance the sales of their titles in the home entertainment market. Immediately after creating Global Independent Media Force, the coalition was joined by smaller labels including Film Threat DVD, Vista Street Entertainment, Key East Entertainment, Global Communications, RGB World, and Cullen Studios.

"These companies bring something unique to our growing list of product," says Ron Bonk, founder and president of Sub Rosa Studios and the driving force behind the coalition. "They offer a great mix of genres, showing the true versatility and commercial viability of today's independent DVD releases. Whether consumers are seeking out action, art, or amusement, they can find it among the DVDs being released by our coalition members. And the distributors in the coalition can find a stronger retail presence through the united effort that the Global Independent Media Force offers."

Under the new Sub Rosa Studios' Global Independent Media Force, independent producers and distributors who've had difficulties dealing directly with the major home entertainment retail channels or the middlemen sources that serve them can now take advantage of an entry point maintained by a major recognized entity in this sector.

"Sub Rosa Studios has been distributing movies for over a decade and we've made great connections with many of the major buyers out there," explains Bonk. "The problem is, many major companies don't want to keep track of a ton of accounts, and thus they make smaller independent producers and distributors go through a third party source to do business with them. At that point, the producers and distributors are at the mercy of those third party sources, which often require constant pressure to push the titles and sometimes even abruptly go out of business or change their title offerings. This leaves many producers and distributors suddenly cut off from the major buyers and forced to scramble to find a new pipeline to get their product out."

In addition, the coalition will provide expert assistance in all aspects of marketing, packaging, publicity, duplication, and design. Financial involvement in the coalition's process is determined by the depth and scope of assistance that is required, thus offering a fair and flexible range to work within the budgets of the producers and distributors joining the coalition.

Another company that has enjoyed theatrical success has been Avatar Films, a New York–based boutique distributor which made a name for itself by presenting foreign films such as Cesc Gay's *Nico and Dani*, Mohsen Makhmalbaf's *Kandahar*, Benoit Jacquot's film version of the opera *Tosca*, and Elia Suleiman's Cannes-honored *Divine Intervention*. Yet Avatar Films actually began its operations in 2000 with an underground film: Jason Rosette's *Bookwars*, a documentary on the quirky subculture of New York City second-hand book sellers who peddle their wares from sidewalks on fold-up tables.

Rosette, an actor and sometime book seller who made his feature film directing debut with *Bookwars*, first came in contact with the late Robin Lim, Avatar Films' founder, when production was screened as a work-in-progress at the Independent Feature Film Market in New York in 1999. "I believe that Michel Negroponte, co-producer of *Bookwars*, had received a call from Robin a day or two after the screening and he had expressed an interest in distributing the film," recalls Rosette.

Since Avatar was a start-up company, Rosette was hesitant about selling both domestic and international rights to the film. He opted to give Avatar foreign rights only to gauge their performance capacity and sought to self-distribute the film in the U.S.

"I continued to attempt to book the movie myself, to give it at least a modest run at an art-house in New York," Rosette continues. "This was my major goal, since reviewers are obligated somewhat to review a film once it has a run in a major market. First, I took it to Anthology Film Archives, where John Mhiripiri (the programmer there) sniffed at it and told me 'it was better that I thought it would be.' But still, he hemmed and hawed about screening it. Shortly afterwards, though, I succeeded in booking it at Cinema Village via the generosity of Ed Arentz (the programmer for the theater), and we had our run there."

The Cinema Village run was unique in that *Bookwars* was presented commercially as a digital projection, a first for New York. Previous shot-on-video films that played commercially in New York had to be transferred to film before securing a theatrical engagement.

"However, at this time I was thoroughly exhausted," adds Rosette. "I mean, I'd made the film, posted the film, and now I was distributing the film and I had somewhat of a working relationship already with Avatar. So I offered Robin the opportunity to climb on board the Cinema Village screening to help establish his theatrical arm while relieving some of the headaches associated with PR, et cetera. We did in fact split expenses 70/30, myself paying the majority, in accordance with the filmmaker/distributor split that would remain after the exhibitor took their cut. To their credit, Avatar tried hard to book the film, which was a niche art picture anyway and a difficult sell, but they were also short on resources especially since Bookwars was their first film. In the end I loaned them my AIVF Exhibitor Guide, which I had been using to book the movie myself, and they used that as the basis for the rest of their theatrical distribution efforts."

Three years later, Avatar earned a reputation for its eclectic catalogue and its successful penetration of the art house circuit. But this was not known to Ben Coccio, who had won several awards for *Zero Day* on the festival circuit in early 2003 and he was ready to move to the next level.

"At that time I had finally gotten a producer's rep for the film — essentially a sales agent," he says. "The sales agent started setting up screenings for distributors, and on the list of people to show this thing to were all the usual suspects: Palm, Cowboy, THINKfilm, Samuel Goldwyn, Zeitgeist, et cetera. But Avatar was not on the list — it was not a company that either I or my reps were aware of. Around the same time, Jason Leaf at Avatar heard about *Zero Day* winning the Atlanta Film Festival and his curiosity was piqued. He got in touch with me, I sent him to my reps and Avatar eventually became the movie's distributor."

Going It On Your Own

Coccio's luck in snagging a distributor was uncommonly easy and Avatar's connections enabled the film to secure a theatrical premiere at New York's Film Forum, a highly prestigious cinema. However, had Coccio's luck been different, *Zero Day* would have been unable to get into any theaters if no distributors signed up and he was faced with the task of selling it as a self-distributed title.

"The spirit was willing but the flesh was weak," says Coccio when asked about self-distributing his film. "I would have wanted to, but after the festival run, I was deeply in debt and not making any money. It would have required me raising funds, which is something I had failed at before I started shooting."

Self-distribution is not a new concept — John Cassavetes did this for his films in the 1960s and early 1970s — but increasingly many filmmakers have taken this route to maintain a sense of control over their work. Even prominent filmmakers such as animator Bill Plympton and documentarians Penelope Spheeris and Arthur Dong have self-distributed even though their films have been much sought after by major distributors.

But while self-distribution gives the filmmaker a strong sense of autonomy and sovereignty, it also comes with hefty bills and killer headaches. Doug Miles discovered this when *Don't Ask Don't Tell* hit the self-distribution trail.

Would Miles recommend self-distribution? "Hell no! Get a major studio behind your film at all costs! Preferably one run by a guy named Weinstein or Eisner. But if you can't do that, then I guess you should go for it. We learned a lot of costly lessons doing this. We thought we were smart because we held out half the money we raised specifically for advertising and distribution. Unfortunately we made some bad decisions on where and when to try to launch the film. If we had been a little more patient, and not blown our advertising budget so early in Seattle (where the film premiered), I think we could have leveraged the opportunity we got later on coming out of a good run in Boston into New York much more to our advantage."

Miles offers some charming zoological and anatomical imagery regarding the success rate of a one-title self-distribution effort in today's film industry. "The little guy in this business seems to have about as much chance as a fresh-fucked goat in a barrel of piranhas. It's really tough, if not impossible to succeed in distribution unless you've got some really big swinging dicks behind you. I guess people do it and pull it off, but my experience — so far — has been as Hunter S. Thompson described the TV business: 'a cruel and shallow money trench where pimps and thieves run free, and good men die like dogs'."

Greg Hatanaka joins Miles in his view of self-distribution for film-makers who cannot get their films picked up. "No! Simply because self-distributing your film means that you'll be living with your film for another one-to-two years in addition to the two years it took to write and produce it, which means a delay in making your next film and losing your creative momentum. On top of that, there's also the major issue of being to collect from exhibitors when they know you have nothing to follow it up with."

DIGITAL DATA DISPLAYS

One problem that kept many underground films out of theatrical circulation has been the fact they are not on 35mm film, the standard projection format for cinematic exhibition, but are on digital video. Even at this late date, many theaters do not project digital video. When filmmaker Ted Bonnitt wanted to release his 2001 documentary *Mau*

Mau Sex Sex, a celebration of the golden age of exploitation movies, he had two things going against him: no distributor and no funds for a 35mm transfer. But this did not stop Bonnitt from not only getting his film shown, but also from making film distribution history.

"Self-distribution was not our first choice," says Bonnitt. "We entertained several offers from notable distributors, which amounted to exclusive rights for them and no money down for us. Our only reasonable choice was to embrace self-distribution, despite the formidable challenges. After all, we had the most to lose and the most to gain. And because *Mau Mau Sex Sex* is a documentary with no marquee talent attached, it was clear that we had to establish a perceived value of the movie. If you want to make money in TV broadcast, cable, and home video sales, the cachet of a theatrical run will make all the difference. We decided that if we opened in New York and got positive reviews, it would launch us out of the gate with some momentum. The trick was to pull that off as a very low-budget enterprise."

Working as his own distributor, Bonnitt started to work the phones. "We cold called three Manhattan theaters with video projection capability and offered them a screener. They all wanted to book it after they took a look. Our critical notices in the New York media, particularly a positive review in the *New York Times* helped us book the movie in theaters across the country, and then internationally. We avoided film festivals, unless they timed to critical events, such our opening in New York for advance publicity purposes. The Santa Barbara Film Fest invited us to play two weeks ahead of our NY opening, which resulted in a *Variety* review, and we also played at the International Documentary Festival in Amsterdam, which stimulated international sales through their market. But two other festivals that we played were useless to us, and we turned down the rest. We would only go to festivals that offer a market program, or something in return for exploiting your movie, such as attending buyers and meaningful press.

"We chose this strategy because of what we encountered as myopic political content correctness in the documentary world. If we should someday distribute a documentary regarding a subject more appropriate (like less funny, happy and sexy — and more struggle oriented — and I'm only half-kidding here) for such venues, marketing may

A sidewalk book vendor earns a healthy profit in Jason Rosette's documentary *Bookwars*.

Daniel Friedman and David Sonney recall the glory days of grindhouse cinema in Ted Bonnitt's *Mau Mau Sex Sex*.

benefit from a more extensive festival strategy. Otherwise, you can shoot your publicity wad in the festival's city when it shows, and enjoy none of the ticket sales. So, if you ever want to open in that city again, you won't get the publicity and have to spend money to buy advertising space to draw fresh ticket buyers. Some festivals overseas are more progressive in that they offer box office splits of ticket sales akin to a standard booking arrangement, and handle the publicity and venue."

Fortunately for Bonnitt, he had a proper budget in place to ensure the costs of opening *Mau Mau Sex Sex* was covered. "New York by far was the most expensive city to open," he warns. "The theaters there demand that you run ads in the *Village Voice* and *New York Times*, which cost a pretty penny. Don't ever expect to make money in New York theaters unless you have a New York–themed doc, like *Dark Days*. New York audiences have so many choices, and unless you pay a fortune in advertising to keep your movie in their consciousness, or have a special interest or ethnic theme to promote on a grass roots level, it can be lost in the shuffle very easily — even when you receive plentiful and positive press coverage and reviews. New York was also the only city where we worked with a publicity firm, which was referred to us by Cinema Village, the theater where we played. They did a great job of delivering all the major press, including an interview in the *New York Times* and even an original art piece on the movie page of the *New Yorker*! Our experience taught us to go with the smaller publicity agencies — they are more scaled to the small movie and will work much harder for you, unlike the big, fancy agencies who didn't even return our phone calls, and would have charged us ten times the amount, and probably delivered less.

"The total New York opening cost was well under $10,000 including ads, artwork, trailer prep, ad space and publicity, hotels, and expenses which is still about a third of what it can cost. Other cities cost us nothing up front, as we made a back end deal with theaters to pay for advertising space out of our share of the box office take. When possible, we booked the movie at what are known as 'calendar houses' where customers are mailed scheduled listings of movies shown at the theater, saving us advertising expenses. We did our own publicity in every city (except New York, of course) by either calling the media directly or going through the theaters' publicity agent.

"One footnote: Distributors warned us that several theaters would not pay us because many distributors only get paid when they threaten to hold back the next picture from them. We were told that as a self-distributor, we would not have that leverage (with only one movie). I'm happy to say that no theater stiffed us, even the most notorious! All of our experiences with theaters were really positive."

While Bonnitt's story had a happy ending, it also signaled a new beginning: the digital documentary was the very first film to be theatrically released on DVD. How did this home entertainment format find its way to the big screen?

"We did not see getting back the 40-plus thousand dollars it would have cost to make a 35mm transfer and prints," states Bonnitt. "I also did not want to degrade the final digital image on film. We called theaters around the country and found that sufficient video projection venues existed to play in the cities that we targeted. This is an independent, art-house movie and they tend to have more diverse projection equipment and put more effort into promoting your run. However, these being the early days of DV, many theaters did not have video projection equipment, and the cost to rent the projector and playback machine was prohibitive. So, we had theaters wanting to book the movie, but unable to do so.

"Our solution came from Sharp Electronics, which introduced a high quality portable LCD projector (P-20) that we were able to ship overnight to theaters. We tested it with a DVD player, and the image was remarkably good, considering the compression on the DVD. Sharp provided the projector in order to introduce their new product to the theatrical marketplace, and we suggested that theater owners bring their DVD player from home and plug it in. We never had a complaint from a customer, and we received big press reviews in every city we played without any mention of how we showed it. It was a successful road-show sleight of hand trick! Theaters were even willing to pay for the projector's $100 shipping cost, because after all, their take of the box office sales is in part to cover the cost of their facilities, which we were in part providing to them with projection capability. Necessity is the mother of invention. It represents a new trend, where independents are getting down to business. They'll make their movies on desktop computers and distribute them on DVDs to art-house cinemas with smaller and more powerful video projectors that look and sound much better than 16mm. It's an elegant solution that helps dispel the stigma of self-distribution."

How did the programmers and exhibitors react when Bonnitt told them the film was available for DVD projection? "The typical response was: 'Huh? Really? Wow. Okay. We'll do it.' Exhibitors are refreshingly down to earth. They'll try anything if they think that it will sell tickets. So, the fact that *Mau Mau Sex Sex* was the first movie to be distributed theatrically on DVD was no problem for a great majority of them, just a cost-effective solution. And, as a result, theaters are buying the Sharp projector, because it costs less than a 35mm projector, which represents a breakthrough for them. It was a win-win solution for everyone involved, including the audience, who otherwise would never have seen *Mau Mau Sex Sex*. And what was required of them to make their projection booths ready for this type of projection? A connection to their sound system, and usually with a simple RCA plug. We included an easy three-page step-by-step instruction manual on how to plug in the DVD player to the projector and point it toward the screen — everything else is automatic."

Mau Mau Sex Sex played theatrically on DVD in over 20 U.S. cities, including New York, Los Angeles, San Francisco, Chicago, Boston, Philadelphia, Seattle, and Salt Lake City. Bonnitt supplemented his distribution profits by selling VHS and DVD copies of the film and its soundtrack CD in the theater lobby to patrons who attended the screening.

An Underground Experiment Gone Wrong

In the spring of 2001, a curious experiment took place in New York. The Den of Cin, a 45-seat video projection lounge (which doubled as a catering hall for private parties) located in the city's trendy East Village neighborhood, was positioned as a new home for underground cinema. Physically it was a proper fit: the Den of Cin was based underneath the Two Boots Video store and was accessed by a slender, rickety staircase. The venue set aside Friday and Saturday nights at 11 p.m. for "Sicko

Cinema," a heading for edgy, unusual, and frequently inane films that no other theater would show during the daytime.

It didn't work. Not for lack of trying nor for a lack of titles. The variety of films offered ranged from comedy (*Everything Moves Alone*) to horror (*Ice from the Sun*) to horror-comedy (*Zombie! Vs. Mardi Gras*) to surreal drama (*Texas Night Train*). Even some rare retro flicks, such as the 1954 burlesque revue *Striporama* starring Bettie Page and the 1974 vampire classic *Lemora, Lady Dracula* turned up.

So what went wrong? Selena Ambush was the Den of Cin manager at the time and she recalls the odd reaction which Sicko Cinema received.

"It's a curious thing about Sicko Cinema and the films it featured," she says. "I worked the Den all week long; everything from birthday parties for privileged children down from Westchester and the Upper East Side, to rollicking live music events and drunken congratulatory post-screening parties for burgeoning filmmakers. Whenever I was asked about the 'Sicko' series, which I often was, or mentioned an upcoming showing, without fail it was met with raised eyebrows and the occasional chuckle. But it was also met with sincere questions about this or that and genuine curiosity. There was always someone who said that they would most certainly be there that weekend, usually promising to bring myriad friends and underground film buffs. 'Oh yeah,' some guy would boast with false knowing, 'My buddy Otto would love this movie, he lives for that stuff.' But strangely only one of these so-called enthusiasts ever surfaced come Friday or Saturday night."

Which is not to say that Ambush had the space to herself all of the time. "Oh sure, there were the rare successes and it was exhilarating," she adds. "When the room was full and people were drinking, these small video-screening events felt like something worthy of rolling out the red carpet and calling Joan and Melissa Rivers. But there were only two or three films that ever built to that pitch. *Striporama* drew the most consistent crowds and by 'crowd' in this instance I mean 10 or 12. It was a film with the pin-up types of the 1950s, showcasing Bettie Page specifically, who has enjoyed such a resurgence of popularity in this recent reach for all things retro. Its appeal was obvious. But for the most part, Fridays and Saturday nights meant four or five people, maybe one would buy a beer. Some of the patrons were those slightly scary but ultimately harmless types (except for the vague acrid odor hovering about them) who only surface after dusk in New York City and have probably been living in the same tiny apartment for 23 years amidst stacks of old newspapers and fifty-cent soda bottles. But just as many of those who showed up were young East Village hipsters out for a casual but amusing evening in their Diesel jeans and well-worn Pumas. One evening yielded a couple of teenagers, most likely from Jersey and foolish enough to think that I'd serve them when they complained that they had left their IDs 'on the train.' But they enjoyed the movie so much, laughter coming easily and heartily — the only sign of life in the room, that I remember refilling their soda cups for free and shoving a brochure with the line-up for the upcoming months at them as they ascended the stairs out of the Den. I hoped they'd bring friends, but I never saw them again."

Sicko Cinema limped through from April to November of 2001 before being withdrawn. "It would be easy to blame the overall failure of this programming on the lackadaisical management of the Den space by the Two Boots corporate owners or the simple obscurity of the films themselves," says Ambush. "But the fact of the matter is that New Yorkers want to be in the know. They want to have seen it all, done it all, and be able to discuss it in a witty and urbane manner. Indie films are all the rage, though they have quickly become as mainstream as anything accused of being 'too Hollywood' and the term 'underground movie' is thrown around the industry like candy. But genuinely underground or independent film efforts are simply not a top priority. They are relics for collectors and true cinema buffs and even then it seems like most people gravitate to a specific genre with little interest in the rest. For instance, there were never any repeat customers on those late weekend nights. To have succeeded Sicko Cinema needed, among other things, at least a few regulars."

THOSE WHO UNEARTH UNDERGROUND MOVIES

Most distributors who release underground films tend to travel the direct-to-video route. This is understandable, given the previously-explained dynamics of the film distribution business. Some, however, have enjoyed a degree of success in bringing these films into limited theatrical release. The major distributors of today's underground cinema can be found here:

Alternative Cinema — The umbrella for three labels: E.I. Independent Cinema (offering sultry horror, sci-fi & drama), After Hours Video (which aims at the naughty side of cinema) and Shock-o-Rama Cinema (which goes for the gore). http://www.alternativecinema.com

Artistic License Films — Aiming more at the higher-end of the underground, this New York theatrical distributor has provided release for eccentric features such as the campy musical *The American Astronaut* and the lesbian crime comedy *By Hook or By Crook*. http://www.artisticlicense.com

Asylum — A feature film production and distribution company covering both American and international releases ranging from the artistic to the extreme. http://www.theasylum.cc

Avatar Films — Primarily an art house distributor for major international releases, this company has found time to bring smaller fare such as *Bookwars* and *Zero Day*.

Barrel Entertainment — A fine source for nihilistic mayhem thrillers, with an occasional art flick to spice the presentation. http://www.barrel-entertainment.com

Brain Damage Films — With a cheery mix of goth, horror, shockumentary, and blood-tinged reality movies. http://www.braindamagefilms.com

Brimstone — Vampires, werewolves, and aliens are the primary stars of this label. http://www.lindenmuth.com

Department 13 — The collected short films of underground director Joe Christ and other assorted madness can be found on this small Georgia label. http://www.dept13.com

Eclectic DVD — With titles like *Dracula's Great Love*, *In Smog and Thunder* and *My Life with Morrissey*, this company surely earned its name. http://www.eclecticdvd.com

Film Threat DVD — The online indie cinema magazine has spun off this DVD line, with a primary focus on off-beat comedies such as *Jar Jar: The F! True Hollywood Story* and unconventional dramas including *Getting Out of Rhode Island*. http://www.filmthreatdvd.com

Hargrove Entertainment — Primarily focused on TV syndication and distribution, this small New York company has found controversy and success in the presentation of edgy political documentaries including *Falun Gong's Challenge to China* and *Yugoslavia: An Avoidable War*. http://www.hargrovetv.com

Leo Film Releasing — Originally a primary source for art and global cinema, this small California label now offers a supersized serving of horror and urban thrillers. http://www.leofilms.com

Margin Films — Filmmaker Quentin Lee released his early films, including *Shopping for Fangs* (co-directed with Justin Lim) and *Drift*, and also provided a banner for small gay-oriented dramas. http://www.marginfilms.com

Microcinema International — The best of the Independent Exposure series of short films are compiled in DVD releases from this touring festival group. http://www.microcinema.com

MTI/Fangoria/Bedford/Artist View — Action, horror, sci-fi, adventure, and even comedy find their way into this company's extensive offerings. http://www.mtivideo.com

New Concorde — Roger Corman's label, with plenty of low-grade action and adventure flicks (which, increasingly, seem more derivative of bigger budget Hollywood epics). Corman himself has not directed in years, but his reputation and managerial imprint makes this stand out from the other straight-to-video labels. http://www.newconcorde.com

Sub Rosa Studios — The reigning B-Movie king, with an astonishing line-up of films that dwell in the worlds of sci-fi, action, urban, thriller, comedy, and even an occasional prestige drama such as John Farrell's film version of Shakespeare's *Richard the Second*. http://www.b-movie.com

Tempe — Another small straight-to-video label offering more horror and sci-fi, although this one scores laugh points via their delightfully snarky Bad Movie Police label that presents so-bad-they're-good B-movies with campy introductions and running commentary. http://www.tempevideo.com

Troma — The grand old master of the exploitation flick, its name is synonymous with no-budget/high-camp tomfoolery. http://www.troma.com

World Artists — Originally focused primarily on art-house fare from both an American and global perspective (early releases included the films of Chantal Akerman, Jon Jost, and the Swedish classic *Elvira Madigan*), this small label has provided video and occasional theatrical release for films by Caveh Zahedi (*I Don't Hate Las Vegas Anymore*), Tom Sawyer (*The Strange Case of Señor Computer*) and the ultimate in experimental nightmarishness, Elias Merhige's *Begotten*. http://www.worldartists.com

INTERVIEW

KIRSTEN TRETBAR REACHES HER ZENITH

When Kirsten Tretbar decided to produce and direct *Zenith*, a documentary on a small and economically depressed Kansas farming town that tries to overcome its emotional malaise by staging an elaborate Passion Play, she wasn't making a movie for the sake of making a movie.

Let's have Kirsten tell her story:

Q: What were the main challenges that you came up against in getting *Zenith* distributed?

KIRSTEN TRETBAR: As all filmmakers who've made a feature film, be it narrative or documentary, I hoped that *Zenith* would play on the big screen. I shot it and edited it with this in mind. All footage was shot with a large range to chop the bottom off of every frame, to eventually blow it up to 16 mm or maybe even 35mm. I paid exorbitant fees to an amazing sound dubber/mixer in Minneapolis, who mixed the entire film in a huge professional sound stage, with Dolby stereo. I even color corrected most of the footage, section by section, with expensive

Avid software. On top of that, I paced the film much more slowly and lyrically, and included huge sweeping visuals, and slow moving shots, keeping more in order with a theatrical film.

Yes, my first hope for distribution was the theater — that *Zenith* would be a landmark documentary like no other — a sweeping cinematic visual film about the land, and farmers, one that harkened back to films like *Man of Aran*, or Agnes Varga's *Gleaners*. In my mind's eye, I hoped that all who saw *Zenith* would die over its brilliance, it would win every award at Sundance, and that Miramax or some equivalent would buy it outright from me for a million plus, and that it would be sent out theatrically, I'd be nominated for an Oscar, and that would be that!

Now, I wasn't so naïve to think that any of this would actually happen. I had been producing documentary films for ITV (the English equivalent of network television in the states) for several years, and my brother, Eric Tretbar (*The Usual, Snow*) was an experienced indie filmmaker. So I'd seen the trials and tribulations first hand of Eric's career in cinema. Also as a producer for television docs in England, I knew that the state of getting good films distributed these days, on TV or in theaters, was at an all-time low. People just weren't, and still aren't, paying the price it takes to make a good film. Even POV only pays something like $550 a minute, for docs, no matter what their original budget — which for me would barely cover my living expenses during production.

After almost three years of struggling to get my film actually distributed theatrically, I finally landed a deal to show *Zenith* on NBC. This is the story of all of my rejections, and final release of my film on television.

To be more positive, never in my wildest dreams would I have thought my first documentary film, a film about Kansas farmers, would show on network television. Although this was not what I'd originally intended for the film, how many first-time directors can say they showed their film to millions of viewers? Not many. So I'm beyond proud that *Zenith* aired on national network TV! Specifically, *Zenith* aired the weeks before, during, and after Easter on 63 NBC affiliates in April of 2003 — the very weeks that America had just invaded Iraq. Trying to do marketing for this airdate was horrendous, and I'm just glad that any stations aired *Zenith* at all — considering that most programmers and newspapers were focusing on the war. They weren't really feeling sorry for the future of American farmers. So, although I was unable to capitalize on the national airdates of my film showing across the country as much as I'd wanted (I'd imagined interviews on Charlie Rose and Oprah and cover articles in the *New York Times!*), I did at least get it shown in a big way.

But even so, I never made a dime back making this film, or distributing it, not one dime. Nor did I make a penny from the NBC release.

The story of how we eventually got the film on NBC is a long and involved one. Most filmmakers won't admit all the bad stuff they've been through. They want to put it all behind them and act like their distribution came magically to them, a result of their brilliant filmmaking! But distribution stories are always much more complicated than you can ever imagine. I feel it's very much a part of a film's history — who liked it, who didn't, and it's important to think about why. Of course, they never tell you why!

Some factoids about the struggles of *Zenith*. It was: shot and directed by a first-time director (me), funded totally independently from start to finish, accepted into IFP's prestigious New York Film Market, but seen by only a handful of distributors, who eventually said NO. The year *Zenith* got into the Film Market, where most films find distribution and get invited to major festivals, was the same year as 9-11, 2001. The market was only about five weeks after the twin towers fell. New York was like a cemetery. It felt sad, scary, and ghostly — and the last thing on anyone's mind was promoting their films, or schmoozing. It wasn't the best market to show my film. People were already so devastated about the events in the U.S., that they could hardly bare another sad story like mine.

Let's talk about who rejected *Zenith*! It think this is quite fun in hindsight, and also, revealing as to how hard a filmmaker works to find distribution. *Zenith* was first rejected as a proposal by ITVS. ITVS is the funding body for most of the documentaries that show on "Independent Lens" on PBS. Then I resubmitted a trailer to ITVS the next year after I funded the shoot myself, and put together a trailer, and with this, it was named a finalist. Then it was rejected a second time!

We eventually finished the film with independent funding, and then my producer Pam Calvert and I spent over $10,000 of our own money trying to get the film into festivals and get theatrical and cable distributors' attention (through various P.R. articles, reviews, mailings, calls, and meetings). Guess what? They all rejected us! (We did get into several festivals, just not the big ones.)

The news was not always bad about *Zenith*. People had always been interested in the subject of my film. "A group of alcoholic farmers put on a Passion Play?... Cool!" they would say. "Kind of a real life *Waiting for Guffman*?" they'd ask. "How funny!" they'd quip. I'd say, "Well, not exactly... kind of a real life *Jesus of Montreal*." And they'd look confused and immediately lose interest. Although I will say that many people in the indie film world: distributors, festival organizers, and programmers, had expressed sincere interest in *Zenith* after the Film Market. There was definitely a buzz about my film.

This was not just because of the market, but also because I early on had supporters in two friends, Thomas Ethan Harris and Richard Raddon. Thomas and Rich had acted as producers, trying to find me funding while *Zenith* was still just some footage, a trailer, and a paper proposal. These two producers were top dogs at the former LAIFF, now known as the IFP LA Film Festival. They knew everyone in the indie film world, and everyone knew them. They had been big supporters of my brother, Eric Tretbar's films, and they "got" what I was trying to do with *Zenith*.

Thomas and Rich had really talked up my film for a year or two, before and during the shoot, and they had even loaned me money to start editing. Rich had meetings in New York, with HBO, on behalf of my film, and Thomas called every onehe knew, trying to find me funding. They hooked me up with other film gurus, like Bob Hawk, who offered to advise me on my edit. I felt a lot of support from within the independent film world, but, eventually, we all parted ways. People weren't really sure what I was trying to do with the film. Someone even commented on one of my initial edits, " Where are we going to show this thing? On *The 700 Club*?"

My real problem was lack of funds. People will only work with you so long for free, and when you start getting rejections over and over again, people often give up. Edits for documentaries often take lots of time, and that means lots of money and energy. I also have to take some credit for this split. I argued that a two-hour earlier edit of my film was the finished film, and Thomas and Rich argued it wasn't done. I sent this version off to festivals, and of course, got rejected. It took me half a year to realize they were right! (Sorry guys!) I re-worked the edit, and eventually came up with a 56:40 version that worked.

Thomas eventually left LAIFF to pursue other projects, and I was busy editing and editing. (We are all still great friends). But even with this support, *Zenith* was still rejected by Sundance, twice! And, with the help of those producers, and a new producer, Pam Calvert, the newer, shorter, finished version of *Zenith* was considered seriously by POV and HBO. But after waiting several months, was again, *Zenith* was rejected by both!

There was a startling lack of reasons as to why no one was saying YES! It was strange, because everyone who saw the film came out of the theaters in stunned silence. Audiences loved it, and laughed and cried all the way through. And I was getting great reviews and endorsements from very respected critics. People also commented that they thought the film looked more beautiful than most docs, and that the cinematography was amazing. Which I feel is a major feather in my own cap, since it was the first time I'd picked up an camera that wasn't a still camera in my life (I shot it myself since I didn't have the money to hire the DP I'd originally planned to hire).

So we kept plugging away. With my new producer, Pam Calvert, and the help of my husband, Ozzy Benn, a talented graphic designer, we all decided to focus on a web site, which would be the hub of a massive grass-roots campaign promoting the film. We also decided to sell tapes. We finally got endorsements from every major national church group in the country as well as endorsements from dozens of national agricultural groups. If the independent film world at large wasn't "getting" what we were trying to do with the film, we knew, eventually, someone would. And we knew that the themes of the film would resonate with rural audiences if no one else.

Maybe I'm just being an optimist, but I like to think that things have a beautiful way of working out for the best. Because, if you think about

Kirsten Tretbar's *Zenith*

it, this film really was a portrait of a dying farming town struggling hard to stay alive, and the ways a local church helps it to do so. It's a film about rural poverty, addiction, and recovery. The message of the film really is for people who live in, or support, rural causes, people who usually either can't afford cable, wouldn't be caught dead watching PBS, and don't go to art-house cinemas. In the end, I'm very glad *Zenith* aired on network TV and was watched by millions of viewers, rural and urban alike.

I received hundreds of phone calls, letters, and emails after the film aired. These calls and emails brought me to tears and humbled me. I heard stories of people who'd lost their farms, or who were trying to keep their small town churches open. I heard about suicides due to bankruptcy. And I heard several positive stories too, about how people saw themselves in my film, and thought, "What can I do to help my community?"

It really made me think this was why I made this film. Not to be cool at Sundance. Not to get meetings with Harvey or Bob. It was for the farmers.

It's a bit embarrassing to brag about your film. It's kind of like a parent bragging about their kids. It's pretty tedious! But I think it's very important that we, as filmmakers, (and especially as independents), admit to others the struggles we've gone through to make our art, and then to allow ourselves to sit back and be proud of what we've done. We so seldom get the social or peer group recognition we seek or deserve, and we even more seldom get any kind of financial payback for our efforts. Often, all we have is our own inner belief in what we are doing, and the message we know we have to bring to others.

Filmmaking takes years of your life, and years off of your life! It's not a hobby. It's like a spiritual calling towards truth. You do it because you HAVE TO! So I say here that Zenith started with an idea, one night while I was watching my cousins act in the town's yearly passion play, and that very night I knew I had to make a film about these people. And I did. And I still can't believe all that's happened! Sometimes it feels like a dream. That's the high that no one can ever understand or take away from you. And that's what keeps me making films! I'm also very proud of my work on my film, since this is the first documentary I ever directed or shot. I am even prouder to have won several nominations. Last year *Film Threat* (and Phil Hall!) gave *Zenith* one of the best reviews I've ever received, and eventually nominated it "honorable mention" for "Top 10 Best Films of 2003 You Haven't Seen". Kind of a bizarre honor, but a realistic one, and I'm damned proud of it!

In 2004, I was nominated for a prestigious "Templeton Epiphany Prize" for the Faith and Values Awards — known in the L.A. film and TV world as the Christian Academy Awards. People like Robert Duvall win this award, so it can't be all bad.

You may wonder what this all has to do with distribution? Everything. Because, if a filmmaker doesn't have constant bits of support throughout the creation of his or her film, at every single stage, they just feel like dying, they may lose their momentum, and the film flops. Other people who work in the industry understand this, and that's why people are usually so helpful when you're an indie filmmaker starting out. They understand that one carefully placed comment could be the difference in your whole edit, or might inspire you to ask that one investor for a few more thousand dollars to finish your edit. They also know that it's terribly difficult to make a film, and drains your energy and your finances, and can really make a person depressed. All the film-maker friends I know are complete wrecks! They have very high highs and very low lows, and their love of truth and cinema keeps them going. They need constant support from everyone, even though they may act like they're invincible!

My brother's friend, a young filmmaker named Betty Teng, who was one of the judges one year at a major film festival, told him when he was upset about getting rejected (mind you, this same year he was nominated for the Independent Spirit Awards for *Snow*) — she said (I am paraphrasing her words): "Eric, snap out of it. You are *amazing*! Do you know how many thousands and thousands of people want to make films? Do you realize that out of those thousands, probably hundreds of thousands, *you* have not only made a film, but also *finished* a film? Do you know how many thousands of filmmakers start making films, and never finish them? Then not only have you finished your film, yours is one of only a hundred or so films that's even being considered for slots at this festival, out of thousands?" (She had picked his film as one of her final choices that year.) She went on to say that if you even complete a film, and it's any good at all, that you are like, one one-hun-dredth of a percentile of thousands of people who want to make films. You are in the top bracket of all filmmakers in the entire world!

Betty's comment to my brother has always kept me going when I was feeling low, or unrecognized, or just plain exhausted with filmmaking! One comment by one person, may spin off energy to do some other part of the project, or find funding, or may help you meet some new person that leads you to another idea, or distributor, or programmer, and each of these little moments creates your finished film.

The process of securing distribution is really all about the life of mak-ing the film. You're looking for distribution from the first day that you come up with your idea for your film — be it documentary or narrative. You need funding to make your film, but your investors won't just fund an idea. They are funding a product that will eventually be sold, or distributed! And from the very beginning, you as a filmmaker have to approach your film project like a Harvard educated MBA — with every single eventuality thought through. Even if you have no idea who will distribute your film, you better darned well act like you know who will buy it! You're selling a product, both to the investor, and to the distributor. And you better get some quick education on marketing and P.R., or get some talented people in your corner. All of my reviews, all of my supporters, all of my funders, my family, my friends, people at IFP, anyone who knew about my film, from its earliest stages, all supported its getting done, and eventually getting shown on TV. It's all related.

Even the rejections I received led me on, renewed me in a way, or brought new contacts into my life.

Which leads me to a wonderful resurrection story that started with a rejection. When ITVS rejected me for the second time after being named a "finalist," I thought my world had come to an end. Everyone was broke. I applied to work at a furniture store in L.A., my editor, Derek Goodall, refused to work any longer for free, and I was sitting on huge books of logged tapes of 100 hours of footage.

Then I got a call. It was Pam Calvert calling from San Francisco. Pam Calvert was, at the time, the Stations Outreach Manager at ITVS, the winner of a Gody Working Group Award for her tremendous Community Outreach Campaign on the Sutherland's *The Farmer's Wife*. I had no idea who she really was at the time, other than that she had emailed me privately, a few months earlier, while ITVS was considering *Zenith*. She had told me that she had loved my trailer, and wanted them to pick *Zenith*. When they didn't pick my film (I won't go into the particulars here) she eventually quit her job with ITVS. Pam had been tired of working within the politics of such a bureaucracy, and I think my film was just the thing she needed at the time to get out of public television (my thoughts, not hers here).

She called me out of the blue, and asked me if I needed a producer. She had lots of experience with *The Farmer's Wife*, and cared about the farm issues in my film. She told me that she was also a Quaker, so she wasn't afraid of any Christian issues addressed in my story that might scare off other producers from the project. I couldn't believe it. Here was a person I'd never even met, an amazing producer with phenomenal credentials, offering to help me find funding, and finish my film. I said, "YES!" Pam eventually hooked me up with another filmmaker, Tracy

Huling, and through the two of them, they found a contact at the UCC (United Church of Christ) — a contact that got me my finishing funding. Without Pam, I don't know how I would have finished my film.

The great part of this story is this. Pam and I worked for almost a complete year and a half, she lived in Berkeley, and I lived in L.A. She wrote grants, press material, sent out trailers, called hundreds of people on behalf of the film, got reviews, helped write the web site, wrote pages of editorial notes, reviewed four different cuts of the film, et cetera. Here's the catch. Pam and I had never met! We didn't meet each other face to face until we met up in New York, at the IFP Film Market in 2001, to launch the film, over two years after my ITVS rejection! IndieWire did a piece about us meeting at the market that week.

The story of Pam and I working, side by side, via the Internet, phone, and mail, is hilarious and heartbreaking, and so much what making this film has been about — the power of art, faith, and commitment to a common cause. Pam's commitment to my film, aside from any connection we had as colleagues or friends, was all that mattered. And her commitment made me a better filmmaker, and re-invigorated me during a time when I felt no one really cared.

You never know who's out there to help you. Keep your mind and your heart open! And, you don't have to live near someone to change his or her life. You don't even have to know them very well!

Back to how I got the NBC deal. It all really came about through Pam, and Tracy, whom I mentioned earlier, my newer co-producers — and through my investor — the UCC. Pam had helped me find funding from the UCC about six months before I finished my edit. I was broke and at a standstill, and was stuck with a two-hour edit that wasn't working and I was in desperate need of more funding. My editor had quit, I was selling furniture in L.A., and the film was going nowhere. Pam hooked me up with the head of communications at the UCC, a wonderful filmmaker in his own right, named Robert Chase. Bob immediately "got" what I was trying to do with my film and wrote me a check right away so I could enter the finished film in the next NY Film Market.

Just a note here: The UCC is a very liberal church group, started by the Congregationalists and the Lutherans back in the 1950s. They in fact are one of the only Protestant church groups out there today that supports gay and lesbian pastors and marriage. I didn't know this initially. It's really funny to me now that I was worried about the UCC putting money into my film. I thought they were some right-wing fundamentalist group with an agenda. Far from it! In fact, the UCC is so liberal politically, that when more conservative church groups have been interested in *Zenith*, I've felt nervous about the fact I got some money from the UCC! It's so dumb! On the other hand, if I'm showing *Zenith* in a more liberal setting, like L.A. or NY, I feel I have to hide the fact I have any money from any faith based group at all — especially a group calling themselves "Christian." The whole world is crazy!

What the UCC was trying to do, with supporting my film, was to support rural communities, not a Christian agenda. In fact, Bob Chase at the UCC looked at several of my edits (more as a friend and less for editorial comment). He was always concerned that the film be as "general" and "objective" as possible when it came to any Christian imagery or message. But it's kind of hard to keep the Christian themes to a minimum, when you're trying to show how a small town church and an Easter Passion Play, full of Christian imagery, has affected an entire community.

My distribution with NBC had a lot to do with Bob Chase promoting and supporting *Zenith* with the NCCC and the IBC, and for this, I will be eternally grateful. Let me give you some background here. The NCCC (the National Council of Christian Churches) and the IBC (the Interfaith Broadcasting Commission) get together every year and produce and release several hours of "faith based" programming which they give for free to the three big networks. One year NBC might get the programming, the next year CBS, and so on.

The IBC is a group of "communications heads" from all of the religious organizations, of all faiths. For example. The Methodist Church has a "head of communications" that gets funding to run his office from the central church board. This person would produce their web site, and make inspirational films, documentaries, and educational pieces. These "communications offices" have a lot of money, and are quite professional. The "heads" are usually producers themselves, who've either been ordained ministers or rabbis, or who've worked in the TV or film industries in the past. I'm unclear as to the exact history of how the IBC was founded, but I do know that the networks at some point in time had to commit to so many hours of "faith based" TV programming given to them each year, produced by faith-based groups.

Thus, *Zenith* was basically "given" for free to the networks. What I'm saying is that I never made a dime from this great opportunity. I'm not upset about this in any way, but it's just important that people understand that the producers often fund indie films, and often, quality programming is given to television for free. Deals like this often get films shown, but often bankrupt the filmmaker. It did me.

Since the UCC had already given me some funding, they pitched my film, *Zenith*, to the IBC, when all the heads of communication got together for their annual meeting. Since my film was already made, and had some partial funding by the UCC, and since it already had major reviews and endorsements, it was an easy, award-winning shoe in for the upcoming 2003 NBC series.

I think the film's distribution life is far from over. I may still try to pitch it to some cable stations, and to foreign networks as well. Ahhh... a producer's job is never done!

Q: Where has the film played to date? And how did you arrange these playdates?

TRETBAR: Most of the screenings of *Zenith*, aside from my NBC release, have been through film festivals. I did have interest from Film Forum in New York, during the Film Market, but the length of my film was, I think, four minutes too short to be considered a feature. These lengths vary from place to place for feature length consideration, which is pretty ludicrous, since the Academy considers a feature film somewhere around 45 minutes in length.

Zenith screened at: the 2001 IFP New York Film Market, the USA (Dallas) Film Festival, the new Central Standard (IFP North) Film Festival in Minneapolis (headed by Ex-LAIFF programmer, Todd Hansen, and it will soon be very hot!), and The Kansas City Filmmaker's Jubilee Film Festival.

Other playdates might not normally apply to this question, as they may seem less professional. But they still mean a lot to me. My favorite screening was at the Ritz Theater, in Stafford, Kansas (the largest town next to Zenith, Kansas — where I shot my film!) I made a promise to the people in my film to come back and show them the film once it was finished. And I kept this promise. After premiering *Zenith* at the NY Market, I took the film back to Kansas. The little small town theater, The Ritz, had recently been renovated, and it had an amazing sound system, and a gorgeous new white screen. I think the film never looked or sounded better and the people in the film loved it!

The film has also shown at several national church synods (huge conventions) as well as several academic conferences throughout the Midwest. Through these academic conferences, I've met many rural sociology professors and farm activists, as well as theologians, and have had amazing support for my film. In fact, a divinity professor from Princeton, and another from Berkeley, are now teaching *Zenith* in their classes! One professor uses it in his divinity class, and another teaches my film alongside *Jesus of Montreal* in a theology in the media course. I think this is phenomenal!

But my favorite, most successful, and largest "screening" — or playdate — has been my GRIT screening at the L.A. Film School. I'm very proud of the work I did getting this event together, and getting some major national press for my film as a result. The GRIT screening was a public event, but some filmmaker friends and I organized it.

GRIT stands for Girls Reeling It Together. GRIT is an informal women's film coop, started by filmmaker, Shawn Tolleson, and others. Shawn and I had met over the years at various LA IFP events, and we ran into each other at the New York Film Market. I loved her soulful short film called *Missed* and she had loved my film. Months later, she called me and asked if I would like to hold a joint screening with her film, under the auspices of GRIT.

We decided to really promote this new women's film group. I was living back in Kansas City at the time, working on another documentary back here, and regrouping after bankruptcy with the help of friends and family. So for about five months, I helped Shawn, and another marvelous woman filmmaker, named Genevieve Anderson (with Gen's short film *The Cone*) put together the GRIT screening in LA. The three of us decided to pool our resources and really try to make this even something major. GRIT had had a very successful screening two years earlier of women's shorts, and Shawn and Gen had lots of contacts.

We revamped GRITS' mission statement, and logo. My husband, Ozzy Benn, made a web site for the group, and developed the logo and postcards, and developed the software to support a huge email campaign, which would be spearheaded by us from our home in Kansas City. Since my film was the feature, and since I had done so much grass roots work with Zenith, I took charge of most of the PR. Shawn looked for a celebrity host, and Genevieve sought out a fabulous venue in L.A. I was very proud of what we were trying to do. Since the screening, GRIT has made dozens of new members, and is being considered a serious new women's film group. Check out our web site (*www.gritfilms.com*) if it's still up and running as of the publication of this book.

You don't put together an event like this unless you do it to get press and renewed interest in your cause, and your films. So we worked like crazy sending out weekly emails to every agent, manager, production company, women's film group, religious groups, activist groups, indie film groups, newspapers, calendar sites, indie film magazines, and online groups like *Film Threat*! We placed ads in papers about our screening. You name it, we did it, in terms of promotion.

We eventually got the brilliant filmmaker, Vicki Jensen, who won the Academy Award for her direction on *Shrek*, to host the event! We set up the screening at the L.A. film school, sent out invitations, got major articles written in the *LA Times* and *LA Weekly*, and waited. The screening basically sold out. I think the night was a huge success. What I found astounding is the number of women working in the film world who came to this event, not knowing our work, or anything about GRIT. We had some amazing conversations after the screening with women in the film and TV world, who, like us, felt sometimes alone, misunderstood, or judged for wanting to make films with a more soulful message. We had a lot of support from men too. I think GRIT is a great group, and I wish there were more groups out there like this, saying, let's put an end to all the racist, sexist portrayal of people, and work harder to make a more profound cinema! It was one of the best nights of my life, and to this day, I have friendships with dozens of women I met that night.

The moral of this story is this. Do not sit around and wait for things to happen. You have to MAKE them happen. If there's a group you wish you could belong to, but it doesn't exist, then start your own group. Get a friend to do a web site. Send out emails to people you don't know. Get a dialogue going. Write some press releases, and get some journalists behind your cause. You can make it happen!

Q: Did you have any difficulty getting the film shown due to the religious nature of its subject?

TRETBAR: I would have to say yes, but honestly, I cannot say for certain. If you look at the number of people who've really loved my film (I've had some pretty amazing reviews) and contrast this with the number of doors that have not opened for my film, distribution wise, you might begin to draw some conclusions.

But it's hard to speak about these things, when really it's all speculation. Filmmakers never really hear why one programmer or buyer rejects their film. They never get a breakdown about why, because the poor programmer has just plain too many films to watch, and it would take too much time. So, like I said, I hate to be angry that my film was rejected because of its religious subject, if this wasn't the real reason. I've heard many other reasons, such as, "We already have a film in our line-up this year about farming (*Hybrid*)." But I've never heard any concern with the religious content.

But I must admit, I've always suspected that this was probably the case. I'm surprised though, since there's such a huge Christian audience out there who supposedly goes to movies, and you would think that some smaller distribution company would get that, and think about promoting *Zenith* in such a way as to make some big bucks. But I could never convince anyone of this; no matter how hard I tried.

What I did find is that for some people, the film didn't fit any kind of agenda, and therefore, people felt it had an agenda, but they just weren't sure what it was! I showed the film to the huge men's motivational Christian group, Promise Keepers. I sent a copy to a man high up in the organization, because I felt that it would be a great film to show at one of their huge conventions, since many of the guys in the passion play in the film talk about going to Promise Keepers. Although my contact there said he watched the film five times in one weekend, and cried his eyes out, he rejected the film. He felt it wasn't "proselytizing enough." Meaning, the overt message of the film wasn't trying to say, "Convert to Christianity and ye shall be saved!" Well, no, my film is not about that. But it does show honest people using faith and going to church to help change their lives.

Another big supporter of my film, who'd been very much behind *Zenith* in the beginning, saw it, and I heard that he said, "Where would we sell it? To *The 700 Club?*" So basically, you just can't win. Either *Zenith* was too Christian for some viewers, or not Christian enough for others.

And then there's the Jewish debate over whether or not passion plays portray an anti-semitic view of the Jewish role played in Jesus' death. A concerned friend of my family had read an article in the *New York Times* about the Oberammergau Passion Play, and problems there politically. She said, "Don't make a film about passion plays! They're anti-semitic!" Well, I personally don't think that this particular passion play out in the wheat fields of Kansas was trying to say something bad about ancient Judea, but I guess people do think this. Look at the flack that Mel Gibson has gotten for his film, *The Passion of the Christ*. Mel, I understand your pain!

As I said before, from the very beginning of making this film, I knew that many people would see it as a "Christian" film, merely by the fact that I was filming an outdoor Easter Drama, with Biblical imagery of Jesus carrying a cross, being crucified, and rising from the dead. I was also following the story of how one small town church seems to be the only thing between many struggling young farmers and their desperation, depression, or even suicide. I never set out to make a film about the important role a small town rural church plays in the lives of it's bankrupt citizens. This story presented itself to me. And like every good journalist, and every good ethnographer, I knew that this was a story I had to follow.

I initially, perhaps cynically, thought I was going out to Zenith, Kansas, simply to make a film just about "The Great Plains Passion Play" and that I would follow the every day lives of the people who had the lead parts in the play. I knew it had "camp" elements, and could be quite funny, but I also knew that I did *not* want to make fun of anyone just for their amateur theatrics. I myself had trained as an actress, had an MFA in theater, and was actually quite impressed by how professional everyone was.

I believe that the humor will always come out in the sheer honesty of the moment. You don't have to force it. And I am proud to say that the film is actually quite funny in parts.

But I never really intended on creating a kind of spiritual story promoting faith. It just happened that this redemption of the town was the real story I ended up telling. It was the story the people wanted to express, and that I saw and felt everywhere around me.

From the very beginning, I made this film out of my own personal love of this town, Zenith, Kansas, where my own farming family is from. My mother and father grew up there, sons and daughters of local farmers. If you know anything about the creation of this country, you will know that church groups founded pretty much every college and university and small town in America. Education and religion have always been pretty much entwined. You will also know that the small town church was usually the social center of every town, and even the tiniest towns may have had five or more churches of various denominations, all working together to create a better, stronger community.

In my *Zenith* interviews, the locals started opening up to me, like confessions, about their struggles with alcoholism, and how playing the part of Jesus or his disciple in the play, and how going back to church (in this case, a tiny rural Presbyterian church) had really helped to heal them. All of a sudden, I saw this story as the story of every small town in America. These withering communities were full of retirees, working so hard to keep the younger generation from moving away, or to stay solvent and strong. My own Aunt Dwilette heads the adult Sunday school class. I'd never imagined that I would also discover a rejuvenation of faith spearheaded by my beloved Aunt Dwilette — the town's funny church lady with the high voice, and a passionate commitment to help her community.

Her story of going out into the community, and personally inviting "hardened" young farmers and their families to come to church, was for me, the real story within this story. (It's also very funny.) That the faith and determination of one person can truly inspire, unite, and change an entire community for the better — is an amazing story! In fact, the whole movie would have been about Dwilette, but she didn't want me to film her. So every second of footage we see in the film about her, is every second I shot!

No one can really make a living farming anymore, due to the increase in prices of machinery and land, and the decreases in crop prices. When people have no jobs, there is poverty, and with poverty, depression, and with depression, most often, addiction. I never thought I'd make a film about addiction and the role played by faith in recovery. But you find that when you're creating a film, it's as much for you the filmmaker, as it is for anyone else. Like the ex-coop manager, Charlie Parker saying of the passion play "It's more for the people who are in it than for the audiences that come to see it," I too felt a kind of healing making this film. You never realize while you're creating a film, that you are also addressing your own questions. You are a seeker. The film was very much a journey towards that as well. And I think that's one reason the film had such honesty — because I empathized with the story so deeply. These people's honest stories of redemption, and their testimonials, helped me grow more spiritually, and as a filmmaker, too.

Although I do not consider myself a "Christian filmmaker," I have in many ways opened my heart more to the Christian message of forgiveness, acceptance, and renewal. I've learned very much the power of prayer, both as a spiritual person, but also for my own crazy life. It centers me as an artist.

This was the first film I've ever directed myself, let alone shot myself. Although I'd produced several documentaries for the BBC, I'd made many films about music and sporting events, with little or no spiritual, or inspirational content. As a woman of budding faith, I'd always wanted to make a film from that point of view — while still being objective and appealing to a wide audience of any religious background, trying to show the powerful influence faith and drama can have on one's life in a beautiful, cinematic, and inspiring manner.

I approached the filmmaking experience from a spiritual point of view. And sometimes, I feel that this intensity of understanding, the honesty of the people in the film about their addictions and problems, that this is the *real* reason many people (or distributors) rejected the film — not really just because of its "Christianity."

There is so little cynicism in the film, just sincerity. And I think this lack of cynicism is hard to deal with if you're busy promoting sex documentaries, or sensationalist films about dwarves. Does all indie cinema these days have to be so sensationalist, so left-wing, so low-brow posing as high-brow?

My film is apolitical, and I think that's another factor that surprises viewers. They're expecting lots of ranting and raving about the state of farming, and I decided to leave that out (even though I do have hours of such interviews). I also left out the keggers and late night dances, and crazy parties held by the sons and daughters, my age, of the leads in my film. No one ever makes a movie about the middle generation in their 40s, or about retirees. I wanted to do this.

I also realized that no one had ever made a film about *why* farmers are so connected to the land, and thus to God. I myself was kind of blown away by the deep "spirituality" of these farmers. It wasn't preachy religion, with a capital R; it was spirituality, the kind that so many of us in the cities yearn for on our walks up the canyon, or during our daily yoga workout. I was fascinated to try and understand where this sense of "spirit" came from. When you spend every waking moment working on the land, with cattle, dogs, horses, on your combine, under the huge blue prairie sky, and your whole livelihood depends on the elements — wind, rain, hail, tornadoes — I think it's kind of hard not to feel some kind of kinship with a higher power than yourself. I feel proud to have shown this in my film as well as I did.

Back to the question asked above. I hesitate to tell this story, for fear of making some people angry, but I think it's an important example of how judges and programmers don't always make their decisions coming from a place of trust and reverence and respect.

Let me just say that I did learn about one judge on a panel who voted against picking *Zenith* for something (when everyone else around the table wanted it) saying that he "just wouldn't feel safe in that town if his car broke down." I asked my contact why he would say such a thing? This person said that this judge was a young man from New York who said, that since he was gay, he wouldn't feel safe in this town, and so he didn't feel comfortable promoting the story of this town. I find this so sad.

What I find telling about this judge's comment is more the "rural phobia" of the judge than anything else. He based his decision either on past bad experiences, or he based his decision on plain ignorance of rural communities. Perhaps this judge has never spent time on a farm with farming people? Whatever the case, this judgment told me a lot, and made me think a lot about the kinds of films that are getting support, and why?

Are we so afraid of the right-wing militant Christian "right" that we reject any thing even vaguely Christian oriented, no matter how mainstream, or even liberal? I feel that films and art are here to expose hypocrisy, not promote agendas. And the only way to expose the bad stuff is to discuss it. By the mere fact of doing a film about racists, we may see how terrible they are. Are we never to expose racists ever again, for fear that it seems like we're promoting them? Perhaps, the more films we make about rural people, even bigots, the more we show their poverty, their lack of education, maybe then the more we can create a dialogue which will promote getting them help, getting them jobs, and ultimately this will help people be more tolerant.

Are we to just ignore our dying farm towns because these people aren't as sophisticated seeming as we? Are we to reject films about rural America, because these people must turn to religion when they have problems, because they have *nowhere else to turn*? Are we to blame them for their ignorance or their faith? What are we so afraid of? This is a bit like the fear I felt when I got my first call from the UCC when they wanted to fund my edit. I was terrified that this was some radical fundamentalist group, then massively relieved when I found out how liberal they were. Why was I so afraid? I can tell you. I was afraid that if people knew I got funding from a church group, they'd see my film as having an agenda. But my question is this. Don't all films have a message? Don't all films therefore have some kind of agenda? Isn't the agenda to help people a good one?

I found that in making my film, the church groups were about the only social-welfare groups in rural communities helping anyone. After learning this, I'm very proud to have any church support for Zenith. The politicians certainly weren't out there with programs to re-train farmers, or bring in new businesses to help out of work people. WalMart had taken over (it's mentioned several times in the film) in a neighboring town, and most of the local shops in Zenith and Stafford had closed. Where was the help and support for all those out-of-work adults?

The churches are struggling and alone too, trying desperately somehow to keep the towns alive. It's not always so much about promoting religion, with these church groups, as it is about promoting activities, just to unite people, and get them out of their houses (as you can see from the passion play practices, building the sets, and the weekly Sunday School classes where people sit around and laugh and eat cookies). There's not a lot of work, and very little to do. Church is about the only thing they have left.

I've often felt that my film would have had more support if it had been more exploitative, or exotic — say — for example, if it was about a group of Hispanic migrant workers putting on a passion play. Do the people in my film remind us too much of our own relatives we've left behind in the small towns? Do we feel guilty as we watch this film, like somehow, we're not doing enough? It's the same kind of issue that surrounds the question of giving charity at home or abroad. We often find it easier to help a child in a foreign country get food and clothing, than a homeless kid in our own city. We feel happier, safer, if we distance ourselves from the real problems that surround us. If we don't have to get too close, but we help someone out there, someone who looks different from ourselves, we can feel better about not helping our own community. That homeless person next door might just some day be us. It's scary to confront our own fears. My film really looked at everyday poverty, depression, and addiction. I think this scared people more than any Christian elements in the film.

For some reason, there's something about these slow talking, Kansas, white-bread farmers that seems scary to people who've never stepped foot in America's bread belt. They are not cuddly. They are not politically correct or exotic. Their form of Christianity is quite mainstream. They do not speak in tongues, or charm snakes, or reject you if you are different. They ask you who you are first, they don't label you. These farmers in my film are Scottish-Irish Protestants, Presbyterians. About as bland (and as kind) as you can get. My cousin is a punk rocker biker chick, with tattoos and crazy hair, who's lived in San Francisco, and even worked as a stripper. She just moved home to Zenith, Kansas, trying to kick some old bad habits. Guess what? The church in Zenith loves her just as she is!

As a filmmaker, and film professor, I am concerned about this new trend towards angry liberalism, and a self-righteousness over simplification, or fear mongering, and a heightened cynicism in media. Where is the imagery? Where is the cinema? Where is the beauty and pathos?

I grew up in a liberal family, watching Joseph Campbell interviewed by Bill Moyers on PBS. Campbell spoke of the Hero's Journey — how all religions and myths were about the same thing, the journey of the individual to find strength and meaning, a journey through trials and tribulations, death and rebirth. I had always approached the subject of my film from this perspective. I had also studied Cultural Anthropology at Grinnell College (where I now teach film every year) and I have a Master's Degree from USC in Theater. My education and upbringing taught me to be inclusive, and to see the archetypes in all religious customs and stories. These academic pursuits had always taught me to look at all theater and religion as a kind of modern day ritual, where man elevates his ordinary life, and sees it more profoundly, adding meaning and purpose to existence.

You can view the passion play in *Zenith*, from a cultural context, as what ethnographers call a rejuvenation ritual. During the post-Civil War years, the Sioux Indians performed the famous "Ghost Dance." This was their last ditch effort, a week-long dance with wailing and singing, performed by the shamans to raise the thousands of warriors up from the dead, to help them fight off the American Army, and regain their land. Obviously their efforts failed. The passion play for me was this kind of a ritual. When all else is lost, we turn to our God, ask for help to find renewal and a hoped for rebirth, to end our suffering.

It is my hope that we can teach a new generation of filmmakers, as well as judges and programmers, distributors, and audience goers, to appreciate documentaries for their symbolic and cinematic aspects as well as for their literal messages.

Q: How did the *Film Threat* review help in (pardon the pun) spreading the word about *Zenith*?

TRETBAR: That's a hard question. Reviews can totally make or break your career. They can inspire the filmmaker to keep going during a time when they have no more energy to survive! They can re-ignite you if you're still trying to find funding or distribution. They can also get your film completely wrong!

Film Threat reviewed *Zenith* right after the GRIT screening. I believe this was before I had the NBC Easter deal in place. At the time, I'd had some reviews from other papers, like the *LA Weekly*, and other people within the film and agricultural worlds. But, I must say, getting this review, and oh what an amazing review it was, totally validated what I was trying to do with my film. It told me that smart people in the *real* film world could get my work as a filmmaker.

I have long felt, and so has my brother, Eric, that the only reviews worth reading these days are in the *New Yorker* and on *Film Threat*! What was so remarkable, is that for once, a reviewer didn't just enjoy my film for its humor or beauty, but instead, the review saw the sadness in my film — the ultimate tragedy — that all this town had was its faith, and nothing else. This had always been the sad truth behind the themes of my film. It's kind of a death march. And if you know anything about Biblical imagery, you'll know that the apocalyptic bell toll over the resurrection at the end of the play isn't the normal noise one would expect during this scene. The *Film Threat* review noticed details like this that no one else had.

Also, *Film Threat* "got" that I was showing mainstream Christianity for what it is, and what it can do, and that is just seemed to come out of the film, rather than being some kind of agenda I was promoting. This was so true, and something, as you know from my last comments, I had worried about and struggled with. And I loved the reference to my *not* having taken the "Michael Moore" approach. I thought that was so funny, because Michael Moore is my hero. I would die to make a film like him. But I knew from the onset of making *Zenith* that his approach was not right for this film.

As to how your review helped me... I instantly copied the review and, like every good producer, sent it out to everyone who'd worked on the film, helped with financing, and as a press release to various papers and other interested *Zenith* followers. You hate to say, "I told you so", but getting a great review like that pretty much makes you want to gloat! I did a bit of gloating (as much as I could do from Kansas City!).

I think the review also really helped Bob Chase in his negotiations with the NCCC/IBC when they were trying to pick films for the NBC series. I know it certainly helped when I was emailing all the NBC programmers, and tried to get them to pick up the film from the satellite feed the week the war started. A review like that is like short-hand — it saves everyone time and energy when they want to decide something quickly I called several of the NBC programmers the week before the film aired, and said, "You might want to give my film the best slot possible, *Film Threat* just gave it a rave review!" And I did get some amazing slots — like twelve noon on Easter Sunday, in Washington, DC.

So reviews really do help to spread the word about a film, more than you can ever imagine.

Q: As someone who teaches documentary filmmaking, what films do you present to your students as examples to follow... and, perhaps, examples to avoid?

TRETBAR: I had spent several years before making *Zenith* working as a producer on documentaries for British Television, mostly producing art and music series for Yorkshire Television out of Leeds, for the main British Commercial network called ITV (like CBS in England).

When we think of documentaries, we often think of historical, educational films with lots of still photographs, and a famous voice telling us about some battle or another. This kind of documentary drives me nuts. When I think of this kind of film, I think of Ken Burns. Sorry Ken, but I hate your kind of filmmaking. I find it to be a history lesson that you may as well hear on the radio. Or you could get a book, and put on a tape or CD to learn the same thing. YUCK! This is *not* filmmaking.

I love filmmakers like Errol Morris, who try to at least create mystery and feeling in exploring a subject. Sometimes his films also drive me nuts, but at least he's trying to do something new, and that's hard!

That's why I'm always so amazed by films trying to tell a historical story, that find a way to tell the story more cinematically, like Shoah. If you can re-create a feeling, with music, and haunting visuals, or use voice over and interviews to achieve an emotional arc, then that, to me, is the best kind of historical documentary.

I was educated to make more "fly-on-the-wall" documentaries mostly through my work with my ex-husband, Derek Goodall. Derek is a British documentary filmmaker, who was trained in the '70s making documentaries through ITV, at Granada TV, and Yorkshire Television. Derek and I are still great friends, and he in fact edited my film, *Zenith*.

I learned from Derek, and my work in England, that there it's much more the norm, even when making a documentary for television, to let the story unfold visually, and use as little voice-over, or pre-written narrative, as possible. Call this cinema verité, or "fly-on-the-wall" filmmaking, or just call this cinema. I have little time for film history or labels. To me, all filmmaking is a visual art form and I expect it to be beautiful, haunting, funny, noble, and entertaining.

Documentaries, for me, are *not* journalism, or visual histories. They are living visual ethnographies, about people alive today — a place where the audience lives through someone's personal experience, guided by music, photography, and sound, not through a litany of educational and historical details.

When I was living and working in England, I would see all these wonderful documentary series that we would call reality TV, but they were so much better. I was always totally blown away by their artistry and beauty. Then I'd come back to Los Angeles, and watch TV, say PBS, and just be sick at all the bad journalism posing as filmmaking. So this is where I learned to make docs that feel more like cinema. Working in England taught me is how lazy American TV producers are — especially with the visuals going along with the news. They're always talking about "B Roll". Meaning, the other roll you shoot to be the visuals underneath their voice over. That's just not the way to look at a scene in my opinion.

I would watch American TV after coming back from the UK, and just die over how the visuals that went along with the written voice over were always just plunked down, to illustrate literally what was happening. In such situations, Derek would teach me, you don't need both the narration, and the visual, if they say the same thing. In other words, you don't even need to make this piece. It might as well be a book or a radio show. This helped me tremendously in my edit. For example, the news anchor might say, "A house was on fire and they rescued a bunny" and then the visual would be of a house on fire and a bunny in the hands of a fireman! Or the visual would have absolutely nothing to do with the narration. Using the narration I just mentioned, the visual might be of men sweeping the street behind the journalist looking on. This is the worst kind of journalism, and journalists and cameramen who work in news could learn lots by taking a film class. So could some filmmakers!

I find a lot of this kind of cheap journalistic documentary filmmaking on TV these days. I know that it's often done this way, because there's a lot of library footage out there, and a lot of very cheap TV companies commissioning new documentaries. These companies don't want to pay for any new footage, interviews, or filming. I myself have been offered some of these jobs, producing documentaries for a company I won't name. This company hires producers (never called directors of course) to write a script. Then the company hands you library footage, and working with an editor, you are supposed to "fit" the film stock they own to your script — say on a film about a battle in World War II. It's so sad! That's why you see so many terrible "original" documentaries on TV.

Making a documentary is kind of like putting together a huge puzzle, made out of shifting holograms. It's different from narrative feature filmmaking in that so much of your finished film comes out of what you actually come up against during the shoot, what you decide to follow, and how it's all edited together.

This is all to say that my favorite documentaries show you the story, rather than tell you. And to show you a story, and create a plot, or any kind of dramatic structure, it just takes time. Which means money. People don't realize how expensive a good documentary can cost. My favorite docs have the same arc as a narrative film, with an Act I, II, and III — they have a premise or problem, they have main characters, and sub-plots, and they follow the lives of these characters through ups and downs, and hopefully through some change or growth. You're not going to film much "change" in a weekend. You must really live with your subjects, get to know their world. It's the same in good "ethnographic fieldwork." You must really get so close to your subjects that they don't see you as an outsider anymore, and they begin to ignore your camera.

One note about the new "reality" shows. Although this is not cinema, it does fall under the guise of documentary work and often feels like cinema if done properly. And I must say, whether you like the subjects or not, a lot of this is pretty decent filmmaking. What I mean by that is that we often see a story unfold visually, and it's fun to tune in each week to "see" what will happen next. We the viewer decides while watching, who's the good guy, and who's the bad guy. Even shorter shows like *Blind Date* have the three-act structure down really well, and that's one reason we tune in. I find their popularity an interesting indicator that "fly-on-the-wall" or cinema verité documentary filmmaking is alive and well, and most people love it!

Now, I mentioned earlier that Michael Moore is my favorite doc filmmaker. I see his films more as essays than documentaries, but he is the main character of his film, and he takes himself on a journey of exploration throughout each film. If you break down his films, you will see all the same plot devices used in narrative features. There's always a downturn, and a crisis, around the mid-point scene, and you fight for him to "win" in the end. He's a brilliant filmmaker, and personality, and I love the way he plays the part of the "innocent fool" in his films. It's fascinating.

I am totally inspired by narrative films too, that feel like documentaries. I've often studied these films to see if I create similar imagery in my documentaries. Good photography is a must, as is lighting, sound, and score. To me, documentaries can be every bit as evocative and cinematic as any narrative film, and I think, they should be. Why not make a beautiful cinematic film… about real people?

9: So You Want to Make Underground Movies?

Our journey through today's Underground Cinema has come to an end. Or has it? Perhaps you have been inspired and intrigued by the films featured in this book and you would like to try your hand at making underground movies.

Underground filmmaking offers a higher degree of independence than Hollywood filmmaking. In Hollywood, filmmaking can be considered as art by committee — you are under the control of the various studios, unions, agents, and test-marketers in regards to what you can shoot, who you can work with, and what you are expected to deliver.

Working underground, however, gives you a greater sense of freedom. But it also demands a higher level of responsibility. In many ways, the underground filmmaker bears an intense burden since he or she needs to be in command of all aspects of the production process — both creative, financial, and even emotional. After all, no one ever said freedom was free!

So what do you need to know in order to get started in the world of Underground Cinema? Let's go over this checklist to determine what is required is you wish to carve out a place in this particular cinematic world.

1. You need to have the right personality. Filmmaking is a collaborative effort and you will be coming in contact with many unreliable and unpleasant individuals. Tact and diplomacy are required if you want to get ahead in this field without devolving into either the internal angst of ulcers or the external rage of violent behavior.

2. You need to know all about filmmaking. Creating motion pictures is a serious discipline that requires a full understanding of all aspects of the production process. Even if you plan to have other people handle the technical and postproduction aspects of your film, you need to have a full understanding of what they are expected to do.

Ideally, it would make sense to study filmmaking in school. For those who are not able, for whatever reason, to attend filmmaking classes then the best alternative is to become as fully self-educated as possible. There are no shortage of invaluable books that details the basics of film production, and these can easily be obtained.

Furthermore, it would help to seek out and watch the classics of Underground Cinema. Many of these films are easily found on video or DVD, such as the works of John Cassavetes or the early John Waters comedies, and it is easy to see how these filmmakers worked within the limits of their budgets to create works of remarkable style and distinct substance.

3. Be realistic with your budget. The true downside to the Underground Cinema orbit is the question of money (or the lack thereof). Filmmaking is not an inexpensive pursuit, and while the cost-effective breakthroughs in digital videography and computer editing have made life easier, there are a multitude of costs that need to be considered when putting a film together.

Never begin a film project without a realistic budget in place. Surprise expenses can and will pop up, so budget in the proper amount of funds to cover possibilities of damage, cost overruns, delayed schedules, or any possible money drainer.

Furthermore, be realistic in keeping your budget aligned with the scope of your production. You cannot make a *Lord of the Rings* fantasy or a *Spider-Man* action flick on a five- or four-digit budget. Trying to use cheap effects and production values to suggest something grander will have the wrong results — similar to Edward D. Wood Jr.'s use of pie tins as flying saucers in *Plan 9 from Outer Space*. Unless you are going for intentional camp results, don't attempt to make a film which you obviously cannot afford to do properly.

4. Have professional-level support throughout. Since no person makes a film in solitude, you will need to work with a cast and crew who work at a professional level. Finding such people may take time and require extensive auditions and reference checks, but in the long run it will work out.

One of the most important people to have around during film production is a professional photographer who can take publicity stills. Too many underground filmmakers forget to have professional-quality pictures taken and wind up belatedly yanking screen grabs, which more often than not are blurry and not good enough for publication. Having a professional photographer taking publicity stills can help in the sales and marketing of the film down the road.

5. Be original with your music. Do not, under any circumstance, "borrow" classic or well-known recorded music for your film without having the problem rights clearances. And if you don't have the rights, create a new score. This may sound like Filmmaking 101, but incredibly many films are not able to be shown because of this issue (including the previously discussed *Superstar: The Karen Carpenter Story*).

6. Get a copyright. When the film is completed, file a copyright for the production with the U.S. Copyright Office in Washington. Without a copyright, your film will be considered public domain and you will have no further rights to it.

7. When in doubt, test it out. If you want to get feedback on the footage, don't be afraid to test your films (either in isolated scenes or as a rough cut) before audiences. Sometimes being so close to a project creates problems in deciding what works and what doesn't — outside opinions from those you respect can provide a degree of balance.

8. Create a web site for the film. Nowadays, everyone and everything is online. Having an online home for your film will help raise its credibility and introduce it to a wider audience. Remember to include high-res

photographs on the site and, if possible, create a trailer than can be viewed online.

9. Create a media kit. Even if you are creating a short film, it helps to have a media kit for the production. A media kit does not need to be elaborate — basic information should include a full listing of cast and crew, a plot synopsis, biographies for the key talent involved in the production, and contact information (telephone, e-mail and URL) for the filmmaker. If you are not planning to include photographs in the media kit, include an online link where such photographs can be located for downloading.

10. Build up reviews. Traditionally, films that are not in theatrical release have experienced problems in getting reviewed. But thanks in large part to the Internet, many highly respected online film review magazines have happily accepted unreleased and under-ground titles for review. Some of these online magazines include *Film Threat* (www.filmthreat.com), *eFilmCritic.com* (www.efilmcritic.com), *B-Independent* (www.b-independent.com), *Flipside Movies Emporium* (www.flipsidemovies.com), *Movie-Gurus* (www.movie-gurus.com), and the genre-specific *Monsters at Play* (www.monstersatplay.com) and *Sex Gore Mutants* (www.sexgoremutants.co.uk). Positive reviews from these media outlets can enhance the pedigree of a film. Negative reviews, of course, will not help — but then again, no film artist has ever gone through the industry without at least one negative review!

11. Plan your future. Do you want to take the film into the festival circuit, or seek out a distributor, or self-distribute, or what? Create a strategy on getting your film into circulation, and do extensive research regarding the outlets where you are planning to send your film for con-sideration.

12. Be patient. The process of creating a film can be lengthy, often last-ing a number of years. It is easy to lose faith in yourself and your work if progress is not rapid. But don't rush — time is your ally and with proper planning, focused determination and a can-do attitude it is not impossible to achieve your goals as a successful filmmaker.

For Further Reference

A ll of the films and filmmakers featured in this book were originally profiled on *Film Threat* (www.filmthreat.com). You are invited
to log on to *Film Threat* to learn more about the titles and talent
featured here, and to keep updated on the latest happenings in the
world of underground cinema.

For further information on the films cited here, or if you are a filmmaker and you have a film that you would like to have included in
future editions of this book, please feel free to contact the author at
input@filmthreat.com (Subject line: Attention for Phil Hall).

About the Author

Phil Hall was born in the Bronx, NY, and was educated in New York's raucous public school system. He graduated from Pace University with a B.A. in journalism; his minor was religious studies and he considered a career as a minister, but did not pursue it because he enjoys sleeping late on Sundays. His career got off to an auspicious start at the age of 19 when he landed an assignment as a United Nations correspondent for Fairchild Broadcast News. Phil is a contributing editor for *Film Threat,* and the book editor for the weekly *New York Resident* newspaper and the online magazine *Here Boston.* His film journalism has appeared in the *New York Times, New York Daily News, Wired Magazine, Hartford Courant, American Movie Classics Magazine,* Tower Records *Pulse! Magazine, Video Librarian, Daily-Reviews.com* and the *Organica Quarterly.* He also serves on the Governing Committee of the Online Film Critics Society and is a member of the National Book Critics Circle. This is his first book.